PROBLEM GAMBLING
in Canada

PROBLEM GAMBLING
in Canada

LORNE TEPPERMAN AND KRISTY WANNER

ISSUES IN CANADA

OXFORD
UNIVERSITY PRESS

OXFORD
UNIVERSITY PRESS

Oxford University Press is a department of the University of Oxford.
It furthers the University's objective of excellence in research, scholarship,
and education by publishing worldwide. Oxford is a registered trade mark of
Oxford University Press in the UK and in certain other countries.

Published in Canada by
Oxford University Press
8 Sampson Mews, Suite 204,
Don Mills, Ontario M3C 0H5 Canada

www.oupcanada.com

Library and Archives Canada Cataloguing in Publication

Tepperman, Lorne, 1943–
Problem gambling in Canada / Lorne Tepperman and Kristy Wanner.

(Issues in Canada)
Includes bibliographical references and index.
ISBN 978-0-19-544528-2

1. Compulsive gamblers—Canada. 2. Compulsive gamblers—Family relationships—
Canada. 3. Compulsive gambling—Canada.
I. Wanner, Kristy II. Title. III. Series: Issues in Canada

HV6722.C3T465 2012   363.4'20971   C2011-907085-5

Cover image: © iStockphoto.com / P_Wei

Contents

Acknowledgments

In a recent survey, a large majority of Canadian respondents (86 percent) said they believed that the individual gambler was responsible for his or her own gambling problem (Hall and Scarpelli 2010). Our hope is that this book will expand your thinking about the present-day gambling problem and, especially, about the many social influences that fuel this devastating addiction.

In writing this book, we have been helped by the co-operation and guidance of our acquisition editor at Oxford University Press, Jennie Rubio. Jennie has always urged us forward; yet she has also understood our reasons for recurrent, even protracted, delays. Moreover, she has given us useful criticism at every stage of the (lengthy) writing process. We hope the book in your hands finally justifies Jennie's patience. We are also grateful to copy editor Deborah Cooper-Bullock for her intelligent and scrupulous efforts to make sure we said everything we wanted to say and justified everything we said with correct references. Finally, we are grateful to Katie Scott, the production editor, for cleaning up the page proofs—a process much lengthier and more complicated than non-authors might imagine.

As to content, we have drawn on the published and unpublished work of many gambling researchers, and we have credited them all accordingly. In particular, we want to thank some associates whose unpublished work proved useful in writing this book: namely, Albert Kwan, Sasha Stark, and Mark van der Maas. We have also received excellent research assistance from undergraduate students at the University of Toronto: namely, Jessica Claudio, Laurel Falconi, Kim Fung, Rose Hrvatin, Mohammed Khan, Komal Somjee, Brianna Sykes, Laura Upenieks, and Hoursa Yazdi. Thank you, assistants, for your energetic intelligence and co-operation. Nikki Meredith checked the page proofs, catching errors and suggesting improvements.

Finally, we have also received useful comments on various drafts of the manuscript from Jim Cosgrave, Amber Gazso, Rob Simpson, Garry Smith, and Sasha Stark, and editing help from Nikki Meredith. Thank you, everyone, for your wonderful contribution to this book.

In the end, we two authors are solely responsible for what we have said and left unsaid in this book. It was an interesting journey for the two of us—formerly, teacher and student; then employer and employee; and now finally colleague and colleague, friend and friend. We hope you enjoy this book and learn something from it.

Lorne Tepperman
Toronto, Ontario

Kristy L. Wanner
Columbia, Missouri

PROBLEM GAMBLING
in Canada

Chapter 1

Gambling:
Its Pleasures and Costs

William Rutsey, director of the Canadian Gaming Association (CGA), has repeatedly declared that the gambling industry in Canada supports the Reno Model of gambling developed by international gambling experts Alex Blaszczynski (Australia), Robert Ladouceur (Canada), and Howard Shaffer (the United States).[1] This model holds that:

- the majority of the adult population gambles responsibly;
- only a small minority of the population experiences gambling-related harm;
- any responsible gambling program rests upon two fundamental principles:
    - the ultimate decision to gamble resides with the individual and represents a choice, and
    - to properly make this decision, individuals must have the op portunity to be informed;
- within the context of civil liberties, external organizations cannot re move an individual's right to make decisions;
- . . . [not only is gambling] a choice, [but] responsible gambling also rests on the principle of informed choice; and
- informed choice should be based on providing relevant, empirical- ly based information to help the players make their decision (CGA 2006).

That's one possible outlook. But to many academic students of gam- bling, anything that emanates from the CGA is suspect, as the group is perceived to be a biased and non-credible source.

According to another viewpoint, also supported by international gambling experts, the more available we make gambling opportunities, the more people gamble; and the more people gamble, the more numerous problem gamblers will be. Currently, hundreds of thousands of Canadians are estimated to have problems with gambling. We will describe and examine these problems in this book. What's more, both the gambling industry and the provincial governments have grown dependent on problem gambling. Research by Williams and Wood (2007) shows that roughly one-third of all gambling revenue is produced by problem gamblers—that is, people who cannot control their addiction to gambling. (Some psychiatrists would claim that these people have an addiction to losing money, the usual and foreseeable outcome of gambling.)

Like most human behaviour, gambling behaviour is learned socially, from other people. Like all human behaviour, gambling behaviour increases in frequency when it is socially encouraged and socially rewarded. Like all activities and substances that entertain people or change their consciousness—movies, television, pop music, professional sports, prostitution, alcohol, and illegal drugs, to name a few—gambling produces huge revenues for private investors. In addition, like all of these entertaining activities and substances, gambling increases the risk of addiction. Some people lose control and need frequent, even constant, pleasure and stimulation from gambling, just like some people lose control and need television, sex, shopping, alcohol, or cocaine.

The reasons some people become problem gamblers while most gamblers do not are complicated and we will talk about this shortly. Likewise, the reasons some people become addicted to gambling but not to, for example, shopping, sex, or cocaine, will also be discussed. That said, it is worth noting that comorbidity—the occurrence of multiple addictions—is common in problem gamblers, concurrently or over their lifespan. As well, most addicts, whatever the poison they choose, are disproportionately likely to show symptoms of depression or bipolar (manic-depressive) disorder. Their addiction is a direct response to their need for emotional sensation, excitement, a sense of purpose, or an end to anxiety. There is a psychological, even psychiatric, component to problem gambling, as there is to all addictions.

Many consider Blaszczynski and Nower's (2002) Pathways Model to be the state-of-the-art explanation for how problem gambling develops. This approach is laudable for many reasons; for example, it recognizes that there are different trajectories to problem gambling. One theory and one treatment does not fit all.

This book will focus on the *social* influences that encourage people to look for emotional sensation, excitement, a sense of purpose, or cessation of anxieties in gambling, including advertisement and media portrayals of gambling with their efforts to glamorize and normalize gambling. A brief look at the social reasons leading many Canadians to experience depression and anxiety will explain why many become vulnerable to the attractions of gambling.

This book will also look at what the gambling industry and government regulators have done both to *promote* gambling and to *discourage* problem gambling. In many respects, this book is about the debate between two points of view: On the one hand, gaming industry officials and government regulators feel that problem gambling is a personal problem, to be solved individually with limited help from either the industry or government. In short, they believe gambling is a matter of personal responsibility and personal blame. On the other hand, public health experts view problem gambling as a publicly induced and encouraged health risk—like selling cigarettes to children or allowing obesity-friendly fast foods in school cafeterias.

The goal of this book is not to find the "right answer" but to air this important public debate—to put gambling on the public agenda for thought and discussion.

The "Gambling Problem"

The practice of gambling can be placed on a continuum that ranges from nongamblers at one end, through recreational gamblers in the middle, to problem gamblers at the other extreme (Currie et al. 2006; Hardoon, Gupta, and Derevensky 2004). Over time, a fraction of the nongambler population migrates to recreational gambling, and others migrate to the problem gambler population. We may eventually come to understand precisely how and why such migration occurs. Until we do, designing effective preventive strategies remains a difficult challenge.

How widespread is the so-called gambling problem, and why should we care? A 2005 Ontario population survey using the Canadian Problem Gambling Index (CPGI)—the CPGI will be discussed in more detail later—reported that:

> the large majority of participants (90.7 percent) had not experienced gambling-related problems in the past year, with 36.6 percent classified as non-gamblers and 54.1 percent classified as non-problem gamblers. Of the total sample, 5.8 percent were classified as at-risk of gambling problems, and 2.6 percent were classified as having moderate problems. Less than 1 percent (0.8 percent) were classified as having severe gambling problems. (Wiebe, Mun, and Kauffman 2006, 14)

While estimates vary between populations and over time, they all suggest that roughly one Canadian adult gambler in twenty has a current or prospective gambling problem. This means that in a population of roughly 32 million Canadians, of whom 75 percent are over the age of 20, some 760,800 have a gambling problem or are at serious risk of a gambling problem.

Before proceeding, we should acknowledge that these estimates are reliable and can be taken seriously. Several decades of research have gone into creating and refining reliable measures of problem gambling. This research effort is evident, for example, in the encyclopedic volume *Research and Measurement Issues in Gambling Studies* (2007), edited by Garry Smith, David Hodgins, and Robert J. Williams (all major gambling researchers in Alberta). Gambling researchers now have a clear idea of what we must measure and how we can best measure it. Though some debate remains around the edges of the measurement issue, by and large gambling researchers go about their research in similar, trusted ways.

Today, the CPGI is a widely used Canadian survey instrument that measures problem gambling. The index includes questions that help pinpoint the extent of a given individual's compulsion to gamble. The questions also provide insight into reasons gambling can become a problem for some people. Often, the problem is revealed in the form of compulsive behaviour, lying, and preoccupation, as we will see in Table 1-1, which presents the Problem Gambling Severity Index, a short-form version of the CPGI.

Most problem gamblers end up disturbing the lives of other people, such as their partners, parents, children, employees, or friends. That means many Canadians are affected by problem gambling. The effects of gambling are the same, whatever the jurisdiction or community size in which it takes place.

The outcomes are also similar across countries, so although the following interesting statistic is from the United States, figures are likely similar for Canada (comparable Canadian statistics are not currently available): reportedly, 41 percent of all working Americans claim to consistently live from paycheque to paycheque (Rassmussen 2007). In fact, this troubling statistic has been updated, and a more recent report by business journalist Michael Snyder suggests that "61 percent of Americans 'always or usually' live paycheck to paycheck, which was up from 49 percent in 2008 and 43 percent in 2007" (as quoted in Wenzel 2010).

A CNN report claims that:

Scrambling to make ends meet is an exercise all too familiar in many homes. Even before the economic meltdown of 2008,

Table 1-1   The Problem Gambling Severity Index
(A Sub-scale of the Canadian Problem Gambling Index)

Problem Gambling Behaviour

- **Bet more than you could afford**
  How often have you bet more than you could really afford to lose?

- **Increased wagers**
  How often have you needed to gamble with larger amounts of money to get the same feeling of excitement?

- **Returned to win back losses**
  How often have you gone back another day to try to win back the money you previously lost?

- **Borrowed money or sold anything to gamble**
  How often have you borrowed money or sold anything to get money to gamble?

Adverse Consequences

- **Worrying about a gambling problem**
  How often have you felt that you might have a problem with gambling?

- **Suffered criticism**
  How often have people criticized your betting or told you that you have a gambling problem?

- **Feelings of guilt**
  How often have you felt guilty about the way you gamble or about what happens when you gamble?

- **Financial problems**
  How often has your gambling caused any financial problems for you or your household?

- **Negative health effects**
  How often has your gambling caused you any health problems, including stress or anxiety?

Source: Adapted from Ferris and Wynne 2001

one-third of workers were reporting they didn't have enough income to live comfortably. To achieve this, more than half said they would need to earn more than $500 per paycheck. Thirty-seven percent of workers said they have one income for their households while 16 percent say they work more than one job just to make ends meet. (Rassmussen 2007)

It doesn't take much imagination to realize that people who live from paycheque to paycheque, or from welfare cheque to welfare cheque for that matter, and who are chronically short of money, would be in big trouble even from small, regular gambling losses. Many of the people we interviewed for our study of problem gambling fall into this category.

At the same time that increased numbers of people are having trouble making ends meet, increased numbers of people are being drawn to casinos, racetracks, bingo parlours, and other gambling opportunities online. Yet, research evidence consistently shows that as gambling *opportunities* increase—at casinos, racetracks, bars, corner stores, or on the Internet—so do gambling problems. Nonproblematic gambling is the pool from which problem gambling emerges. So to prevent problem gambling—that is, to reduce the risks of onset—we must consider the larger environment in which gambling is structured and marketed by an aggressive global gambling industry.

Gambling has become a major global industry in the last 20 years, and it continues to grow rapidly. Gambling is no longer restricted to colourful characters and exotic locales, as it was a century ago. Gambling is advertised everywhere as fun and entertaining. What's more, national, provincial, and municipal governments are helping to promote gambling to raise their own revenues. Governments reason that people are going to gamble anyway, so it makes sense for them to regulate gambling and take a cut of the revenue.

As with alcohol and drugs, gambling has historically also been a major source of revenue for organized crime. For this reason and others, in the second half of the twentieth century, many governments moved to legalize and regulate gambling and take a share of the profits. From here, it was a small step to promote gambling and increase those profits, which are seen as "nontax" revenues or even "voluntary taxation." A small fraction of this money is directly reinvested in public goods such as charitable foundations. (In fact, some of the money raised this way is even spent on problem gambling research.)

The gambling industry has done its best to highlight the positive economic and social effects of gambling, as in this newspaper story reported in the *Toronto Star* in April 2008:

> Canada's largest and most financially significant entertainment industry is gambling, accounting for 267,000 full-time jobs and contributing $15.3 billion a year to the economy, according to the Canadian Gaming Association.
>
> The industry group's report . . . says 57 per cent of gambling revenue—$8.7 billion—supported government services and charities.
>
> The other $6.6 billion "was spent to sustain operations, paid out as salaries, and used to purchase goods and services."
>
> The gaming association's research . . . found 135,000 people are directly employed in the industry, and indirect gambling-related

employment such as food and entertainment services swells the total to 267,000 full-time jobs . . .

[Association president William Rutsey says,] "It is now demonstrably clear how the majority of spending in the industry goes directly back to Canadians in the form of paycheques, construction in communities, and revenues for the programs and services and charities that we value." (Canadian Press 2008)

A more recent article in the *Toronto Star*, cited in the July 2011 issue of *Canadian Gaming Business*, has highlighted the great financial contribution that gambling has made, and continues to make, to Ontario's economy:

The Ontario Lottery and Gaming Corporation [OLG] has reported revenues of $6.7 billion for the 2010–2011 fiscal year, resulting in a $2.068 billion profit—the largest take for the province since 2003.

In a recent press conference, OLG chair Paul Godfrey said this level of contribution was "unique among provincial agencies, boards, and commissions," and that proceeds would be going towards provincial schools, charities, amateur sports and culture.

OLG's new president, Rod Phillips, was also on hand to congratulate the agency's staff for contributing to the successful year, saying, "Management and employees set clear targets for providing measurable improvements to our business (and) they . . . exceeded them." (*Canadian Gaming Business* 2011)

At the same time, the gambling industry has promoted an image of gambling that is fun, exciting, and often dashingly naughty. The international gambling centre, Las Vegas, has championed the idea that "what happens in Vegas, stays in Vegas." This slogan suggests that any secret mischief can be "left behind" after your vacation. Nobody will find out, for example, if you went to bed late, ate too much, drank too much, smoked too much, or slept with someone other than your usual partner. Gambling, by definition, is a game of chance and the Las Vegas slogan suggests that life should (occasionally) be a game of chance too. It suggests that people—in gambling and in life—might do well to sometimes take exciting chances and try to beat the odds.

Thanks to aggressive advertising and marketing, gambling has become an overwhelmingly popular pastime for many North Americans (Ladouceur 1996; Shaffer, Hall, and Vanderbilt 1999; Canadian Partnership for Responsible Gambling 2007). Yet this expansion of interest in and access to gambling has led to a corresponding increase in concern about the health issues associated with gambling (Currie et al. 2006).

Gambling has become a public health issue in the sense that it has social causes and harms the health of many people. Gambling is more than the expression of personal taste, individual psychopathology, or genetic inclination. It is a behaviour that is learned socially through observation and experimentation in social surroundings, influenced by the examples set by social role models. Often, as we will see later, people first learn the essentials of gambling within their families during childhood.

Family life is a significant source of learning and encouragement for many gamblers and, as it turns out, a key risk factor for later problem gambling. Families supply beliefs about gambling and reward or punish would-be gamblers. Cultures encourage gambling when they portray it as an activity that tests skill, courage, luckiness, or intelligence. (Cultures may also discourage gambling by viewing it as foolish or wasteful.)

Currently, mass media advertising supplements cultural messages with positive images of gambling. So to understand a person's gambling—and even his or her problems with gambling—we have to understand both the family and socio-cultural messages the person brings to a gambling event. Failure to consider these contributions makes therapy and behaviour change significantly more difficult.

Just as gambling has social causes, it also has social (and health) effects for families and communities. As we will see, gamblers can lose in many ways when they play the odds at games of chance. Many who took part in our study suffered disastrous financial losses at the track, the poker table, the bingo hall, or the slot machine—and they lost much more than money. Imagine children growing up in a household in which mom or dad periodically loses the month's grocery money. Imagine a husband or wife who suddenly finds that the family bank account has been emptied, the house has been mortgaged, or the children's college savings have been spent.

It is difficult for most people to imagine the precariousness of life with a problem gambler. These gamblers are financially out of control; every day they risk everything their family has worked for years to earn, save, and buy. Many spouses feel powerless as their partner steals family money or pawns family possessions to gamble. Some families must sell their homes and move to rented accommodations because a parent has created more debt than they can carry. Some families live as "afterthoughts"—second priorities after gambling. Occasionally, partners get fed up and leave the gambler to protect themselves and their children.

This book gives voice to gamblers and their families who have faced these situations. Their stories, in their own words, show that excessive gambling can cut a wide swath of destruction through families, careers, relationships, and future prospects. For these reasons, problem gambling becomes deeply important to the community, as does the fact that it is growing. As a society, we neglect these problems at our peril. Further, we shouldn't suppose that the people most directly affected can solve the problems on their own. Often the people most at risk are least able to protect themselves.

This book takes a mainly sociological approach to problem gambling. Up to now, much of the social science research on gambling has taken a psychological approach: it has focused on the thoughts, emotions, and behaviours of problem gambling, without considering their social milieu. For example, some researchers have viewed problem gambling as the product of cognitive distortions—errors in thinking—about the likelihood of winning and the merits of chasing losses. Related cognitive-behavioural counselling has encouraged gamblers to think and act differently, whatever their personal inclinations. This psychological model of behaviour change places the onus for "responsible gambling" on the shoulders of the particular gambler. Many policy-makers, industry representatives, and the public seem to share this viewpoint, and it is reflected in everything from government gaming policies to treatment and prevention programs.

Notably missing from gambling research is a sociological perspective. Sociology goes beyond an analysis of just the individual to include the social context in which the gambler is embedded. Its underlying logic is that, even in instances when the act of gambling is solitary (as with online gambling or video lottery terminals [VLTs]), the results echo throughout the gambler's social network. And since people's gambling influences the lives of those around them, the reverse is a possibility: people around the gambler may exert influence on their attitudes and habits.

The Lure of Gambling

Almost everyone gambles at some time or another—if not with bets at a racetrack, at a casino, or online, then with lottery tickets, real estate transactions, or risky stock buys. People gamble for various reasons and in various ways. Mainly, they gamble to make money without investing much effort.

 Why do people gamble? Because, given the choice, most people would rather gain money quickly and easily. They dream of winning a lot of money, just by luck. Most people would love to win a large pot of money and be without financial constraints on where and how they live. Gambling dangles that promise before our eyes.

That is not to say there is no psychological or psychiatric component to problem gambling; we know there is from the Pathways Model cited earlier. However, problem gambling has many components: cultural, social, psychological, chemical, and even genetic. Statistically, each has some explanatory power. However, therapeutically, each contributes little to the prevention or cure of problem gambling, and more research is needed. All we can say with certainty is that many factors contribute to a general understanding of problem gambling, and researchers need to study them all. But we must not allow social and cultural factors to get lost in the mix. These social and cultural factors are things we can manipulate and control, if we (as a society) want to.

The people who graduate from gambling to problem gambling are betting their lives—their incomes, jobs, marriages, friendships, and even health—on winning a lot of money, just by luck. In short, this book hopes to make a difference by focusing on social and cultural factors that we can discuss and engineer through legislation.

The Idea of an Addiction

What do we mean by addiction? We are used to hearing, and even using, the word *addiction* to refer to behaviour that is uncontrollable, repeated or frequent, socially disapproved of, and possibly harmful. For example, people talk about alcohol addiction and alcoholics (who are alcohol addicts) or drug addiction and drug addicts as people who cannot stay away from alcohol or drugs, even though these substances are harming their bodies and their social relationships.

More recently, we have started to hear about other addictions that describe socially censured behaviours, such as sex, shopping, Internet, or eating addictions. So far, there has been too little research on any of these topics to discuss them here, and it is unclear whether they should even be included in a chapter on addictions.

Perhaps they are not addictions but habits, hobbies, minor sins, or what people used to call "personal weaknesses." By calling them *addictions*, we give them a medical label and imply that they are as important as other behaviours labelled addictive, which perhaps suggests that they should be dealt with medically. Besides, even if we think these are symptoms that can be "treated," we wonder whether they should be called *addictions* or *obsessions*, terms which imply a different set of symptoms and treatments.

These questions are especially pressing for problem gambling, which has come closest to proving itself as a new important form of addiction (Griffiths 2009a). The medical definition of addiction, based on criteria used by the American Psychiatric Association (DSM-IV) and the World Health Organization (ICD-10), has seven criteria (see Table 1-2). (The Diagnostic and Statistical Manual [DSM] describes the identifying

Table 1-2   Aspects of Addictive Behaviour

- **Tolerance**
  Has your use of drugs or alcohol increased over time?
- **Desire to cut down**
  Have you sometimes thought about cutting down or controlling your use? Have you ever made unsuccessful attempts to cut down or control your use?
- **Withdrawal**
  When you stop using, have you ever experienced physical or emotional withdrawal? Have you had any of the following symptoms: irritability, anxiety, shakes, sweats, nausea, or vomiting?
- **Difficulty controlling your use**
  Do you sometimes use more or for a longer time than you would like? Do you sometimes drink to get drunk? Do you usually stop after a few drinks, or does one drink lead to more drinks?
- **Negative consequences**
  Have you continued to use even though there have been negative effects to your mood, self-esteem, health, job, or family?
- **Putting off or neglecting activities**
  Have you ever put off or reduced social, recreational, work, or household activities because of your use?
- **Spending significant time or emotional energy**
  Have you spent a significant amount of time getting, using, hiding, planning, or recovering from your use? Have you spent a lot of time thinking about using? Have you ever hidden or minimized your use? Have you ever thought of schemes to avoid getting caught?

Source: Melemis n.d.

Credit: http://www.AddictionsAndRecovery.org; *I Want to Change My Life: How to Overcome Anxiety, Depression and Addiction* by S.M. Melemis

features and favoured treatments for a very large number of mental illnesses; it is aimed at the medical and therapeutic community but is widely known outside that community because of its important cultural assumptions and practical consequences.)

Deciding whether a person has an alcohol or drug addiction, therefore, requires asking and answering questions in only seven categories.

A person answering "yes" to questions in three or more of the categories shown in Table 1-2 meets the medical definition of addiction. As we have seen, researchers use a similar instrument to detect gambling addiction. Note, however, that in the definition outline in Table 1-2 there is nothing about how often a person uses the drug or alcohol. The issue is whether people have trouble controlling their use, and whether there are negative effects whenever they use the substance.

Why is addiction a social problem? Alternatively, what turns this personal trouble into a public issue? In part, the answer is that the social effects of addiction—whether by drugs, alcohol, or (as we will see) gambling—are extensive. For example, gambling can result in broken families, poor health outcomes for addicts and their loved ones, lost days at work, and a cost for treating and "fixing" the addicts. In addition, crime and safety issues are created.

Broadening out from a purely medical, psychiatric, or psychological understanding of addiction, we can take a sociological or public health approach. Then, we can see there are *social causes of addiction* that turn this personal trouble into a public issue. Whereas the medical approach focuses attention on the addicted individual and his or her personal pathology, the sociological and public health approaches focus on social forces that increase the risk that certain people, or groups, will develop addictions (Hammersley and Reid 2002). This point of view argues that we need to understand what it is about our society, and our social policies, that promote harmful, addictive behaviour, and how we can change society to reduce these risks.

There are factors in our society, our communities, and our families that predispose people to gambling problems. However, before we look at these factors, let us formally define and measure problem gambling. Gradually, researchers have developed a sociology of problem gambling that takes into account not only genetic, chemical, and psychological aspects of the problem, but also social causes and consequences. In this book, we will touch briefly on many of these sociological issues; a brief history of this approach can be found in the seminal paper "Sociologies of Problem Gambling" by Bo J. Bernhard and Frederick W. Preston (2007), both sociologists at the University of Nevada, Las Vegas campus.

A central concern of the sociology of problem gambling is the cultural and institutional framework, including advertising of the practice. Gambling has become a major global industry in the last 20 years, and it continues to grow rapidly (Moodie and Hastings 2009). Gambling is advertised everywhere as a source of fun and recreation. Yet, as we will see, it is universally associated with social, psychological, and health problems. The problems, and connections between problems, we discuss in this book are not restricted to Canada. Indeed, a recent book by Sam Skolnik, *High Stakes: The Rising Cost of America's Gambling Addiction* (2011), makes similar points about problem gambling in the United States and about the US government's investment in maintaining, or at least permitting, this problem to grow.

Features in society and the gambling environment contribute to gambling problems. These include game features—for example, features in the design of slot machines or VLTs (such as speed, noise, and flashing lights)—that get us to bet more than we planned. These features also include advertising and other mass media messages that shape our views about gambling and normalize it, making gambling seem cool, fun, and desirable (L. Valentine 2008). They include the widespread and growing availability of gambling in casinos and online, twenty-four hours a day, seven days a week. And they include casino promotions and incentives, such as free buses to the casino, free meals and drinks, and even free hotel rooms and other perquisites for high rollers who play (and lose) often. We will discuss this environment—and its associated cultural values and social institutions—throughout this book.

A social approach to gambling does not deny the importance of psychological factors in gambling behaviour. A large body of research has identified links between gambling and mood disorders, including depression, anxiety, and bipolar disorder (Di Nicola et al. 2010), which suggests there are genetic bases to problem gambling, as there are to these mood disorders. Equally, research has found that problem gambling, more often than by chance, is found among people who are impulsive or display anti-social behaviour, who drink too much, who are lonely or socially isolated, or who display excessive or inappropriate anger.

However, the psychological model of behaviour change places a burden of "responsible gambling" squarely on the shoulders of the individual gambler. It neglects the role of advertising, for example. Would we allow auto makers to advertise that their cars easily break the speed limit, thereby encouraging drivers to do so? Or encourage distillers to advertise that their alcoholic beverages help drinkers get drunk and rowdy more quickly than other beverages? To do so would be socially risky. Yet, gambling advertisements routinely encourage people to risk their money on very unlikely gambles, on the supposition that risking money is fun and sexy. The advertisers—both private and public—know that the majority of gamblers will lose most of their money; nonetheless, we permit such advertising. The problem governments face is determining how they can keep encouraging such behaviour so they can continue to reap the profits.

As Cosgrave (2010, 113) notes in an important new paper on the topic, "Embedded Addiction: The Social Production of Gambling Knowledge and the Development of Gambling Markets":

> While gambling expansion is predicted on the provision of "entertainment," and where gambling is marketed as the consumption of safe risks, there is also the possibility of risky consumption and the production of problem gamblers . . . The risks posed by the problematic gambler (e.g., to "state-owned gambling enterprises") must be solved to enable the legitimation of markets and the ongoing quest for profits/revenues.

Accordingly, in the next chapter, we will consider the view of gambling that is promoted by our mass media—a view that is complicit in the promotion of behaviour that, in many instances, leads to addiction and distress.

Chapter 2

Gambling in a Historical Perspective: Canada and the World

Do all "normal" people gamble in the same way? Are gambling problems unique to our own society? The answer to both these broad and important questions is no. It is precisely for this reason that we need to understand gambling—and problem gambling—as a cultural phenomenon that varies over time and from one society to another.

What follows is a brief, selective, and necessarily superficial look at the history of gambling. This section's goal is to whet the reader's interest in learning more about the history of this long-standing human practice and to situate current Canadian gambling practices (and beliefs) in a larger human context. For a more detailed account of this important topic, see David G. Schwartz's *Roll the Bones: The History of Gambling* (2006).

People gamble in all societies, but they gamble in different ways. Betting games have existed since the earliest of times in all cultures, but these games—their rules and skill levels, for example—have varied over time (Kulig and MacKinnon 2005). Gambling is a multicultural phenomenon that has evolved through history. As long ago as the 1600s, a casino opened in Venice, Italy, named Casini (Kulig and MacKinnon 2005). Whether the buildings where gambling occurs are called casinos, Casinis, or even Kasinos (as in Indonesia), they all operate in the same way and include common elements.

One similar element of gambling throughout many cultures is chance. In games of pure chance, physical skill and strategy play no role in deciding the game's outcome. Dice games, roulette, and bingo are three games whose outcomes rely solely on randomness—the "roll of the dice." They appeal to people because the game's uncertain outcome mirrors the uncertainty of life itself. Reith suggests that games of chance are especially appealing in large, complex societies such as our own. By voluntarily engaging in these games, modern players can gain some small measure of influence by at least choosing the arena in which their chances will play out. They may not be able to control fate, but they can choose which game to play and where to play it.

Chance can also be involved in games of strategy, such as mah-jong and poker. Roberts, Arth, and Bush (1959) assert that these types of games also mimic the social world of the people who play them. They are considered forms of gambling if money is bet on the result, since there is an element of chance—as well as skill and strategy—in each of these games.

Games of strategy simulate the complexity and calculated nature of social life—for example, of military combat. Societies with games of strategy may not be advanced industrial societies, but they will typically have advanced subsistence patterns, sophisticated technology, and high levels of political integration, judiciary organization, social layering, and labour specialization (Sutton-Smith and Roberts 1970). In other words, they are built on the notion of complexity and planning.

Most games played in large, complex societies such as our own mix chance and strategy. Take the game of football, for example, which combines strategy and chance with great physical skill. Gamblers recognize the element of chance or luck inherent in a football game, yet often approach the game with a strategy in mind. In some games involving chance, such as poker, strategy plays a significant role. Winning at poker depends to some degree on chance (i.e., the "luck of the draw"); however, depending on the variant played, strategy—in the form of selectively bluffing, folding, or drawing cards—also plays an important part in winning.

Another common element in gambling is a preoccupation with winning and losing. Schwartz (1977) likens the Western attitude toward games to its attitude toward business. The media often compares the activities of businesspeople to games that can be "won." Think of the following often-used business saying: "It's a zero-sum game; somebody wins, somebody loses." Despite its stated concern with rationality and merit, our society is fascinated and seduced by the appeal of luck and the need to win.

A Brief History of Gambling:
From Pre-industrial Communal Societies
to the Pre-modern Period

As far as we know, people have always gambled. Early games of chance took the form of casting lots and dice. The Babylonians, the Etruscans, and the ancient Chinese all played gambling games. Flipping a coin, possibly the simplest game of chance known today, began with the ancient Greeks. *Bones*, a slang term for dice, originates from *astragali*, the knucklebones of sheep and cows, which were used in primitive gambling games. Early players of games of chance saw the game's outcome as evidence of their deity's existence. In short, they attributed social, cultural, and occasionally even spiritual meanings to the chance outcomes of games and contests. All of these interpretations were socially constructed, in the sense that the players invented interpretations that were culturally meaningful at that particular time and place.

Equally important was the social role played by gambling. This role is obvious when we examine the practices of gambling in pre-industrial, preliterate, or primitive societies today. Naturally, these societies are pale reflections of the way people in small preliterate communities may have gambled thousands of years ago. However, they suggest the diversity and social significance of gambling.

While gambling for many in the Western world has become a pursuit motivated mainly by idle pleasure or monetary gain, other cultures continue to engage in games of chance for entirely different reasons. Consider the gambling attitudes and behaviours of the tribal Gende people in Papua New Guinea, where card playing is serious business. Some games last only a few hours, while others last an entire week. In this community, gambling contributes "to a more equitable distribution of cash throughout the community" and participants are as concerned to "decrease *relative* income differences between themselves and others as they [are] to increase their gross income" (Zimmer 1986, 247; emphasis in original).

With few cash crops available, little revenue flows into the community. Given this harsh and unstable economy, Gende card playing has become an innovative exchange system that redistributes cash throughout the community to lessen income differences. The exchange of winnings through gambling also ensures that social relationships are reinforced and debts repaid. Nobody ever really loses in a Gende card game, because no one associates losing the game with losing money. Once money is introduced into the game, there are no longer any legitimate claims to it. Simply put, all participants play for the available money and as they keep playing, the money is redistributed to those who need it.

As hunter-gatherer societies changed gradually over thousands of years to feudal societies through the development of agriculture, gambling began to serve different purposes. Yet some common elements remain. Gambling, for example, remained a primarily social activity, played face to face with other people. It was seen as a leisure activity for all (Reith 2007). It continues to have a social and cultural meaning, even if that meaning is no longer the same as it was in communal, tribal societies.

What makes gambling different in feudal societies is, first, the overlay of multiple cultural traditions: Christian and pre-Christian, Eastern and Western. Second and more important is the development of social stratification or layering: feudal societies, though primitive by modern standards, are much more differentiated than tribal societies. They contain multiple social classes, and people in these societies are preoccupied with living up to their social status.

For example, over time, gambling in court society (especially in France) became more than a mere opportunity to display one's noble character and indifference to money; it was a firm social expectation. What mattered above all else were one's actions during a game and one's reaction to the outcome. Winning, after all, was evidence of one's superior skill, and so winning was better than losing. However, winning was thought honourable only if certain conditions were met: a player must never win by cheating and, more importantly, must never gamble for material gain. Losing, meanwhile, was no source of shame, since it provided more opportunity to display a player's social graces than winning. Losing money graciously showed a healthy indifference toward money. Since debts incurred through gambling were not legally binding in seventeenth-century France, payment relied solely on the integrity of the debt-holder's code of honour. Therefore, paying a debt on time revealed one's good character.

King Louis XIV of France, or "The Sun King" as he was known, occasionally paid off the debts of those who gambled and lost in his court (Kavanagh 1994, 37). The not-so-implicit message from king to courtier was: "Money is no concern for people like us. Lose it all, gain it all back—it matters little either way." Louis XIV's court at Versailles was so feverishly taken over by all sorts of players that the palace itself became known as *ce tripot* ("the gambling den"; Reith 2002, 65).

The aristocratic gambling spectacle was not limited to French nobility. It was practised by aristocrats wherever feudalism continued to hold sway over the commercial (and then industrial) middle classes. Another example is nineteenth-century Russia, which in many respects copied pre-revolutionary France. There, poet Aleksandr Pushkin and many other writers loved to gamble, and they wrote at length about gambling. The most famous literary example is Fyodor Dostoevsky's novel *The Gambler*, which is about a young tutor employed by a formerly wealthy Russian general. Dostoevsky's own addiction to roulette was in many ways the inspiration for this book, which he completed under a strict deadline in order to pay off gambling debts. For a detailed account of gambling in nineteenth-century Russia, the reader is directed to what has quickly become the classic work on this topic: *The High Stakes of Identity: Gambling in the Life and Literature of Nineteenth-Century Russia* by Ian M. Helfant (2002).

Seventeenth-century England, however, was significantly different from pre-revolutionary France and Russia. In England, a much more dramatic growth in the social significance of commerce and science brought the new middle class to prominence and power. Though gambling had been a popular pastime through most of recorded history in England, it became an obsession in the 1600s, and took on particular social meaning. Suddenly, gambling was everywhere. The interest in games of chance was higher, the amounts wagered larger, and the condemnation of gambling more violent than ever before.

Three discrete but interrelated types of gambling became prominent in England, and some other parts of Europe, during this time: (1) speculating in economic ventures; (2) gambling on games of chance; and (3) betting between individuals (Reith 2002). To understand this spurt in gambling, we must look to the rapidly growing mercantile economy.

As wealth increased among the new middle class, people had more opportunities to take part in the games of chance once reserved for the nobility. As well, people came to see parallels between making money in commercial ventures—an activity with its own inherent risks—and making money through games of chance. As mentioned earlier, betting between individuals also became popular. Almost any incident whose outcome contained some element of chance provided the opportunity for a wager. Some bets were ridiculous (for example, in 1735, the Count de Buckeburg bet that he could ride backwards on a horse from London to Edinburgh), while others were morbid (such as betting on when people would die). However, most betting was trivial and focused on the details of daily life. Anyone struck with the sudden urge to bet could easily find or devise an event to bet on, as well as someone to bet against.

The start of gambling as a widespread cultural practice in the seventeenth century encouraged the commercialization of games of chance in the years to follow. Gambling as a source of recreation for the working class, and as a money-making industry, had come to stay. Meanwhile, the common folk gambled mainly for entertainment and occasionally for the chance to earn some quick money, though the bourgeoisie condemned gambling as a horrible social ill distracting the masses from more fruitful pursuits.

As the Industrial Revolution spread across Europe, its characteristic bourgeois class gained power and influence. With the bourgeoisie embracing money as the most valued thing in business society, members of the old nobility tried to distinguish themselves from the social classes below by implementing a crackdown on gambling.

Gradually, in Europe, tolerant gambling attitudes began to come to an end, even among the aristocracy. In England, the nineteenth-century Victorian era had strict moral and religious codes of conduct that fostered an atmosphere of condemnation of social vices, especially against engaging in games of chance. Gambling stood directly opposed to the principles and values championed by the Victorian middle class.

Upper-class women gamblers in particular were singled out for criticism, since they undermined the Victorian ideal of the virtuous and pious woman. Men addicted to gambling were portrayed publicly as weak, undisciplined rogues who had abandoned their duties to family and society. Women problem gamblers were portrayed even more severely, as having betrayed not only society but their own better nature as well.

Munting (1989) suggests that the abolition of English state lotteries in 1826 marked the shift in official gambling attitudes from one of vague disapproval to one of harsh denunciation. Certainly, this effort reflected a growing public view that gambling was to be shunned. There was a concern then that the poorer ranks of society were especially vulnerable to the dark side of gambling. This paternalistic attitude toward the lower classes repeats itself throughout the history of gambling regulation.

Several acts were introduced in the mid-nineteenth century to lessen the prevalence of gambling, acts which primarily targeted the working class. The first act, in 1845, removed gambling debts—mainly because of bets on horse racing—from legal enforcement. While this act was intended in part to decrease street gambling, it inadvertently encouraged it, as well as the development of betting offices. The second act, in 1853, attempted to mend this mistake, forbidding the operation of betting houses. In response, more gambling moved to the streets, and permanent or temporary betting houses commenced their operations.

So even as the government made concerted efforts to curb gambling among the working class, England witnessed the birth of a full-scale commercial gambling enterprise. Itzkowitz (1988, 8) calls the industry of gambling a "very Victorian institution," by which he likely means that every public effort was made to (appear to) do the right thing, while people secretly continued doing what pleased them. In time, gambling would become a central part of working-class leisure (McKibbin 1979), and street bookmakers would be viewed by their peers and community as hard-working, upstanding entrepreneurs (Itzkowitz 1988). This was, indeed, the beginning of the modern age of gambling, though contemporaries did not know this at the time.

Gambling in the Modern Era: Commercialization and Expansion

To understand how gambling changed from a diffuse and local pastime into an organized, government-regulated, national industry, we must consider the place where large-scale gambling first occurred: the racetrack. Betting on horse races was the first true form of organized mass gambling.

As we have seen, betting and gambling of all sorts have taken place throughout history. Placing wages on racing dates as far back as the Roman era, when betting on chariot races was common across the empire. However, in Roman times, gambling was mainly a local event, for technological and practical reasons.

Larger gambling spectacles had to await the development of much larger, more complex forms of organization. In the nineteenth century, alongside early industrialism and urbanization, racetrack betting became the most popular form of gambling in the Victorian era. Unlike public betting houses and street betting, racecourse gambling had not been made illegal. Then, the arrival of the railway transformed horse racing, just as it transformed so much else. Trains could convey horses, owners, spectators, and punters from one racetrack to the next. Meets could be organized into annual schedules. Major races with large prize winnings and other high-profile events that were sure to attract audiences (and profits) from everywhere could be organized and widely advertised. As a result, the number of active racehorses doubled between 1837 and 1869. By 1845, a mass gambling industry was clearly developing around horse racing.

Turning from the racetrack gambling operation to the bettors who supported it, we find once more the class-based double standard that has long characterized the gambling public. Working-class gamblers in the late Victorian era were usually the target of legislation on gambling between the 1850s and the 1950s, rather than the middle and upper classes, partly because people from the middle and upper classes were the ones making the laws.

Most of the working classes placed their bets through bookmakers. Since doing so was illegal and unmonitored, it is difficult to describe beyond anecdotal accounts the gambling habits of the working classes, and it is impossible to know exactly how many gambled on horse races. However, several modern observers have suggested that gambling, along with alcohol and tobacco use, likely played a significant part in their leisure lives (see McKibbin 1979; Itzkowitz 1988; Clapson 1991; Davies 1991).

Yet critics remained ignorant of the actual gambling behaviours and attitudes of the working classes. A study by the Royal Commission found that most ready-money bettors who placed wagers through illegal bookmakers staked paltry sums compared with better-off participants. The poor were more likely to save their winnings than to gamble them away. It seems what enraged the opponents of gambling by the lower ranks was the public nature of their gambling.

The contradiction here was that the middle class never denied with any real conviction their own interest and participation in gambling. Most of the spectators at the racetrack were of middle-class origins; working-class punters stuck to bookmakers on the streets. Educated and wealthy bettors also had at their disposal a network of subscription betting houses that accepted wagers on credit. When all else failed, they could take their business to illegal street bookmakers. In accepting bets from customers, bookmakers did not distinguish among social classes (Huggins 2000). Thus, the middle class, despite their constant emphasis on respectability and honesty, were hardly models of virtue when it came to gambling. Inflated and falsified odds, insider tips, and rigged races remained common features of horse racing, and illegal gambling continued to benefit the upper-class owners and bettors.

In the end, the public's overwhelming interest in gambling would prove too much for the government. Changing social attitudes toward work, leisure, play, money, and religion all played important roles in the legitimization of gambling. As a result, today we are surrounded by legal gambling. In England, Canada, and throughout the economically developed Western world, there remain links between gambling and class. Scratch-and-win tickets and lottery ticket sellers, for example, are much more readily available in working-class communities than in more well-off neighborhoods (Nibert 2000).

As we have seen, people's attitudes about gambling have changed throughout history. Even though it is an acceptable and inevitable part of Canadian culture, many Canadians still believe that gambling may be more harmful than beneficial. Campbell and Smith (2003) note that gambling has always been a tenuous activity in terms of public acceptability; however, attempts have been made to soften public perceptions. The public has come to accept it, but whether or not they see it as contributing positively to greater society is still in question.

Often governments have tried to limit gambling, even while aristocrats set a contrary example by gambling to extremes. This conflict of attitudes has also characterized gambling in Canada. As we shall see, the British debate about gambling—and the role of the government in gambling—has continued throughout Canadian history.

Gambling in Canadian History

From Confederation to the end of the nineteenth century, gambling in Canada was surrounded by an aura of moral and legal uncertainty (Campbell and Smith 2003).

Consider the reasons for this: Canada has several social and cultural features that have given it a unique history of gambling and gambling legislation. First, it has a British and French heritage, which means that cultural traditions of gambling—and thinking about gambling—are rooted in pre-nineteenth-century European conceptions and concerns. However, Canada was never a feudal society, so its cultural values have been shaped mainly by middle-class commercial and industrial values.

Second, Canada has always been a nation of immigrants, so it has always had to grapple with widely differing ideas about gambling. As John Porter showed in his sociological classic *The Vertical Mosaic* (1965), ethnic immigrant differences overlapped with class differences in Canada. As a result, much of the discussion about gambling in Canada conflated prejudices against immigrants (including prejudices against non-Christians and non-white people) with prejudices against poor and working-class people already evident in Britain and other parts of Europe.

Third, Canada, like the United States, was settled through the seizure of a vast, ever-extending western frontier. Early settlers in Canada were mainly young men, out to claim land or profit by extracting natural resources. These young men in new frontier areas posed particular problems of social control largely unknown in Europe. Here, problems associated with drinking, prostitution, violence—and gambling—flourished. In the United States, institutions to bring law and order developed locally, one community at a time. In Canada, these institutions were controlled centrally by the government in Ottawa, the Royal Canadian Mounted Police (RCMP; formerly the North West Mounted Police [NWMP]), the banks and industrialists in Toronto and Montreal (and London and New York), and by the established churches.

Thus, gambling in Canada has a long, historic relationship with the State and the Church that is unlike those found in the United States, Britain, or France. And the sheer variety of competing interests (and beliefs and prejudices) around gambling has ensured a continued debate about the merits of gambling, and what to do about problems associated with gambling.

Throughout Canada's history, two facts about gambling have remained constant. First, gambling has always been a popular and widely enjoyed pastime. In 1497, John Cabot found a First Nations population that played various games of chance that had social meanings that were important to the spiritual, emotional, mental, and physical development of Aboriginal nations. (For more on the role of gambling among Aboriginal peoples, see the work of Yale Belanger [e.g., his books *First Nations Gaming in Canada*, *Gambling with the Future: The Evolution of Aboriginal Gaming in Canada*, and *Toward an Innovative Understanding of North American Indigenous Gaming in Historical Perspective*].)

Second, the laws on gambling and their enforcement have often been ambiguous and irregular. Gambling has never been completely illegal. However, what legislators defined as legal has changed over time. Also, public attitudes toward games of chance have varied over time and across regional, socio-cultural, economic, and ethnic lines. Today, the rights and opportunities to gamble are far more extensive than ever before in Canadian history.

Canada's earliest gambling laws evolved from the country's British roots, beginning in 1388 when the English monarch banned all games except archery for fear of losing his skilled archers to "idle games of dice" (Glickman 1979). However, even in Britain, people's legal rights to gamble varied over time, from place to place, and from class to class. What's more, there, as in Canada, people gambled even when it was not legal.

When the Criminal Code of Canada was enacted in 1892, public gambling was officially outlawed, with only a few exceptions. The most glaring exception to Canada's legal policy on gambling was the provision allowing organized betting to take place at government-chartered racetracks. In Canada, as elsewhere, the elite enjoyed betting on horses, an aristocratic activity with echoes of the old military mode of war in which cavalry mattered. Given that Canada's Criminal Code evolved from the British statute and common law imported through colonization, it is no surprise that the values and ideas of the old country continued to flourish legislatively.

Despite the legislation, gambling in Canada continued, legally and illegally. People of different social classes bet on different games in different settings. Gambling of one sort or another could be found in every part of society, a fact that is well-documented in an excellent social history of gambling in Canada by historian Suzanne Morton (2003).

Gambling practices were strongly distinguished by social class, both in type and visibility. People with power, standing, and influence—mainly white Anglo-Saxon middle-class men—found ways to justify their indulgence in the eyes of the law, as with horse racing and private men's clubs. Those lacking these resources—the working class, ethnic minorities, and, to some extent, women—were forced to exercise secrecy and caution, and remain vigilant against the occasional police crackdown.

The opposition to gambling came from several directions. Many from the business community expressed concern that gambling houses lured recreation-seekers away from more legitimate settings such as movie theatres. Others scorned gambling because it violated the fundamental principles of Canada's emerging capitalist free market economy, which celebrated the virtues of labour, enterprise, and merit.

Most arguments, however, were moralistic rather than economic, emerging from the Protestant beliefs of the Anglo-Saxon middle class. This religious tradition placed a high value on hard work, delayed satisfaction, and humble pleasures. Many in positions of power in Canada, born into this moral background, questioned the work ethic and moral virtue of the common labourer. They believed working-class people rejected conventional social norms in preference for the thrills and promises of instant fortunes offered by gambling games.

Many antigambling advocates—most of whom were white Canadians with a northern European ancestry—associated gambling problems with ethnicity. Racial and ethnic stereotypes often accompanied condemnations of gambling. So scornful attitudes toward gambling often reflected popular views about Canada's immigration policies and various minority groups as much as they expressed views about gambling behaviour. When it came to gambling, there was clearly a social double standard.

Liberalism, as well as Protestantism and capitalism, shaped the political culture of Canada's early history and Canadians' attitudes toward gambling. Liberalism was like Protestantism in its opposition to gambling—at least at this stage. Both sets of ideas encouraged self-discipline rather than state intervention. Both held that self-control and personal responsibility were central to a well-functioning society. As a result, the average Canadian was assailed by moral ideas rooted in Protestantism, capitalism, and liberalism that laid the blame for poverty, weakness, and impropriety at the feet of individuals themselves. It was the job of individuals to avoid causing themselves and others economic or social problems. As such, gambling was considered a personal matter and a personal vice.

Clergy and moral reformers put themselves at the forefront of the antigambling movement in the nineteenth and early twentieth centuries. They stirred up public fears with claims that gambling, already stigmatized, was spiralling out of control and threatening the basic social institutions of family, religion, and community. For much of the twentieth century, this ideology informed the central arguments put forward by Canada's antigambling advocates.

Ethnicity and gambling

Throughout the history of gambling in Canada, we see evidence of discriminatory attitudes against poor minority groups. In the white male Protestant-dominated debate on gambling of the nineteenth and twentieth centuries, criticisms were levelled against those groups considered to be of low social status, chiefly Roman Catholics and racial and ethnic minorities.

Strict Protestants—for example, Calvinists—took a hardline stance against gambling, declaring it a violation of an individual's responsibilities toward work and family. "It undermined the protestant work ethic and threatened the accumulation of wealth that formed the basis of capitalist societies" (Reith 2007, 34). Further, Protestant objections were codified into law, because Protestants were the dominant social and religious group in (English) Canada. Gambling and gamblers were thought to be a threat to the Protestant ethic and all that it represented (Campbell and Smith 2003). The Protestants based their lives around hard work and discipline, so the idea of gambling—which appeared to reward people for practically no work at all—demeaned their way of life.

By contrast, the Roman Catholic church, while not unanimously in favour of gambling, recognized their local parishioners' financial needs and conveniently turned a blind eye to bingo games and other chance-based fundraising. The continuing clashes between religious groups—especially between Protestants and Catholics—resulted in a low-level tension that permeated all levels of Canadian society and continued through the first half of the twentieth century. It is ironic that gambling was associated in the public mind with immigrant communities. In truth—whether legal or illegal—gambling was variously popular in all parts of Canadian society.

The relationship between gambling and ethnicity reflected larger issues about immigration and minority groups in the country. Like other New World countries populated first by colonialists and later by successive waves of immigrants, Canada has long grappled with its own history of institutional and popular discrimination against ethnic minority groups. At the root of Canada's problem was its long-standing preference for Nordic Protestant immigrants, which is reflected in Canada's history of immigration.

The group most associated with gambling in the early half of the twentieth century was made up of the Chinese, who first came to Canada in the mid-nineteenth century to build Canada's railroads. This stereotyping is evident in discussions of gambling from that time. "John Chinaman," the derisory name for the typical working-class Asian immigrant in Canada, was seen as a fanatical gambler, an opium fiend, a visitor of brothels, and a petty criminal. Such descriptions, as well as other factors, prompted Parliament to pass the Chinese Immigration Act in 1923, barring almost all Chinese people from coming to Canada (this act was repealed in 1947). Gambling, then, was associated with the hated Chinese immigrants and this ethnic stereotype added to the moral turpitude associated with gambling.

We cannot deny the Chinese community supported a gambling-friendly culture. Chance and fortune are central ideas in many Asian rituals and celebrations, and gambling as a recreation in China can be traced back millennia. Asian cultures are fascinated with the concepts of luck, fate, and chance, and consider gambling an accepted practice to be enjoyed with friends and families at various social events (Glionna 2006).

As well, demographic characteristics of the Chinese in Canada were also important. Economic and political discrimination prevented labourers from bringing their families over from China. As a result, the Chinese quarters in Canadian cities soon became bachelor communities, overflowing with unattached, working-age men with little to do for leisure except gamble, drink, and socialize with one another. The Canadian host population was therefore at least equally guilty of creating an environment in which gambling provided a rare outlet for marginalized foreigners (Morton 2003).

It is important to note that although most claims against minority groups are of a stereotypical nature, "there is some evidence that certain cultural groups are more vulnerable than others" to high rates of gambling and even problem gambling (Godot 2010, 3). The literature contains many discrepancies, but even today it suggests that indigenous groups in the United States, Canada, and New Zealand exhibit substantially higher rates of gambling than the general populations of those countries (Godot 2010).

Contrary to stereotypes, not all minority group members are confirmed gamblers, but it is also true that many minority group members *do* gamble, and they do so for various reasons. Two theories have been proposed as possible explanations for the relationship between gambling and ethnicity. One theory is that, because of barriers to opportunity, minorities are forced to seek out alternative—and occasionally illegitimate—avenues for achieving wealth, prestige, and other markers of success in life. The other theory is that marginal populations reject the core values of the dominant group. Their own subculture within the larger community evaluates gambling and other pleasures more sympathetically than Calvinist Protestantism.

There is support for both theories. Illegal gambling may indeed have been an important channel of upward mobility for new immigrants. Daniel Bell (1953) notes that American immigrant groups often advanced economically through entrepreneurial criminal activities. Consider the clichéd but relevant example of the Italian-American mobster—a mafioso—of the early and middle twentieth century. When legitimate business opportunities were hard to come by, enterprising members of some immigrant groups created their own businesses, building capital through crimes such as prostitution, gambling, bookmaking, and smuggling.

Deepak Chhabra (2007) examined the idea that ethnicity plays a significant role in determining some aspects of leisure behaviour—a topic we will return to in a later chapter. She focused on two theories, similar to those noted above: (1) the marginality theory, which postulates that black people face monetary constraints that restrict their ability to enjoy leisure time or afford certain things, and (2) the ethnicity theory, which states that minority racial groups have values and norms that are distinctive from the North American mainstream culture. Chhabra (2007) discovered an upward trend of nonwhite participation in casino gambling. Notably, in Alberta, the majority of patrons in the casino were black or Asian people. Overall, Chhabra found that more black people lost money in the several-hundred-and-above categories and participated more frequently than other gamblers; they also travelled farther to gamble.

We need to consider this kind of data suggestive, not conclusive. So far it has been impossible—too costly—to conduct a systematic, random sample survey to reliably document the influence of ethnic culture, or immigrant status, on people's gambling practices. However, the results of numerous studies point to a few likely conclusions. First, exclusion following immigration tends to promote gambling.

Groups excluded from lawful opportunities who are motivated toward criminal activities also had less encouragement to embrace the dominant group's culture and values. The Chinese, Jews, and other excluded minority groups had little stake in the dominant culture's view of gambling (Morton 2003, 110). If the values and institutions of Protestant and even Catholic Canada denigrated minority groups, minority groups had little reason to embrace these mainstream values and institutions.

Made "strange" by a hostile Canadian society, the Chinese were especially likely to play this role of stranger. One of the most enduring stereotypes about early Chinese immigrants was their unassimilable nature (Ward 1978). Life for the Chinese in Canada in the early half of the twentieth century was often rootless and transient. The Chinese Immigration Act was intended to control the foreign population in Canada, but it also hindered those Chinese people already here, keeping them from adopting Canadian values and identities.

Gambling was especially acceptable among the "strangers" in Canadian society—for example, the Chinese—who Canadians had kept at arm's length for generations. For them, gambling was symbolic of their rejection of mainstream Canadian culture. So gambling laws that were made in part to control strange, marginal, and excluded members of society ironically increased these people's lack of connection to the host society.

Changes in gambling attitudes and laws

In 1969, prohibitions on gambling in Canada were repealed and the government took a more permissive approach. At this time, the Criminal Code of Canada was amended to allow the provincial and federal governments to conduct lottery schemes, broadly defined as "games of chance." In 1985, the provinces consolidated control over gambling provision with an amendment giving them exclusive jurisdiction. Gambling was to be strictly licensed and regulated, not ignored and deplored. This new approach to gambling was consistent with an emerging new citizen ideal that supported pluralistic social, religious, and economic norms. With the secularization of Canadian society, even social and commercial activities on the Sabbath eventually became legal (Morton 2003, 169).

The new secularism was concerned with social inclusion and social justice, and this had implications for gambling. Fueling the new openness to gambling was a change in Canadian views on pleasure in general, and gambling in particular. With immigration continuing strongly throughout the twentieth century, colonial elites and their traditional Anglo-Saxon values no longer held sway in Canada's largest cities. The traditional status politics—that struggle between groups for prestige and social position around issues ostensibly connected with gambling—were no longer dominant. Staunch Protestant moral conservatism slowly gave way to pluralism and secular permissiveness.

Progressively pluralistic, secular values compelled the Canadian government to amend its policy on gambling, among other restricted activities. Official tolerance in turn led to even greater public acceptance.

The momentum of change would eventually lead to a widespread acceptability and availability of recreational and commercial gambling opportunities. Increasingly, the standard of acceptability for gambling, as for alcohol and other vices, was one of moderation. With widespread acceptance and participation in gambling, the government could also begin to use gambling as a revenue-generating tool.

Cosgrave and Klassen (2001) suggest that much of the trend toward legitimizing gambling was engineered by the governments themselves. The impetus for this, in their view, was economic: governments' need for revenue to pay for social services. Since direct taxing of citizens is always politically unpopular, the best thing to do is to convince the public to voluntarily give up their money. The establishment of a close connection between gambling and fundraising has been critical in swaying public and political opinion in favour of liberalized gambling laws in Canada and elsewhere (Morton 2003).

Thus, gambling has now been redefined by the State as a form of what Cosgrave and Klassen (2001, 8) call "productive leisure." This phrase refers to any adult play that offers amusement while producing revenue for governmental and political agencies. This revenue was the leading cause of the legalization of gambling. The government could increase revenue without extra taxation (Korn 2000). These authors observe that "the legalization of a variety of forms of gambling has contributed, at least tacitly, to the social acceptance of gambling activity, and for many citizens, lottery players and sports bettors for example, gambling has become a routine aspect of everyday life" (3).

The current state of legal gambling in Canada

Today, gambling has made the transition from prohibition to legalization. There is a greater responsibility and authority over gambling matters by the provincial government, with relaxed regulation (Campbell and Smith 2003).

Western societies have moved from industrial production economies toward those organized according to consumption and the provision of services (Reith 2007). As a result of this notion of consumption over production, Reith (2007) suggested that individuals are presented with a paradox: On the one hand, people are encouraged to consume and give in to self-fulfillment. On the other hand, they must exercise self-control and restraint.

In regard to gambling and consumption, the government legalized gambling institutions and promoted this social activity in hopes of gaining revenues; but, at the same time, it demanded responsible and self-regulating players. "The individual was responsible for his or her own fate at the tables" (Reith 2007, 40). Problem gambling seems to be a problem of inappropriate consumption, namely lack of control (Reith 2007). It appears that governments had assumed that changes to the gambling rules would produce an individual, who—given freedom—would be able to manage that freedom through self-control (Reith 2007).

Gambling in Canada's Aboriginal communities

Recent research in the field of gambling has noted the complexity of cultural variation in gambling behaviour. However, there is a dominant trend in the prevalence of problem gambling among Aboriginal communities. Smith and Wynne (2002) found that Aboriginal respondents showed a higher-than-average risk for developing a gambling problem. Other studies involving Aboriginal subjects have produced corroborating results, supporting the theory that problem gambling is a significant social issue in many Aboriginal populations (Wardman, el-Guebaly, and Hodgins 2001; see also Patton et al. 2002).

Historically, Aboriginal people gambled as a component of religious events and ceremonies (Kulig and MacKinnon 2005). Government-run gambling began in the Aboriginal community in 1984 when the Cree Nation at The Pas, Manitoba, held a federally sanctioned lottery. The first Aboriginal casino was the White Bear Casino in Saskatchewan, which opened in 1993 (Kulig and MacKinnon 2005). It is true that 10 to 15 percent of Aboriginal adults are problem gamblers, which is 3 to 4 percent higher than other ethnic groups. A study by Marshall and Wynne (2003) found that off-reserve Aboriginal gamblers were significantly more likely to be at risk (18 percent) of problem gambling than non-Aboriginal gamblers (6 percent). This is the case because many Aboriginal communities experience high rates of substance abuse and have lower-than-average levels of income and education.

Statistics from the Northwest Territories' 2002 Alcohol and Drug Survey show that among Aboriginals, who make up slightly less than half of the population in this territory, 50.8 percent gambled more than $20 per week, compared with 13.9 percent of non-Aboriginals (Northwest Territories Bureau of Statistics 2002). And, in Wynne's (2002) prevalence study of Saskatchewan gamblers, Aboriginal players were more likely than others to either already have a gambling problem or be at risk of developing one in the future.

Closing Remarks

We've seen how historical and anthropological research shows that in small, relatively classless societies, gambling has little economic, political, or moral significance. However, it has great social significance. By contrast, in feudal societies—which are marked by greater differences in social class and status—gambling is invested with noble qualities. There, it continues to have little economic significance but is used for self-display and contests with Lady Luck. The goal is not to redistribute wealth but to provide a continued context for social interaction and entertainment.

Meanwhile, in individualistic, commercial societies such as our own, gambling continues to give people a way to win a fortune or display courage and luck. Increasingly in our society, gambling has great economic and political, if not moral, significance. And increasingly, gambling here is solitary, not social.

This brief history of gambling in Canada recalls how gambling was prohibited or despised according to its connection with low-status immigrant groups, who gambled more openly than others (notably the Chinese immigrants of the early nineteenth century). However, today more people than ever gamble, regardless of ethnic ancestry. An increased access to gambling signifies not only a growth in Canadian rights and freedoms, but also a desire by governments to receive steady and significant funding from gambling profits.

Recent research also shows that certain social groups, particularly Canadian Aboriginals, appear to run higher risks of problem gambling. This fact poses an intellectual challenge for social researchers and a practical challenge for policy-makers. If research finds a need for legislation to oversee and control gambling, and to reduce risks of problem gambling, such legislation must be guided by systematic research. It must not grow out of racial prejudice, moral superiority, or class exclusivity, as it has through most of our country's history.

However, we would be wrong to view gambling as mainly or merely an activity of marginal, desperate, or disadvantaged people in search of money, though it is often that too. In his excellent recent collection of sociological writings on risk and gambling, Canadian sociologist James Cosgrave reminds us that gambling has historically engaged with a variety of cultural and economic themes. First, gambling has engaged people's seemingly innate desire to play and, when playing, to compete, sometimes for monetary rewards. Second, gambling has engaged people's desire for entertainment and spectacle—the kind of glamorous escapism that gambling meccas such as Las Vegas provide in spades.

Third, gambling engages modern-day people's preoccupation with risk and risk-taking. In a capitalist society, risk-taking—whether in the form of casino gambling, stock market speculation, real estate investment, or otherwise—is viewed as normal and even laudably courageous. The capitalist's world is populated by winners, losers, and bystanders. In this context, gambling is a fault only if it is done badly—that is, if it results in avoidable losses, without inside information or some control over the wagering process. From this standpoint, poker gambling makes as much sense as insider trading, but lottery ticket buying or roulette playing makes no sense, except as a mindless habit of risk-taking.

As sociologist Erving Goffman (1967) said in a classic piece on American culture, everyone wants to be "where the action is." And "wherever action is found, chance-taking is sure to be." Goffman approvingly quotes high-wire acrobat Karl Wallenda: "To be on the wire is life; the rest is waiting." Ironically, members of Wallenda's own troupe plunged to their deaths in efforts to defy the law of gravity. This fact of life (and death) can serve as a sobering note for the discusions of problem gambling that follow.

Chapter 3

The Voices of Problem Gamblers

Who are problem gamblers? How do people become problem gamblers who learn to accept gambling losses almost endlessly? While such behaviour seems crazy, or at least incomprehensible, social researchers have taught us that very often when a given pattern of behaviour seems unfathomable, we are failing to understand it from the point of view of the human actors themselves.

A psychological or individualistic approach may lead us to ask what is going on inside the heads of gamblers. By contrast, a sociological approach leads us to ask questions in another direction: Where did the gamblers learn to gamble, and wherein lies their enjoyment of it? How are their actions shaped by the world around them?

People learn to think about gambling from others, often those they admire or care about, such as parents, siblings, other relatives, and friends. A fuller understanding of gamblers' behaviour requires an understanding of gamblers' knowledge, attitudes, practices, interpretations, and cultural experiences. Usually, asking these questions takes us back to childhood, to the family home, and to the local community.

Gambling Variation by Culture

In 2003, a group of researchers led by Lorne Tepperman and David Korn (a gambling therapist and researcher), funded by the Ontario Problem Gambling Research Centre (OPGRC), carried out a sample survey of the members of six ethnocultural groups in the Greater Toronto Area. The data were collected in face-to-face interviews by trained members of the local community, in the interviewees' first language.

A more detailed description of this study and its findings can be found on the website of OPGRC; the study is also discussed in the book *Betting Their Lives: The Close Relations of Problem Gamblers* (Tepperman 2009). In brief, 60 Toronto respondents were interviewed in each of six ethnic communities. The interviewees were recruited in a variety of non-random ways—for example, through advertising, referral, or a personal connection to one of the interviewers. Because of logistical (especially cost) problems inherent in enumerating and sampling ethnic communities, there is no completely reliable study of ethnic gambling in Canada. The study reported here is widely cited as being among the most credible and reliable of ethnic studies done to date in this country.

The people we interviewed were recruited through a combination of advertising, postering, and snowball sampling (in which one participant recommends another participant, and so on). In the resulting research, we looked for ethnocultural variations in beliefs about gambling, as well as what respondents in different communities had learned about gambling during childhood. We found that gambling beliefs often varied according to the ethnocultural origin of the gambler; the findings that reflect these cultural patterns are presented below. Clearly, these snapshots can only suggest the range of variation. Many other important social factors, such as age, region, religion, education, and socioeconomic status, also influence gambling. However, we must recognize that ethnocultural communities exercise an early and profound influence in shaping gamblers' ways of thinking.

Aboriginal respondents[1]

We spoke to a sample of Aboriginal people living in Toronto, reflecting a mixture of different First Nations and locales. These respondents noted that many members of their group gamble. In fact, most of them reported either having a gambling problem themselves or a family member with a gambling problem. Almost half of those we spoke with reported that gambling has led to financial and other problems in their family.

A few respondents said they believe that gambling is part of Aboriginal historical and cultural heritage (though different groups might have different cultural patterns with regard to gambling):

[Traditionally, there were the] stick games, like when they had celebrations in the northwest, they would have pow-wows, they would have a log, and a lot of these people would sit around and each one would have a stick, it is like the log was a drum. They played a song on it, and with the other hand they would pass a baton around, like behind, and they would bet on where it would stop, when the song was over.[2]

Others claimed that Europeans introduced gambling, or traced the current gambling problems of Aboriginal peoples to the new presence of casinos on reserves. Several Aboriginal respondents linked problem gambling to other addictions such as alcoholism and connected both of these addictions to feelings of alienation, despair, and a desire to escape chronic poverty:

> There are addictions that go together, and it is almost as though all of those things are an escape from the deeper problems [our] people experience.

> The majority of Aboriginals are living in poverty, they have this hope of getting out of that . . . having money for once, so gambling probably does appeal to them.

Aboriginal respondents are more divided on the question of gender differences in gambling. Some reported that Aboriginal men and women engage in different kinds of gambling games. Others believe that men are more aggressive gamblers than women are. Some pointed out practical issues such as transportation and safety risks:

> More women would play Bingo than go to the casino, because Bingo is more accessible than the casino. If someone doesn't have the transportation, they can hitch a ride with someone else to the local Bingo hall. It would be harder to go to the casino. I think men are more comfortable going to a lot of places by themselves. Women might feel more comfortable going with a friend.

British Isles respondents

Like the Aboriginal group discussed earlier, our respondents from the British Isles contained a mixture of origins. Though we did not track the origins, some may have come from England, others from Wales, and still others from Scotland or Northern Ireland. However, none called attention to local variations in UK attitudes to gambling.

Only about a quarter of respondents of British ancestry reported that they have, or one of their family members has, a gambling problem. Some do worry about their own gambling and admit that gambling has led to problems within the family, and particularly to worries about finances.

Though these respondents vary culturally and socially, they mainly self-describe as Christian and draw links between Christianity and gambling. The following quotation reports that gambling is at some level un-Christian:

> In that kind of Christian—in the sense of Catholic or Protestant Anglican—background, [gambling] was a behaviour that was not condoned. It would have been frowned upon and looked at as a weakness, a sin, and all those kinds of things.

Other respondents, however, see their own gambling backlit by an illustrious history of aristocratic and social gambling in Britain:

> When you get to the track, you get the women with their beautiful hats. The racetrack in that situation is more of a social [event]. Men take their wives with them. The Queen [went] with the Queen's mother . . . This is part of a social thing.

That said, British respondents cited various motivations for gambling. Some named poverty as a factor, but others listed excitement, stress relief, and addiction:

> It's a thrill . . . I do it for the excitement, really.

> I know doctors that gamble; they're addicts and they are gamblers . . . and they say it's stress related—it's a stress release for them.

Two-thirds of these respondents described cultural gambling gender differences. Like the Aboriginal respondents, they too link women to bingo, claiming women are more suited to casinos and men to horse racing. Whatever their gambling choice, women are expected to be more modest and more moderate given their traditional family and gender responsibilities:

> I've known a lot of women who like to gamble. But women have been the ones to try to maintain the peace in life, in their relationships, in their families, et cetera and that's such a heavy responsibility. So they've squashed that down a bit, whereas men are just allowed to do it.

> In terms of my generation, gambling was worse for men because they had the money and they probably gambled the rent. Women didn't used to work so they could only gamble the egg money.

It should be noted that respondents reported that these traditions are changing, and some suggested that more women are gambling now because of more access to gambling opportunities. This change in opportunities may also reflect changes in education and social class.

Caribbean respondents

Like the British and Aboriginal respondents, the Caribbean respondents were from a mixture of origins, reflecting a variety of birthplaces and cultural backgrounds. That said, they shared beliefs about gambling that were clearly different from those voiced by the Aboriginal and British respondents discussed earlier.

For Caribbean respondents, gambling is a social activity shared among friends as a form of entertainment. As such, they did not link it primarily to poverty, stress, or excitement. Less than one in five of our Caribbean respondents reported that they or someone else in their family has a gambling problem. Roughly 20 percent reported concerns, claiming that gambling has led to family, monetary, or other problems.

Some Caribbean respondents pointed out that gambling games have a long history as a social event in this community. This is particularly true for men:

> In my culture it's maybe more acceptable for men to gamble. It's a social thing, so that when they get together and have a few beers, they play dominos.

Yet, nearly two-thirds said there are no gender differences in gambling. Those who think there *are* differences invariably said that men gamble more than women; largely because they have more opportunity (in particular, they have more money). However, gender expectations also shape attitudes and practices:

> My uncle would go ballistic if he found out my aunt gambled. Male domination, that's the way it is.

> Women are supposed to have more financial sense . . . they know more about family finances, what is needed, so they can't afford to take money and spend it uselessly.

Chinese respondents

The Chinese people we studied were somewhat more culturally homogeneous than the other groups; though some had come from the Chinese mainland (where, until recently, gambling was prohibited), and others came from Hong Kong, Singapore, or other locations where gambling was practised. Despite this variation in geographic origins, we were struck by the cultural uniformity.

Among the Chinese people we interviewed, gambling is a well-established, traditional social activity. Only 3 of the 60 Chinese gamblers we interviewed reported gambling alone; generally, gambling takes place with a spouse or partner, or with other family members.

Some respondents described gambling on card games (e.g., pai gow and fan-tan) and horse racing; but, mah-jong is by far the most popular traditional Chinese betting game:

> It's thrilling. Men and women, old and young, they all like to play this game, despite their educational background. Playing mah-jong is acceptable to all. In China, these people include senior officials, intellectuals, housewives, aged ladies, and those without jobs. It seems people from all walks of life can accept this form of gambling.

Various reasons are behind the Chinese love of gambling. Some respondents listed the need for group leisure activity after immigration to Canada. Others named the long history of gambling in Chinese culture and gambling patterns that were passed down in the family from one generation to the next:

> Gambling in China has a long history. This is partly because there are not enough ways of entertainment. Also gambling has become trendy as a kind of recreation activity. Gambling behaviour also passes down from one generation to another. Many families have a gambling history.

Chinese respondents appear to be less likely to see gambling in terms of profit, or even as a way of dealing with stress or anxiety. For some, it is a status symbol marking financial success:

> Many people believe showing up in a casino is a symbol of distinction. Many rich people go to [the] casino [to] eat, drink, and play.

About one-third of the Chinese respondents did not believe there are gender differences in gambling. Those who did usually framed their views in terms of risk-taking or daring:

> Men generally like taking risks so they are more likely to [be] involved in gambling.

Linked to this gender difference is the idea that women, as caretakers, must be more considerate of their families than men. Like the other respondents, the Chinese interviewees credited women with more reserve.

Though gambling and daring are valued, family duty carries a higher value. So it is not surprising that when asked what would lead respondents to quit gambling, some said only the threat of family destruction could have that effect:

> The best way of helping people to quit gambling is to let them know the consequences of gambling, which often lead to a broken family. It is a disaster for the family, and also for family members.

Few of the Chinese respondents reported worrying about their own gambling. However, we found indications, through our use of the standard South Oaks Gambling Screen (SOGS) instrument, that problem gambling was far more common in this ethnocultural group than respondents were prepared to admit.

Latin American respondents

Again, the Latin American respondents—like the British, Aboriginal, and Caribbean respondents—came from mixed geographic and cultural backgrounds. However, all came out of an Iberian (chiefly, Hispanic) cultural milieu, which showed attitudes to gambling quite different from those in the other cultural groups we studied.

Over half of our Latin American respondents said they grew up with a close friend who gambled. Yet relatively few—only about one in eight—reported that they or a family member currently has a gambling problem. Nearly one-third believe that gambling has led to family problems; but, very few of our Latin American respondents worried about financial difficulties because of gambling.

On the contrary, most of our Latin American respondents drew a link between gambling and poverty, seeing gambling as a response to poverty:

> Gambling is a way of life for many Columbians, because everyone is so poor. If you want to make money quick . . . the boys learn to gamble at twelve, sometimes nine. And there are cockfights, dogfights, even fights with the bulls . . . and cards on Friday, and spin the wheel, pool and soccer. In a way, there's more gambling in Columbia than here in Canada.

When asked why Latin American people gamble here, some respondents mentioned the desire for easy money. These respondents associate the possibility of winning easy money with the general openness and generosity of Canadian society:

> As a Spanish person, when you come from a third world country you always see Canada and the United States as a city of gold, and you always want to reach that limit. You want to be categorized as first world and have your own house. I believe that's everyone's dream. They don't want to live anymore in poverty; they want to advance. And some people take those steps in gambling believing that in a one shot kind of a deal they'll do it.

According to these respondents, it would take poverty or the threat of losing their family to keep them away from gambling.

Gendered differences in gambling were related to traditional ideas about masculinity and femininity. One respondent noted, "Cockfighting is a very male thing; no ladies come. Dice, poker, cards are male oriented." Many respondents discuss gambling as an exclusively male activity, and the theme of machismo often emerges. Gambling is widely described as a way to bolster or prove masculinity. As such, women who gamble are considered not properly female or even perhaps a threat to masculinity:

> Women don't gamble because their husbands don't allow them. Besides, women are more responsible with the money; we stick to our budget. Women are not like men.

> The gambling in Ecuador is mostly for men, for the boys, it's a macho thing. [Women don't gamble] unless they're prostitutes in the red light district and the old French ghetto area. So women are not expected to gamble.

Occasionally, there are exceptions to these deeply entrenched gender roles. The few women who gamble in public are sometimes said to belong to richer classes:

There are a lot of women at the casinos over there, but of course only rich women. Regular housewives don't go to the casinos and they also don't go to horse races, which are more for men. But there are a lot of women at the casinos.

Gambling, for Latin Americans, is rooted in traditional culture. Along these lines, several respondents from Cuba and Argentina noted the role of superstition in gambling:

In Argentina . . . if one dreams something it is equivalent to a number, so for example 48 is dead man talking, 15 is a pretty girl, 22 is ducks. And when one dreams [numbers], one can check this index that has been printed and can be obtained at variety stores and public spaces where there could be gambling.

Russian respondents

Many of our Russian respondents came to Canada with high educational and occupational aspirations, in addition to a love of gambling. These respondents do not see gambling as an easy way out of poverty or a demonstration of daring and masculinity. Instead, gambling is much more about skill, strategy, and brainpower. It is also a social activity: most Russian respondents reported that they usually gamble with friends.

Yet even in this social context, many develop gambling problems. One Russian respondent in five reported a family member with a gambling problem. Many respondents worry about the financial implications of these gambling addictions. These respondents appeared to us to be less willing than members of other groups to discuss gambling, largely because they grew up in a country where it was illegal:

Attitudes to gambling in our ethno-cultural group differ from attitudes to gambling in other groups because all of us used to live in a closed society. We tried to hide any involvement in gambling. Here it is open.

Given their love of gambling, Russian respondents mention many games that form a part of their culture, including lotteries, dice, chess, cards, dominoes, and billiards. The type of gambling uniquely associated with Russian culture—Russian roulette—is rarely mentioned, though it is also a part of this gambling culture:

In Russia, there is a very cruel kind of gambling, like Russian roulette. It is of [a] Russian nature, I mean a game for life or death. Such an extreme is common for Russians and gambling leads to suicides and tragic consequences.

Nearly half of the Russian respondents denied that men and women gamble differently: "Gambling cannot be differentiated according to sex. Gambling thrills both equally, men and women." Some, however, claim that generally women prefer less complicated games, such as the lottery, while men prefer more complex games. And like other groups, they believe men are more likely than women to take risks and lose control.

When asked why people of Russian extraction might choose to gamble, and what would persuade them to quit, the answers varied. They mentioned their immigrant status, a need to make money, and family and cultural histories of gambling:

First of all, they want to distract [themselves] from everyday problems. Then, everyone hopes to improve his or her financial state. Besides, many people in the Russian community don't speak English well, and consequently they don't have many places for visiting. They can't go to theatres or movies, as they won't understand a thing there. And not everybody has friends to communicate with. That's why people choose this way of entertainment and spending spare time . . . I don't think it is possible to convince them to quit gambling.

While most gamble, some talk about it negatively, in light of the damage that it does to families. Few according to our research felt that it is possible, or even important, to stop gambling. They see it as a central part of their national character, their self-expression, and their lives as immigrants in a new country:

As for convincing a person to stop gambling, I don't think anything could convince a person to stop doing what he likes, even if it does harm to him. If it doesn't do harm, why should he stop doing it?

The survey results from this research suggest that there are a range of different attitudes about gambling, which reflect social experience and cultural learning. Making sense of gambling and associated problems requires an understanding of social learning and the social contexts in which these attitudes can be enacted.

Gamblers' Erroneous Beliefs about Gambling

Central to the approach of cognitive psychology is the idea that problem gambling grows out of erroneous beliefs about the operation of chance (e.g., what happens when two dice are rolled dozens of times). Indeed, many incorrect notions are included in this category, including the so-called gambler's fallacy, the illusion of control, selective retention, and others. In this brief section, we touch on only a few of these.

In a 2005 study, the same team of researchers explored gamblers' beliefs and opinions. The results yielded interesting information about the ways gamblers define and justify their own gambling.

First, as expected, we found that many problem gamblers hold irrational or even superstitious beliefs about gambling, some of which are cultural. (Arguably, in fact, these beliefs tell us more about the gamblers' cultural background than about gambling per se.) Psychological research shows that problem gamblers reason differently than nongamblers (Toplak et al. 2007). Irrational beliefs are particularly common (Moore and Ohtsuka 1999a), and erroneous understandings of the economics of gambling lead some to act against their best interests.

For example, many of our interviewees reported feeling certain that they were able to beat the odds to win in gambling. The reality, however, is that the odds are always against the player, and accumulating money over the long term is rare. Some recognize their illogical reasoning but continue gambling anyway:

> I tend to gamble for the wrong reasons. I think sometimes that I can just win money to get out of financial problems when I should be responsible and do the right thing.

Another gambler provided clear insight into what many of these problem gamblers are thinking:

> You always hope to win. You may go through a bunch of losses. And every loss you think maybe the next time, maybe the next time, maybe the next time. I'm sure everyone who gambles says the same thing . . . you always hope that the next time is going to do it. [But] it doesn't happen, or if it does, it's not a humongous huge win where you can say "I got all my money back that I've ever gambled, so I'm happy."

Several respondents credited winning to factors that lie beyond the gambling table itself. For example, some cited superstitions or a supposed ability to assess the "feeling" of a winning opportunity:

> When I am playing roulette, [it's] something as stupid as imagining whether it is going to be red or black or watching how it comes up . . . If I don't think that it is going to come up the way I want it, I hold off from betting.

> I get a vibe whether or not it's gonna be a good night. I get that feeling; it's really hard to explain but [last night] I didn't get it, so I didn't go.

No superstition or erroneous belief is more common than the "50-50 theory." Almost half of our respondents reported an understanding of gambling in which they always have a 50-50 chance of winning whenever they gamble, because there are only two outcomes—win or lose: "With all [games] you have the same chances of winning—fifty-fifty."

Many gamblers correctly believe the odds of winning depend on the game they are playing, since some games rely more on skill (e.g., poker), while others rely entirely on chance (e.g., lotteries, slot machines, and roulette). Still, many people believe that even though their chance of winning is low, they might win big someday:

> Chances of winning? Very low. You always hope to win. You may go through a bunch of losses. And [with] every loss, you think maybe the next time, maybe the next time.

Gamblers in this study often said they thought they could influence the outcome of a game of chance through various strategies or habits. These superstitious beliefs about luck and skill gave them a false sense of control that kept them feeling likely to win.

Why Gamblers Gamble

Erroneous beliefs aside, people gamble for all kinds of reasons, and it seems likely that these reasons influence the likelihood of crossing the line from controlled to uncontrolled gambling. In our 2005 study, we asked gamblers to describe what they liked about gambling as well as their most memorable gambling experience. Some reported that gambling is mainly an opportunity to go out with friends, meet new people, and have fun:

I enjoy it. It is just fun. I guess that it is also a social thing. My partner and I gamble with his friends once a week and it brings everyone together.

Many, however, seek a feeling of excitement or rush of adrenalin from their gambling. Many described the excitement of gambling in terms of the physical changes they experience while playing:

The feeling when you're winning is indescribable. Your heart races, you're excited, you feel on top of the world.

It's just a rush. The rush of . . . I am going to get this card and I am going to win this pot. Nuts.

Such elation leads otherwise cautious or even passive people to become aggressive risk-takers, feeling incredibly confident of their ability to prevail. Respondents often describe an inability to control this elation:

[I feel] more excited, more confident, I feel that I own that space there.

There's an excitement that I will win and I can have more money, so I can buy more things. [You feel] more excitement, like when you play slot machines and look like you are going to win but you didn't notice that you lost all your money.

The high of the moment quickly turns from feelings of extreme happiness and excitement to great frustration and anxiety when the gambler becomes aware of money lost. For those who gamble to reduce stress, losing often increases the stress, leading to a self-perpetuating cycle. For those who gamble for the thrill, gambling serves as a substitute for something missing from their day-to-day lives.

Others gamble because it is an escape from everyday boredom and routine. This escape is made easy by casino incentives such as free buses and meals. Whether as a psychological escape—a way to get their minds off their problems—or a physical escape from their house or family, gambling appears to offer a ticket to freedom, however brief:

It gets you out of yourself, so you don't have to focus on yourself.

The minute I go there, I feel so free. I feel that there is nobody to ask me anything. I am the master of that whole place. At home,

I have to be on my toes, like I cannot tell anybody that I have a migraine. I cannot tell anybody that I am in pain. I have to rush to make food, so that when they come there is food.

While escape is an important factor for many gamblers, others say they gamble just to win money they need. Their obsession with winning leads to increased gambling, in time creating additional stress that often harms their health. But they continue in hopes of reaching the big win that will recover past losses, make them a profit, help them achieve financial stability, or even win them a fortune:

I'm not working. For me, [gambling] brings a different kind of financial stability that being on disability can't do.

It's pretty exciting when you read in the newspaper about people winning four million dollars. My eyes light up for them, but I wish it was me.

Characteristics of a Gambling Problem

Remembering that most adults gamble at some time or other, the question of interest becomes not why do people gamble, but why do people gamble beyond their means, losing control of their behaviour? This in turn suggests we must compare what we know about problem gamblers with that of non-problem or controlled gamblers.

The most common form of gambling in Ontario, according to Wiebe, Mun, and Kauffman (2006), is the purchase of lottery tickets, with 52 percent of surveyed Ontarians having done this in the previous 12 months, followed by raffle (29 percent) and scratch (25 percent) tickets. Fewer people report participation in sports-related gambling than casino gambling. In Wiebe's study, the least common forms of gambling were Internet-based (2 percent) and sports betting with a bookie (0.4 percent). Many gambling practices—such as the purchase of raffle tickets, and the use of casino slots, racetrack slots, non-Ontario casinos, and other slots and VLTs—grew between 2001 and 2005.

According to Wiebe's study, on average gamblers spend 2.2 percent of their personal income on gambling. People determined by the Canadian Problem Gambling Index (CPGI) to be "moderate problem gamblers" spend an estimated 8 percent of their personal income, while "severe problem gamblers" spend 21 percent.

While the average gambler reports spending only between 1 and 1.5 hours per month on casino or racetrack slots and casino table games, "severe problem gamblers" report spending between 3.2 and 4.6 hours per month on these same activities. Less commonly discussed forms of gambling—on stocks, options, and commodities trading—proved to be the costliest gambling activities in both time and money, with a mean expenditure of 58 hours and $5,450 per month.

As we saw earlier, all cultures view gambling as a gendered activity, with women and men gamblers described in different terms. The Wiebe study (2006) grants some credibility to these beliefs, showing that gender is the single most important factor distinguishing gamblers in Ontario. For example, 6.3 percent of Ontario men reportedly engage in games of skill, as opposed to only 1.2 percent of Ontario women. Participation in bingo is twice as high for women (6.5 percent) as it is for men (3.1 percent). Men are also roughly seven times more likely than women to bet on sports games, five times more likely to take part in speculative investment gambling, and three times more likely to gamble with card or board games.

Other social characteristics—education, income, and age, for example—also play a role in shaping people's gambling. On the one hand, younger people are more likely to gamble at bingo, card and board games, scratch tickets, and casinos. On the other hand, lottery purchases increase with age and then decrease dramatically after the age of 60. Rates of participation in bingo decrease as education levels increase, with the lowest rates of participation among people with a postgraduate degree (just over 2 percent). Higher income Ontarians are more likely than lower income Ontarians to purchase lottery tickets, gamble in Ontario casinos, make speculative investments, and bet on horses.

These social and demographic variations suggest that factors other than individual psychology likely explain people's proneness to gambling, and to problem gambling.

Family Influences on Gambling Behaviour

In our research, while problem gamblers tend to gamble on their own, many associate gambling with family life. Nearly three of four respondents reported gambling or playing gambling games while growing up, with 17 being the average age at which they started gambling. Most of the current gamblers in our study were exposed to gambling at a young age, had family members who gambled (some of whom may be problem gamblers themselves), or are part of a social network of gamblers.

These findings are not surprising. The habit of gambling, like drinking and smoking, often passes from one generation to the next within families. Oei and Raylu (2004) suggest that parents often pass on their beliefs about gambling to their offspring, and these beliefs either promote or discourage gambling in the younger generation. As well, people who witness their family members gambling often imitate these activities, incorporating them into their own behaviour (Gupta and Derevensky 1997).

In adolescence, having friends who gamble can play a significant part in one's introduction to gambling. Over half of the respondents in our study (59 percent) said that their close friends gambled. Others recall attending gambling outings with family members or being taught about gambling by friends. The influence of family and friends has, in many cases, continued into adulthood. Some respondents reported that friends and family still encourage them to gamble even more often than they already do:

> When we [my family] go down, the six of us, something we have to do is all get out to bingo together.

> His family again, they're big on it. Like his aunt, she had to ban herself, she had to go into security and say, "Don't let me in, I have a problem." So, it's in his family, and they all talk about it, they think it's great. They go to the casino . . . I guess to them, it's acceptable.

In the 2003 study of ethnic gambling described earlier, we also found that family influences on gambling often begin in childhood and persist through adulthood. People who become problem gamblers typically begin gambling at a moderately earlier age than non-problem gamblers. As well, hearing or seeing parents gambling or following the gambling of close friends during teenage years influences the likelihood of problem gambling in adulthood.

Some respondents recalled learning that family members considered gambling a social activity that was fun, exciting, and enjoyable regardless of winning or losing:

> My grandma said it was lots of fun . . . going out and socializing and playing bingo.

> My grandfather was at the racetrack everyday . . . He made it seem really exciting. He'd come home sometimes and show us a thousand dollar bill.

In many cases, this way of thinking about gambling influenced later gambling behaviour:

> I think that is why I used to go gambling twice a month when I was younger. She [mother] described it as going out with the girls . . . they just went out like other people go somewhere with their friends . . . [like] going to the movies.

Part of the excitement, in some families, was the imagined possibility of winning big. Children learned to think about what a big win would do for their lives:

> I heard conversations of my parents and their friends when they'd come to play cards . . . Those conversations were full of excitement and dynamics. Besides, we often bought lottery tickets. Every jackpot was followed by excitement and discussions about what could be done with money in case we won.

> My father was a gambler . . .[He] would openly send us out to get his lottery tickets and his numbers. He would say, "This could be our lucky chance to get the big one" and if he won the money, we would get a lot of things—our education would be paid for, our car, computer, what have you.

Others learned from their families to avoid gambling and were told that gambling was avoided by "good people" or that gambling could have unwanted results. Sometimes, this view was associated with religious beliefs or ethical ideas about the comportment of decent, responsible citizens. Sometimes these suggestions backfired, while other times they effectively steered people away from gambling behaviour:

> They said, "Don't gamble, stay away from gambling, live a clean life. Keep yourself clean and don't get involved."

> Gambling was evil, that's what we were brought up to believe . . . I don't know, maybe that's why we flipped, got intrigued . . . I had to see how "evil" it was.

Some learned from these early experiences to keep their own gambling secret from their children. Many, however, did not try to hide their gambling. They reported that their children were learning about gambling by watching their own or another family member's habits, or by talking to their parents about gambling:

They [the children] said, "Get out mom; go have a good time." They've heard [gambling] is like an entertainment, socializing, getting out, something to do.

Sometimes, children become directly involved in a family member's gambling, helping to open lottery tickets, for example, or celebrating a big win together. Some parents, concerned that their children are learning bad habits from themselves and other family members, take steps to teach their children about gambling:

I told [my daughter] "You see how daddy plays and he's spending so much money when it would be possible to buy things for that money. See, it's a hundred dollars. For those hundred dollars, you wanted that Barney cassette—we could buy this many Barney cassettes and he lost it—he just threw it in the garbage." . . . I translated it into material things, so that she could understand what that was.

Many people—including many problem gamblers—learned to gamble as children, learning to associate gambling with hope, excitement, and happiness. In addition, many pass similar ideas along to their own children, which may explain why many children go on to gamble as adults. However, this does not fully explain why some of these children developed a gambling problem. Little is known about the reasons why some graduate from non-addictive gambling to problem gambling in adulthood. Yet part of the explanation undoubtedly involves *what* people learned to think and believe about gambling while children.

One of the difficulties of studying people with problems is that we risk blaming their problems on blameless, or relatively blameless, factors in the people's history. It is probably for this reason that psychiatric theories of addiction and mental illness tend to be overdetermined—that is, characterized by too many intertwined causes.

Equally, there is a risk of failing to note the benefits that accrue in "normal" lives from experiences that sometimes produce problems in less "normal" lives. For example, not all family socialization that occurs because of gambling is bad. Many nonproblem gamblers have learned from family members how to gamble temperately and how to use gambling as a safe and salutary leisure experience. Perhaps the take-home message is that we need to help families find ways to teach their children temperate ways of gambling in adulthood.

In the next chapter, we will discuss the role gambling plays in the adult lives of problem gamblers, especially in their relationships.

Chapter 4

The Gambling Career

This chapter describes the downward spiral that occurs in the classic problem-gambling career and how it affects relationships in the gambler's household. We first consider the route this spiral typically follows, and then explore its impact on relationships.

A classic work on this aspect of problem gambling, by Henry R. Lesieur, is titled *The Chase: Career of the Compulsive Gambler* (1984), so titled because chasing losses is a defining feature of problem gambling. This chapter will discuss this and other defining features of problem gambling on which Lesieur elaborates, such as the problems associated with getting money, hiding money, moving money, and dealing with debts when the money is all gone. And, most important, we will see, as Lesieur did, that compulsive gambling interferes with work and creates stress—even disaster—for families.

The downward spiral of problem gambling is a process of progressive status loss, destabilization, and disconnection. We can think about this process as a *gambling career*. Here, the word *career* suggests a sequence of life events that, to varying degrees, is both socially structured and open to personal choice. The word *career* used in this context is morally neutral, implying neither blamelessness (on medical grounds) nor blame (on moral grounds). It means, merely, that people's lives—in gambling and otherwise—often follow patterns, and are rarely completely unique.

The pattern described here represents a typical downward spiral in the career of a problem gambler. Clearly, different individuals have a range of experiences. As well, problem gamblers may pass through these conditions in different sequences and at different rates. Yet, despite these variations, it is possible to discern some key stages or turning points in the experiences of long-term problem gamblers.

Researchers and therapists have been talking about the problem gambling career for centuries now. Bo Bernhard's doctoral dissertation on this topic, *From Sin to Sickness: A Sociological History of the Problem Gambler*

(2002) showed that theories about problem gambling were prominent centuries ago and that these early theories even foreshadowed what eventually became the DSM criteria for diagnosing problem gambling.

Early Theories about Problem Gambling

The theories most familiar to us today are those that began in the psychoanalytic tradition with the work of Sigmund Freud. These theories about problem gambling were seemingly crafted to explain the kind of downward spiral that we describe below. Psychoanalytic theorists viewed problem gambling as a neurosis—a form of mental illness in which the individual was driven by unconscious forces to seek his or her own destruction.

In the psychoanalytic tradition founded by Freud, sexuality—especially the parental punishment of infantile sexuality—was the cause of self-destructive behaviour. In his famous essay on the problem gambling of Russian novelist Fyodor Dostoevsky, "Dostoevsky and Parricide" (1928), Freud showed the connection between self-destructive behaviour and Dostoevsky's troubled relationship with his father. Dostoevsky's father—an abusive, yet oddly beloved, alcoholic—had created strong feelings of guilt and duty in all his offspring. As children, Fyodor and his siblings were always under surveillance and were made to feel they were never doing enough to warrant their father's approval.

According to Freud's theory, Dostoevsky's problem gambling was an adult version of masturbation, presumably a behaviour Dostoevsky's father had proscribed. Instead of acting on his wish to kill his father, a desire revealed in several of Dostoevsky's books, Dostoevsky supposedly flouted his father's control over his sexuality by masturbating symbolically (i.e., by gambling).

Today, Freud's theories of infantile sexuality and the Oedipal struggle are held in low regard, even by many psychoanalysts. No doubt, Freud overused this theory. Sometimes, in the words of a saying attributed to Freud, "a cigar is just a cigar," and things are just things, not symbols of other things. There is no way to test and reject Freudian theory, in whole or in part, so we cannot do more than speculate about its veracity, however interesting.

In the mid-twentieth century, Edmund Bergler, a follower of Freud, provided a somewhat more widely accepted theory of problem gambling. His theory also focused on the causes of self-destructive behaviour. Like Freud, Bergler concentrated on guilt and neurosis, often a result of the conflict that arises during childhood out of the gap between social norms (the superego) and anti-social (or non-social) impulses.

Bergler spent more than five years analyzing problem gamblers and their behaviour. His work gave rise to the first systematic model of behavioural traits associated with problem gambling. Bergler's (1958) six key observations about problem gamblers were as follows:

1. The problem gambler habitually takes chances, feeling alive only when the odds are against him. His real thrill is not in winning but in taking and meeting an impossible challenge.
2. For the problem gambler, the game overrides all other interests. Gambling is the sole object of attention, and everything—the gambler's family life, friendships, thoughts and conversation—centres on the next game and the next bet.
3. The problem gambler is blindly optimistic and never learns from past defeats. In this sense, he never learns from experience, no matter how disappointing. Seemingly, he is irrational—beyond the reach of all logical argument.
4. The problem gambler never stops when winning. Healthy gamblers know when to quit; problem gamblers get themselves in deeper and deeper when they are winning, and finally lose everything.
5. Despite caution at the outset, the problem gambler eventually risks too much. Motivated by irrational urges or perceptions of invincibility, the gambler finally throws all caution to the wind and raises the stakes disastrously high.
6. The problem gambler experiences a thrill between the time of betting and the outcome of the game. In that brief period, he or she feels a delicious, thrilling tension that is quickly gone and has to be repeated.

So according to Bergler, it is the pleasure and thrill associated with *uncertainty* that is exciting, perhaps even overshadowing the desire (or need) to win. Bergler says this shows the problem gambler subconsciously wants to lose. Whether motivated by feelings of guilt, masochism, or a death wish, problem gamblers do not want to stop until they are ruined and do not stop until they have no more money.

As with Freud's theory, there is no way to test Bergler's view that the problem gambler is driven mainly by an unconscious, self-destructive desire to lose. Again, Bergler's ideas provide nothing more than an interesting speculation. Moreover, like other Freudian reasoning, it proceeds from the assumption that unconscious forces drive all behaviour. (Here, remember Freud's famous thinking about the role of the unconscious in parapraxes—mistakes and accidents that reveal unconscious wishes—as well as jokes and double entendres.)

It is easier for us to believe that problem gamblers misguidedly gamble to win (or at least to feel the thrill associated with possibly winning), than to believe they play to lose. Again, often a cigar is just a cigar, not a phallic symbol.

Dostoevsky himself, the source of Freud's earliest interest in problem gambling, viewed problem gambling as the repeated attempt to achieve freedom in an overdetermined world. Only in this way could an individual feel truly alive, despite also being truly at risk of the most desperate and long-lasting harm. Though they might know the odds are stacked against success, problem gamblers feel liberated by the freedom of flying in the face of chance and of, possibly, prevailing over it.

These theories, though difficult to test, remain attractive to many. They help us better understand why problem gamblers are repeatedly willing to undergo the biggest risks, suffer the biggest harm and degradation, and injure the friends and family they love in pursuit of the successes rarely attained through gambling.

Cognitive theories—which proceed from the assumption that problem gamblers (merely) harbour mistaken beliefs about gambling outcomes—help people, in some instances, to understand their current behaviour and its irrationality. In some instances, it helps them to change their behaviour and redirect their impulses. However, by ignoring the root causes of people's self-destructive behaviour, cognitive therapists often promote the exchange of one compulsion for another (e.g., gambling for drinking, having sex, or shopping).

For at least the past century, there has been a tendency to medicalize problem gambling. We will discuss this tendency's influence on the public debate about gambling in Chapters 11 and 12. However, the reader can also consult Brian Castellani's book *Pathological Gambling: The Making of a Medical Problem* (2000) for a useful discussion of how problem gambling became medicalized.

We want to emphasize that there are benefits to studying gambling from a variety of different approaches. We agree with sociologist Bo Bernhard's (2007a, 135) argument that much can be learned from taking an interdisciplinary approach:

> Within the spheres of mental illness studies [including addiction studies], productive social and individual change is best effected by bringing the fields of sociology and psychology together . . . Though a broader-based, sociologically informed approach would no doubt be dauntingly complex, we should push forward to incorporate sociological understandings into our psychological and psychiatric practices. Although the medical model sharpens our

ability to perceive the internal and immediate causes of human suffering, a sociological model helps us paint a more holistic portrait of these afflictions.

Nowhere is this fruitful combination of fields more evident than in the development of longitudinal or "career-based" notions of deviance and illness. Then, whether we take a medical approach or otherwise, we can see that a downward spiral is associated with problem gambling. We examine this career pattern briefly in the following pages.

Initiation into Gambling

Problem gamblers often start their gambling career as social or recreational gamblers. Then, a particular event—such as a coincidental series of wins or one large win—often starts the individual on a path to uncontrolled gambling by creating a false sense of control.

Other gamblers are looking for a social life, and they associate gambling with friendship and company. We saw in the last chapter that many gamblers come from households or cultures where gambling is seen as a main basis for social interaction among family members and friends. Occasionally, gamblers seeking sociability progress to more frequent gambling episodes, perhaps out of loneliness.

Yet others begin to gamble as a way of dealing with anxiety, stress, or loneliness. They find gambling relaxing. Often, women are the most likely to seek relief through gambling; for them, gambling is a way of marking off their personal time from family duties and escaping from the drudgery and boredom of their household.

From the beginning then, each gambler launches into problem gambling for a unique set of reasons, and then lives out a personal downward spiral. The shift from social or recreational gambling to problem gambling often occurs quickly, within weeks or even days. What begins as harmless excitement rapidly turns into a set of physical sensations that the gambler comes to need and that are provided only by the act of gambling. Whatever the origin of their need, problem gamblers often increase the frequency of their gambling to experience the thrill of a win sooner and more often.

Negative Reactions

Not surprisingly, gamblers love to win—and expect to win—and they hate to lose. When they lose, they experience negative emotional reactions. Since losses are more common than wins, negative reactions become more frequent than positive ones. In addition, because wins and losses are intermixed and unpredictable, extreme, uncontrollable mood swings result:

> Your mood changes . . . It changes so fast that you don't even see it changing . . . One minute you're in a great, great mood then all of a sudden, bang! You don't even notice it; you're in a bad mood all of a sudden.[1]

While gamblers report simply getting more intense while gambling, and especially after losing, partners claim they turn into different people:

> I find the minute she walks into the casino her personality changes just like that and a lot of the time, I just can't stand the person she becomes.

Problem gamblers, usually aware of the mood swings they experience as a result of gambling, are willing to risk the financial losses and emotional lows to gain the excitement of the next win. This seems to be not simply a *willingness* to take a risk but a *need* to take it. It is this apparent compulsion to take risks (and the readiness to suffer the frequent pains of losing in hopes of occasionally winning) that leads researchers to liken problem gambling to an addiction, like alcoholism.

Increased Neglect

Despite the losses and the negative emotions they experience, problem gamblers find themselves devoting more of their time and money to gambling. As the emotional attachment to the gambling thrill grows, the frequency of gambling naturally grows too. In search of money and excitement, problem gamblers begin to neglect other aspects of their lives. The most often neglected aspect is family, a result of the long hours, or even the successive days, spent gambling. Family ties are weakened and strained, and uncontrolled gambling becomes a problem shared by the entire family.

As well, gamblers begin to neglect their school or work, resulting in lost skills and poor job performance. With reduced performance, the gambler's educational and occupational opportunities are strained, making him or her increasingly reliant on gambling as a source of income. Problem gamblers often become so absorbed that they may even neglect their health:

The last six or seven months I have been doing it [gambling] again very frequently. I have no care for family or even food.

Compulsion and Loss of Control

In time, the aspects of gambling that were enjoyed early in the gambling career are replaced by feelings of anxiety. Problem gamblers lose control, and are swept into the high of winning. The low that follows can be devastating. This high is similar to the high experienced in alcohol or drug addiction; recent research using brain imaging shows that the pleasure centres stimulated in the brain by a gambling win are the same areas stimulated by drugs and alcohol. No wonder, then, that problem gamblers feel great when they are winning, excited when they are about to play, distraught when they are losing, and depressed when they are prevented from playing.

Worry and guilt increase in severity as gambling-related problems worsen. Problem gamblers describe ever more negative gambling experiences, characterized by stress, fear, and anxiety, and a loss of personal control:

> [Gambling's] good in small amounts, but when I get in the rush, it takes over, and again . . . it's more than I can handle sometimes. I did try to figure out how to get away from it, but I always get back into it somehow.

For problem gamblers, no amount of winning is ever enough; likewise, no amount of losing is too much. The emotional extremes reflect a desperate compulsion.

Though problem gamblers may be aware that they are out of control, they are unable to make themselves quit. The physical and emotional need to gamble overrides the ability to frame the activity as unnecessary or harmful.

When not gambling, problem gamblers experience unpleasant emotional and physiological reactions that have been compared to withdrawal from an addictive drug:

> It was really out of control years ago. It was like jonesing for drugs. Trying to get money [to gamble] was like trying to get a fix.

Problem gamblers may get to a point where they have physically uncontrollable and insatiable needs to gamble.

Comorbidity

Problem gamblers often show signs of comorbidity, the presence of two or more disorders at the same time (Petry, Stinson, and Bridget 2005). For example, they might combine problem gambling with excess alcohol or drug use. Comorbidities contribute to the downward spiral by worsening personal health and encouraging addictive behaviour.

Comorbidities can come about in any of the three following ways: First, problem gambling may cause the other disorders (e.g., by creating excess stress that is soothed by alcohol or drugs). Second, other disorders may cause the problem gambling (e.g., by serving as a pastime for people mainly engaged in drinking alcohol). Finally, both gambling and the comorbid disorder(s) may share some other common cause, such as clinical depression or mood disorder. Certain personality traits, such as disinhibition and inadequate stress management, predict both problem gambling and other behaviour disorders. Certain psychiatric disorders associated with attention processes and impulse control, such as attention deficit hyperactivity disorder (ADHD) and bipolar disorder, may stimulate gambling desires (Winters and Kushner 2003).

Research supports more than one causal explanation of comorbidity. Several of our respondents report smoking and/or drinking *only* when they gamble; others admit to smoking or drinking more than usual when gambling:

> *Respondent:* [I've been smoking] since I was 17. But I'm a social smoker and I'm not an every-minute smoker. I'm not going to bingo today until ten o'clock or midnight tonight, and I won't smoke until I get to bingo.
> *Interviewer:* Was there a worst [gambling] experience that you can remember?
> *Respondent:* Yeah, just recently. I mean, basically, not even remembering what I did or how I did or where I gambled. It is, basically, alcohol involved in it.
> *Interviewer:* So you drink usually when you gamble?
> *Respondent:* Yeah. Most of the time . . . All of the time. It is a trigger.

For these individuals, gambling causes or aggravates substance abuse. One respondent admitted to using cocaine, alcohol, and cigarettes as stimulants to stay awake while gambling for three days straight:

Sometimes you're up, you can't sleep, what the fuck, so you go out and have a cigarette, smoke some dope, and "Fuck this . . . I fucking have to do a little line here or a drink . . ." Some [gamblers] drink like a fish, so I got out of those games, I don't like those guys, they are too intoxicated, too stupid.

A secondary result is that problem gamblers who abuse substances are often not at their best when playing games of skill that involve wagering large sums of money.

Yet gambling locales such as casinos and racetracks often promote drinking by their patrons. Casinos, for example, will often offer patrons free alcoholic drinks:

The drinking just makes you stupid. You don't think about what you are doing, so that's a huge influence. You go to the bar and everything is so perfect and so central in the casino. The bar is right there and the tables are right there and they walk around and serve you drinks, so basically it's a bad mix.

While it is already difficult for gamblers to abstain from gambling, alcohol makes it even easier to abandon all caution, and potentially to indulge in other substances as well.

The Financial Downward Spiral

Problem gamblers constantly need money to continue betting. Given that they lose more often than they win, however, they are always running short, resulting in a financial downward spiral. Once gamblers have exhausted all personal resources, they begin to look elsewhere. Whether by gambling more in hopes of a big win, turning to illegal means, or taking loans from friends and family, ultimately the gambler ensures negative outcomes for all concerned.

Often, problem gamblers first look for money by making personal sacrifices. These sacrifices may include small changes in buying habits and budgeting, or large changes such as selling prized possessions (e.g., musical instruments, vintage cars and motorcycles) or even cherished memorabilia (e.g., medals and cups):

I save my weekly and monthly expenses and add it to my gambling secret account. For example, I'll walk and save my TTC tokens and put that towards my secret account. I'll avoid eating out and I'll bring my own coffee.

Some gamblers are dogged by concern about money they have lost and hope to regain it through further gambling:

> The first day I lost $1500, I went home and thought "How did I lose it and how do I recover it?" I was stressed out. I ate no food and just thought about how to cover this up. I thought about how I should tell my family. I thought about how to sort out this mess. How to recover the money haunted me. I made a plan for the next day. I said that I would play more sensibly. I told myself I would play some games at less risk . . . I stepped into the casino and for the first hour I was well behaved. Then I lost the money and started saying that I would have to make it up.

Other gamblers take on an extra job to earn money that is solely theirs, money that they feel allows them to continue gambling without supervision. When another job is not feasible, or large sums of money are needed immediately, some problem gamblers take out a loan. They may seek loans from banks, loan companies, or relatives:

> I spent seven hundred dollars one night and I just blew it all . . . playing slots and blackjack. We just borrowed and borrowed and borrowed from a couple of people . . . [We borrow] probably once a month . . . Usually do those payday loan things.

Problem gamblers often come to rely on this source of funds, so borrowing can become as habitual as gambling itself. However, with the habitual need for loans, gamblers increase debt, worsen relations with friends and family, and ruin their credit. People who were once friends come to distrust and dislike them.

Efforts to find money to gamble become less legitimate, as gamblers become more desperate. Gamblers will often lie about needing emergency help so they can secure loans from loved ones while concealing the truth. While not wanting to hurt or lie to friends and family, gambling remains the priority:

> I keep losing money, so I keep having to borrow from Peter to pay Paul. It is this circle that I get involved in, where you are forever lying to do this, to do that, to cover that. You forget who you are lying to. You know that there is $10,000 owed here so you've gotta do that, so you go here and do that, but you've forgotten that you've already paid . . . You end up lying and manipulating things.

Often there is a move toward illegality to finance the habit:

> A lot of times, the only times I was gambling regularly, I was em-
> bezzling money from work to gamble . . . I eventually got fired,
> because I started trying to pull money from people's credit cards.
> Gambling also led me to a shoplifting addiction, because I was just
> too proud to go to food banks and whatever. I got caught twice in
> one month and sent to jail.

Gamblers also steal indirectly. By gambling away all their household's
money, gamblers rob their family, placing their own needs before family
needs:

> I used to spend the whole paycheck, the rent, the food, the bill
> money, everything . . . then I lied about it. She caught on when I
> lost so much in a month . . . like close to $1800 in a month.

Once gamblers have exhausted all available means, they are often forced
to declare bankruptcy. However, even this may not end the underlying
problem.

Alienation

When betting persists even after a gambler has hit financial bottom,
problem gamblers put their families at enormous risk. Many problem gamblers respond by lying about the frequency of their gambling
and the funds lost. Serious financial trouble becomes difficult to
hide; partners start asking questions and often demand that the spouse
stops gambling. Concealment results in alienation for both the gambler and his or her partner. Some gamblers even steal from family and
friends.

Partners who are kept in the dark by lies are unable to help, and the
spiral continues. As a result, problem gamblers feel adrift; they are isolated from the world outside of gambling:

> There is a gambling help line . . . but I never . . . talk about [gam-
> bling]. It's good to talk about it. [But] most of my friends they
> don't gamble, I'm the only one. So I don't talk about it. They will
> not understand me.

Gamblers often find themselves confused and broke when they hit the
bottom of their downward spiral. They have lost their financial resources,

and lied to or even stolen from friends and relatives. As a result, they feel that they have no one to whom they can go for help.

While gamblers experience a downward spiral, their marital and familial relationships decline. Problem gambling affects both the gambler and his or her family by increasing the stresses on the family. Families must address new issues associated with financial difficulty or poverty, caregiving responsibilities, secrecy, and the resulting distrust.

All families face sources of stress. For example, most families undergo life transitions such as birth, death, marriage, divorce, retirement, the empty nest, and migration. These transitions all have disruptive, stressful effects, even though they are common and foreseeable. Chronic stressors confronting families also include poverty, racism, inequality, and unemployment. In addition to stress, these factors reduce resilience and hinder the family's well-being, including the physical health of its members.

Introducing a gambling problem into the context of these normal family stressors has a range of implications. Well-functioning families— families that are usually cohesive and flexible, with good patterns of communication and conflict resolution—are always better equipped to deal with new stresses. Flexibility and cohesion helps some families overcome the considerable strain that results from problem gambling. Other families, however, are pushed to the breaking point.

The effect of a gambling problem on familial relations emerges gradually and in stages. First, primary problems of time and money present themselves. Marital relations gradually worsen as a result of the deception, emotional withdrawal, negative health effects, and a lack of shared activities. Finally, these problems result in increased conflict or excessive conflict avoidance, and thoughts of divorce.

Money issues

A partner often feels that money spent on gambling could have gone toward other household items or family activities and, therefore, should not be wasted on a gambling habit. Even small amounts of money are significant because they signal an inability or unwillingness to give up a habit that periodically grows out of control:

> I would say to him, "you've got to stop with the ProLine stuff, 'cause it is getting way out of hand. You know, sometimes you spend $2.00, sometimes it's $4.00, sometimes it is $6.00. And I think you are spending way too much money doing it."

The money problems affect the financial and emotional stability of the relationship. Even partners who keep a separate bank account or live away from the gambler often become the primary source of loans (which are not always paid back).

Partners are not the only family members who feel the negative financial effects of problem gambling. Children, who view money in a relative sense, are also affected:

> *Interviewer:* How do you think your gambling has affected your daughter?
> *Respondent:* I know it has affected her a lot. When she was about thirteen or fourteen, she wanted a pair of jeans and I said, "I don't have the money." "If you wouldn't spend three nights in bingo I could have had my money for my jeans." . . . So she knows.

Conversations between children and parents on these issues gradually increase the stress level in the family, potentially undermining parental authority.

Partners often find it difficult to remain committed to a relationship that is so deeply undermined by a gambling problem. Usually it is the partners, not the gamblers, who begin to develop a realistic view of the future:

> We haven't bought a house, we don't have enough savings, I don't think we can have kids, which is something that I want. You can't bring up kids with that, you know. You need a new car, there's a lot of new bills.

Unlike their partners, gamblers minimize financial issues: "No major problems, just sometimes money problems . . . bills don't get paid on time, that kind of thing but nothing . . . too major."

Often, gamblers don't fulfill their partners' expectations as mates or parents. As a result, budgeting and other financial responsibilities are added to responsibilities the partner may already be carrying. This often leads to partners being overburdened, taking on an almost parent-like role toward the gambler, to protect their family lifestyle from the gambler's habits:

> Then we had people [creditors] phone constantly . . . But he wasn't paying them. He didn't have the money to pay them back . . . You are not there emotionally for each other, because he is too busy thinking about going gambling. Mentally he is not stable. You

know, we can't get ahead, because I am busy covering his tracks. How can one get ahead in life, if I am busy doing his part? Kids see that and the arguing—the arguing and the constant bickering for money. The kids see that. It destroys the family.

Time issues

At their most basic, marital problems associated with problem gambling grow out of a shortage of time and money. Money aside, one way problem gambling hurts intimate relationships is by reducing the time a couple spends together:

> My family is basically Irene. All of my [other] relatives are in Scotland; I've got thousands in Scotland. Irene is very, very against [my gambling]. A lot of it has not so much to do with the money, but [also] the hours. You can disappear for 2 or 3 days. I don't want to come home after 8 or 9 hours, I want to stay there.

Another adverse effect of problem gambling is a lack of time spent with children. One gambler reported, "I don't give my kids the time they need, especially on weekends . . . Once a week, on a minimum, I'll go to the casinos." When partners propose shared activities other than gambling, gamblers often disengage:

> I've encouraged horseback riding, or bowling, or hiking or that kind of thing. But she says she's been thrown off a horse, she twisted her ankle while hiking, and this kind of thing, so going to a casino, other than [those that] used to allow smoking, is pretty safe. [Laughing.]

Many of our respondents admit that time spent gambling is essentially a waste that leads to many other issues.

Emotional Ups and Downs

As we have seen, the gambler often gives gambling a higher priority than relationships, leaving partners hurt and feeling rejected. This results in an intensification of emotional volatility in the household, making emotional explosions likely and frequent.

One respondent described a situation at home when her partner was watching a game he had a bet on: "If we're in the house and he's watching sports, you cannot talk while the game is on." Another interviewee goes so far as to claim that his primary emotional loyalty is not to his partner but to gambling: "I really, really love the cards more than him." Other gamblers recognize how destructive the single-minded focus on gambling can be:

> Where everyone else grew up and matured and took care of their responsibilities, I just got heavier and heavier into gambling. All my energy was going into that. It was all the energy I was supposed to be putting towards our relationship, putting towards work, my brothers and sisters and the family, [and] other things. There was no balance whatsoever. Everything went into gambling.

However, gamblers often reveal that they feel their relationship problems are, at most, of secondary importance. Taking second place to gambling leaves partners feeling disconnected, neglected, and emotionally abandoned:

> It's what I call the "gambling zone," where he's constantly preoccupied with it, he's constantly disengaged from his family and the kids, and he's disengaged from positive feelings—having a distinct lack of emotion and [being] hard to get through to and [not responding] to questions.

Partners who do not gamble find it difficult to share the experiences of gamblers:

> When she loses, it creates an unnecessary barrier between us . . . Nobody wants to admit when they've lost, so it creates an unnecessary bad feeling because it makes her feel responsible for losing . . . I can't share complete joy with her highs because I know it will be followed by another low; and when I suffer through another of her lows, it's another unnecessary low that she is feeling.

Even deeper than the immediate monetary issue that arises from gambling is the emotional issue: problem gambling drains emotional energy away from the relationship and toward the gambling. Eventually, a great many relationships are eroded and often even ruined.

Gambling deeply undermines intimate relationships. Couples no longer share common interests, activities, or conversations, and partners begin to feel they have little in common with the person they once knew.

Gamblers often say they do not feel understood by their partners or that they have little to share. When the two members of a couple feel they have reached an impasse, and they no longer have anything in common, they often decide to part ways.

The intent and willingness to leave the gambler is often preceded by an ultimatum, which usually fails and the stress becomes too much: "I'm not going to be on the roller coaster ride with him. I refuse."

In short, the lives of problem gamblers are full of emotional highs and lows, both directly related to the gambling experience and indirectly related to it, by its effects on their health, jobs, and family relations. Many gamblers do not take note of their social and economic losses until it is too late. Many have to lose everything of value before realizing the full extent of their problem.

In closing, we should note that this brief chapter has ignored some distinctions that are important for academic understanding but slightly less important for a general appreciation of the problem. For example, we have not distinguished between the various gambling formats in terms of how hazardous they are, nor have we distinguished between continuous and noncontinuous gambling formats.

All things are a matter of degree. Games of skill (e.g., poker) are different from, and pose somewhat different problems from, games of pure chance (e.g., a slot machine). Games that promote a sense of continuous urgency and excitement (e.g., slot machines) are different from, and pose somewhat different problems from, games that are casual or even companionable (e.g., lottery tickets or bingo).

That said, our goal has been to examine some of the problems of addiction common to all types of gambling. A longer, and thus more thorough, book will provide a more detailed analysis of the variations.

In what might be viewed as a bit of ironic levity, Lesieur ends his classic work *The Chase* (1984) by noting that, in sociological analysis, we are often inclined to look for hidden positives—that is, benefits that are concealed to the naked eye but which help to explain the persistence of an otherwise harmful behaviour. Accordingly, Lesieur (1984, 250–52) looks for and finds some hidden positive functions of problem gambling, as follows:

1. The increased part-time and overtime work by some problem gamblers is necessary to help them meet their debts. This extra work increases society's net productivity.
2. Gamblers make a major financial contribution to the gambling industry and its employees (and, as we will also see, to the provincial government).
3. Gamblers make a major financial contribution to organized crime and its associated bookmakers, loan sharks, and money launderers,

thereby assisting the upward social mobility of less-privileged people.

4. Some of the revenues generated by gambling are used to make a significant contribution to valued social programs and public initiatives.

5. Gamblers contribute financially to the profitability of banks, credit unions, and loan companies, which help to finance the gambler's financial desperation.

6. Through frequent defaults on gambling loans (see above), the gambler contributes to the employment potential for insurance investigators, credit agencies, collection agencies, police officers, and lawyers.

7. The negative example that gamblers set and their visible suffering provides an opportunity for other members of society to reaffirm their commitment to moral values of hard work and thrift.

8. The medicalization of problem gambling has provided a growing opportunity for professional therapists, counsellors, and researchers to prosper by helping and studying problem gamblers.

9. Finally, the actions of gamblers supply a growing justification for the building of prisons to house people who run up gambling debts they cannot pay and who do criminal things to pay them.

Chapter 5

Gambling and the Workplace

This book has explored the wide-ranging effects of gambling. Although gambling can be entertaining, it can also lead to significant losses of money, personal integrity, relationships, and employment, drawing individuals into a downward spiral of debt and despair. Research suggests that each problem gambler negatively affects between 11 and 18 others (NCPG n.d.), reaching well beyond the immediate family/friend circle to include co-workers, employers, government officials, and employees of financial institutions. This chapter will look more closely at the social structures in the workplace that support and reinforce gambling behaviour, the impact problem gambling has on employees and employers, as well as prevention efforts and best practices for organizations. The chapter will close with a look at those employed by the gambling industry itself.

In 2002, Alberta released the findings from its extensive employee survey on substance use and gambling. This workforce survey revealed that 2 percent of employees were moderate-risk gamblers, while 1 percent could be classified as problem gamblers. The study also found that 30 percent of employees gambled at work in the past year, which equates to roughly 502,100 people. Of those, about one in five, or just over 100,000, reported gambling weekly on the job.

Another interesting finding from the study was that only about 22 percent of workers regularly gambled together after work, and invitations to gamble were rare from co-workers (6 percent) and supervisors (3 percent). This suggests that gambling in the workplace may be more of a solitary and hidden activity, with little social protection for those in serious trouble. Industries that reported higher than average gambling prevalence were forestry/mining, utilities, public administration, financial/insurance/real estate, and health care, while social services, education, and agriculture scored below average on gambling prevalence in the workplace.

An important part of work is income. Henriksson (2001) found that people with lower socio-economic status are more inclined to divert to gambling as an alternative source of income. A recurring explanation for this in research literature suggests that gambling offers a means to pursue a desirable economic outcome that people feel they deserve but are unable to attain through conventional means, such as work (Callan et al. 2008). It is often people in low-income brackets, middle management, or employees doing undesirable work who feel the most distanced from the "Canadian Dream." Employees who are dissatisfied with their pay in relation to the pay of others (or to their own perceived economic value) may feel disenfranchised from their job and potential promotional opportunities, and frustrated with the overall fairness of the workplace (Callan et al. 2008). In these situations, and to make ends meet, it is easy to be drawn in by promises of glamour and winnings, especially when they are coupled with easy access to gambling opportunities. Advertising spreads the message of quick riches and gambling venues are often conveniently placed in economically disadvantaged areas (Callan et al. 2008).

Types of Workplace Gambling

Gambling is often associated with casinos and horse racing, but other forms, such as lottery tickets, poker, and Internet gaming, are becoming increasingly popular. Even carnival games, scratch tickets, and community raffles can contribute to compulsive gambling, and most of these forms of gambling are possible in the workplace.

Sports pools and pools for life events such as birthdates or birth weights are the most common gambling activity in the workplace (Hoskins and Tessier n.d.). For example, many employees have shown an increased interest in participating in March Madness. This National Collegiate Athletic Association (NCAA) basketball tournament has created a "booming office pool phenomenon" (McCarthy 2007b). Gambling on March Madness is a seemingly harmless activity, but it can be the first gambling experience people encounter, particularly if they begin gambling later in life. The danger with this form of gambling is that office pools are often company-sanctioned, so they introduce people to the excitement of betting in a "safe" environment. For those 5 percent of people who cannot handle social gambling, the impact can be devastating (McCarthy 2007b).

In one American study, 58 percent of respondents reported that employees at their organizations have participated in Super Bowl pools, while about 55 percent were engaged in regular season pools. Pooling money to buy lottery tickets is also popular (SHRM 1999). These pools are typically short-term social activities that have some team-building value to them, but they also have the potential to create a workplace culture in which gambling is seen as an acceptable activity (Griffiths 2009b).

Telephone betting is an easily accessible avenue for gambling in the workplace where bets can be placed quickly over the phone with a bookie. Many employees also have their own computers with unlimited Internet access. The Internet is one of the newest gaming opportunities, and usage seems to be rising, according to a 2007 study that examined gambling behaviour in North America. Researchers found that 74 percent of those surveyed online preferred Internet gambling to land-based venues. In addition, 16 percent reported Internet gambling at work, and 4 percent indicated the primary computer from which they gamble was located in the workplace (Wood and Williams 2007). People's interest in "in-play betting" is increasing, especially among cricket and soccer fans. This type of gambling is particularly problematic given that bets can be placed over the Internet throughout the event, increasing the temptation for employees to follow the game during work hours, decreasing their attention and focus on the job.

Another gambling-related message and behaviour that is propagated in the workplace is betting on personal games of skill, particularly golf. Business deals and negotiations have historically taken place on the golf course; young executives are encouraged to learn the game for this reason. Betting is also entrenched in golf culture and plays a role in the game for professionals, businesspeople, and leisure golfers. The idea that betting can spice up the game is a commonly held belief among golfers and sports wagerers, so it should be no surprise that betting occurs during work-related golf fundraisers and business deals on the course.

A final form of gambling that is so embedded in business culture that few recognize it as such is the stock market. The main goal of "playing" the stock market is to maximize profit while minimizing investment. There are other shocking similarities between the stock market and more traditional gambling: the euphoria and adrenaline that leads to an addiction is the same for both (Goldberg 2001), gambling professionals make money in a similar way to investment brokers (Jayashanker 2007), and both can be considered zero-sum games.

Many people feel they have more control over their stock market investments than the money they put into slot machines, given their ability to research their investments (Olson 2009). While this thinking may be true in this comparison, people who play games of skill, such as poker, display a similar logic. These gamblers spend a significant amount of time researching strategies and studying human behavioural trends to make the best possible "investment" for each hand they play. In reality, both activities have a degree of chance, rely on educated guesses, and involve monetary risk.

Even with these obvious similarities, many argue that playing the stock market is significantly different from gambling. According to the law, the three elements required to classify any activity as gambling include consideration, reward, and chance (Campbell, Hartnagel, and Smith 2005). The stock market requires some investment upfront (consideration) for the opportunity to gain more money later (prize/reward) and the outcome is not guaranteed (chance). In an online case study, a former problem gambler shared that he experienced an adrenaline rush every time he invested which fuelled his compulsion: "It became an addiction to risk" (as quoted in Goldberg 2001). For some gamblers, the greater the risk, the more excitement they experience, increasing both the appeal and potential for addiction.

According to Looney (2003), some of the preferred areas of stock market gambling that attract serious gamblers are penny stocks, index investing, bonds, and government securities. Likewise, day traders gravitate toward other types of wagers, eager to apply their "gambling skills" to other domains (Griffiths 2009b). The attraction of gamblers and traders to other forms of wagering implies a strong similarity among these activities. In a short excerpt from an online article by Sharon Lem (2010), a Canadian man shared his story. He began gambling on school games and buying lottery tickets at the young age of 11. His gambling escalated to secretly betting at racetracks when he was 16 years old. After a long battle with debts and his withdrawal from school, he eventually overcame his compulsion and got his life back on track by the age of 24. However, once he was introduced to the stock market, the same urges and behaviours were sparked, costing him his family and new career. It is often the belief in one's personal "system" or "investment strategy" that leads to illegal activity within the workplace (Looney 2003).

The stock market may be more dangerous than traditional forms of gambling since investing has always been regarded as a legal activity (Olson 2009). In many ways, the stock market is a wolf in sheep's clothing: well hidden and supported from the depths of business culture, but with the potential for disastrous outcomes for individuals, families, and organizations.

The forms of gambling that we have mentioned so far are particularly conducive to office-related atmospheres or what we might consider white-collar jobs. However, the surge of cellphone and smartphone ownership makes it easier for people to gamble from a range of jobs, including blue-collar positions. In addition, playing cards or dice games, or making personal bets with co-workers are other forms of gambling found in any workplace. A gambler needs only one other willing participant to bet on games, project outcomes, or even the boss's mood. In a culture of betting, it is particularly difficult to control and monitor wagers between employees. Although office pools and group-purchased lottery tickets may provide the benefits of group cohesion and good morale, the outcome of a gambling-friendly atmosphere may on balance be more negative than positive for employees and the organization.

The Impact of Gambling on Employees

When employees experience stress from gambling-related behaviour, their health, overall work life, and job performance are often affected. Increased internal anxiety and concern from gambling losses can produce increased stress levels and fatigue, suppressing the immune system and placing the gambler at risk of illness. In fact, mental and physical health issues such as depression, anxiety, lack of sleep, ulcers, and high blood pressure often accompany gambling problems (Oregon Department of Human Services 2011). These secondary or stress-related symptoms are likely to lead to increased absenteeism, sick days, and poor job performance. Within the workplace, sanctions or self-disclosure of the issue may expose the gambler to stigma, discrimination, or loss of job status or respect from co-workers. In addition, disciplinary and legal action from the employer or the police can further affect employees' emotional and physical well-being (Hoskins and Tessier n.d.).

Problem gambling has its tentacles in many facets of life, and no addiction depletes people's savings accounts and equity faster. Add the loss of a job to this equation, and the results may be disastrous for families, businesses, and society as a whole. It is estimated that one-third of problem gamblers lose their jobs as a result of related problems (Game Planit Interactive 2006). Those who do lose their jobs may commit other crimes to help provide basic necessities for their families, or they may be pushed further into the gambling world as they try to win back money to help pay their debts and ward off threats from loan sharks (Henriksson 2001).

Financial strain, divorce, and job loss are some of the most stressful events in life. Problem gamblers are at risk of all three, on top of the strain of hiding their secret lives. Family members can be seriously affected, creating conflict and tension in the home and adding relationship issues to the gambler's mounting concerns. These worries can feel so overwhelming that suicide appears to be the only escape.

The colleagues of gamblers often experience negative effects as well. Co-workers may be manipulated into lending money to the gambler, and they are often not repaid (RGC n.d.). This can lead to a financial loss for co-workers, tension in the workplace, and loss of friendship.

The ripple effect extends well beyond the individual gambler. Family members often feel the financial burden from lack of income and property loss. For example, they can experience a drop in work productivity due to financial stress and conflict at home as well as preoccupation with worry. As a result, both the gambler and his or her partner may experience job loss, compounding the issues caused by problem gambling.

It is important to note that even individuals who do not meet the diagnostic criteria for problem gambling can experience acute problems that may temporarily affect their lives for a day, week, or month. Organizations may wish to believe that people check their personal lives at the door when they get to work, but plenty of evidence demonstrates the spillover effect between work and home (Byron 2005). For example, social gamblers who experience a big loss often have no idea how they will pay for rent or food in the coming weeks. Under these circumstances, they are likely to experience increased stress and anxiety, as well as a preoccupation with solving the problem. In fact, non-problem gamblers can experience negative consequences that affect their work life in a similar pattern to those experienced by occasional binge drinkers with hangovers. Research shows that social drinkers—not problem drinkers—are responsible for the greatest loss of productivity in the workplace caused by alcohol use (Buddy 2003). In other words, acute problems may affect individuals and the workplace as well.

The Impact of Gambling on Organizations

Most problem gamblers are hard-working, and they are employed in all types of organizations. Through lateness, absenteeism, illness, and crime, employees with an addiction often affect the functioning of their workplace. The Alberta Alcohol and Drug Abuse Commission (2002) estimates the annual cost of absenteeism and lateness resulting from substance abuse to be close to $400 million in Alberta alone. The Alberta Substance Use and Gambling Workplace Study (AADAC 2002) estimates costs associated with gambling to be about $7 million, not including health care costs and wages for the temporary workers who relieve those with this problem.

Although the social and economic impact of gambling is difficult to measure precisely, several studies have attempted to measure its effect on businesses. Griffiths (2009b) placed the effects of gambling-related behaviours on organizations into four main categories: time exploitation, productivity loss, financial corruption, and criminal activity.

The exploitation of time includes arriving late and leaving work early to gamble, long lunch breaks to accommodate betting, gambling during work hours (which includes telephone and Internet misuse), increased absenteeism, and unusual or unpredictable sick leave. It is estimated that gamblers cost employers five hours per month in late time. Similarly, 14 percent of gamblers reported missing entire days from work (Game Planit Interactive 2006). We saw earlier how physical and emotional problems associated with gambling can further reduce work performance and attendance. Stress-related illnesses brought on by gambling, such as depression, anxiety, high blood pressure, and a compromised immune system, can contribute to absenteeism. A workplace solutions firm estimates that job stress costs the Canadian economy $12 billion per year (Morrow, Crossdale and Associates n.d.). Some of this stress is a result of gambling, particularly from those struggling with compulsive gambling.

Gambling-related behaviours that lead to productivity issues include poor concentration, moodiness, unfinished projects, missed deadlines, and poor overall work quality that often puts excess burden on co-workers and managers. Bensinger, DuPont & Associates, a Chicago-based provider of employee assistance programs (EAP), reported that 66 percent of callers to the EAP during the month of March (2006) were from employees that gambled in their workplace. More than half reported that gambling negatively affected their work productivity (Bensinger, DuPont & Associates 2006). In addition, gamblers may become engrossed in betting well into the early morning hours. While this gambling does not occur on work time per se, fatigue affects workplace performance. Lack of sleep decreases cognitive and physical capabilities, and can undermine performance and increase risk of injury. Furthermore, sleeplessness and increased anxiety are experienced by non-problem gamblers who have had a rough battle with luck, not just by problem gamblers. In this context, workplace performance may be affected more than we previously thought.

In a study evaluating the voluntary self-exclusion program in Missouri (a program in which patrons can ban themselves from casinos), less gambling did equate to better work performance. Researchers interviewed 113 participants who were enrolled in the program for between four and ten years. Participants reported improvements in their job performance and job satisfaction during the time they spent in the program. Many also reported better emotional health, better relationships with family and friends, and an improvement in their self-image (Nelson et al. 2010).

Problem gamblers typically experience a preoccupation with the act of gambling: planning their next opportunity to gamble, figuring out how they will find financial resources to gamble, or puzzling over how to make up their losses. All of this mental energy likely contributes to lower engagement with their work, which has been found to negatively impact business-related outcomes (Harter, Schmidt, and Keyes 2003). In fact, it is estimated that low satisfaction and engagement cost the Canadian economy more than $28 billion per year. The financial costs of disengagement increase even more when stress and mental health problems develop (Shepellžfgr Research Group 2007).

Organizations are further hurt financially by gamblers who borrow money from co-workers, request cash advances, and participate in criminal activity. Employees sometimes commit illegal acts for the cash that will allow them to "stay in action." These are usually nonviolent crimes such as illegal bookmaking, stealing money or personal property from colleagues, making fraudulent expense claims, or embezzling (Griffiths 2009b). Often, gamblers rationalize that they are borrowing the money from their workplace and plan to replace it once they win (Oregon Department of Human Services 2011).

Henry Lesieur (1992) found that 75 percent of non-imprisoned and 97 percent of imprisoned gamblers reported engaging in illegal activities to finance their gambling. More than one-third of pathological gamblers reported stealing from their employer (quoted in Ladouceur, Dubé, and Bujold 1994). In one case study report, one woman addicted to video lottery terminals (VLTs) stole roughly $200,000 from her job; in another instance, a public official stole from his workplace by using his seniority to obtain kickbacks from individuals (Fifield 2010). In a more recent case involving Fry's Electronics in the United States, the vice-president of merchandising and operations is alleged to have embezzled close to $65 million to pay gambling debts by creating a covert kickback scheme. The Internal Revenue Service claim in court papers that almost $18 million was used to pay off gambling debts to a Las Vegas resort casino (Associated Press 2011; Telegraph Staff 2008).

At times, it is not only the employees who have gambling problems but the employers themselves, leading to dysfunctional business practices. Family-run businesses can be particularly affected. Deceit and manipulation can create even deeper wounds and family members (who are also co-workers) often enable a gambler's behaviour to help keep both the business and the family together (Berman and Siegel 2008).

Rules and Regulations in the Workplace

Problems with employees gambling in the workplace have been documented in Canada, United States, Europe, and the United Kingdom. The trust in an employer–employee relationship is particularly tested when problem gambling arises because of the potential for embezzlement, its impact on other employees, and a decrease in productivity (all previously noted; Griffiths 2009b). In Manitoba, problem gamblers are generally seen as a liability that must be removed from the workplace; however, the province does make an effort to provide appropriate support for gamblers so they can return to work. The Addictions Foundation of Manitoba suggests that it is not part of the employer's job to look into employees' personal lives; it is merely their duty to make sure the employees can perform the tasks they are hired to do (AFM 2010). In comparison, Looney (2003) claims that employees in New Jersey who are found to have gambling problems are immediately fired or told to resign.

These approaches take a simplistic and individualistic perspective that ignores the possibility that the work environment may have been the original source of the gambling behaviour. Organizations that ignore office pools and day trading at work, yet reprimand employees when gambling becomes problematic, create mixed messages and unfair standards in the workplace.

What options are available to help protect organizations? Two general approaches are available: surveillance practices that monitor and sanction behaviour, and harm-reduction practices that prevent behaviour or reduce negative consequences.

Surveillance practices

Geist (2002) addresses workplace surveillance in Canada. He notes that Canadian employees waste nearly 800 million work hours each year surfing the Internet for personal reasons. With hundreds of computer-enabled employees, overseeing Internet use may become necessary to ensure productivity for many organizations. Because of technological improvements, gambling is easily accessible over the Internet and people can access inappropriate websites and games unrelated to work. Large companies have fired employees for inappropriate Internet use, specifically related to installation of unlicensed software. In Quebec, an employee was dismissed after spending more than 50 percent of his work hours surfing the Internet (Geist 2002). Computer monitoring technologies can now detect abuse early to help prevent costs to companies.

Two types of programs are being used to monitor Internet misuse in the workplace. The first is a server-based program that is installed on the employer's network; the second is a client-based program that is installed directly on the computers used by employees. These computer-surveillance technologies produce customizable reports that disclose how employees use their computers, signalling any misuse.

Fox and colleagues (2003) have suggested various filtering techniques from research that focuses on workplaces in the United States and Europe. These include firewalls, proxy and cache servers (which store web pages that users are likely to use), and Employee Internet Monitoring software. Many organizations have already restricted employees from accessing social media sites. Blocking gambling sites can be difficult, given the cost of buying the software or having IT professionals track frequent changes in gambling site IP addresses. Nonetheless, Fox and colleagues take the stance that companies reserve the right to recover and review any message or file composed, sent, received, or stored via their network. Although the Canadian perspective on computer surveillance in the workplace is significantly influenced by US jurisprudence, a more balanced perspective on this issue is emerging in Canada.

The main concern with the use of these monitoring technologies is whether surveillance infringes on an employee's right to privacy. Canada, while recognizing the need for some monitoring in the workplace, also recognizes an individual's rights as well, as indicated by the Personal Information Protection and Electronic Documents Act. Generally, in Canada "surveillance is permitted only where a substantial problem has been identified, and it is likely to solve a problem" (Geist 2002, 28). However, in British Columbia, a court decision ruled that electronic surveillance by the State is a breach of an individual's right to privacy (Geist 2002). There are multiple opinions as to what constitutes a breach of rights in surveillance outside of Canada as well as inside. Obviously, problem gamblers pose a threat to the company for which they work, other employees, and themselves. Nonetheless, many provinces and countries are still conflicted about whether surveillance is the best approach, although it may be the most reliable solution (Paul and Townsend 1998).

It is clear that precautions to protect companies must be balanced with a supportive environment that values employee health and safety (CCSA n.d.) and fosters engagement and trust in the organization.

Few people like to be micromanaged and watched at all times. The majority of employees must not be punished by the actions of a few. Thus, organizations must weigh the benefits of surveillance with the potential costs of lower morale and engagement. Recovery-oriented approaches adopted in US university settings may serve as a helpful model for all organizations. This model stresses care and concern about students through recovery rather than punitive action for (noncriminal) violations of conduct (NCRG 2009). The economic value of human capital in terms of loyalty and productivity must be factored into issues of monitoring and surveillance among Canadian organizations.

Harm-reduction strategies

There needs to be balance between preventing problems and adequately addressing those that already exist (CCSA 2011). Electronic monitoring is effective at detecting only certain types of gambling. As a result, organizations may be better served by increasing their attention to this specific health and occupational issue. For example, possible approaches include a policy statement, awareness training (to teach employees to recognize the warning signs), cash flow monitoring (to search for irregular patterns), and financial and problem gambling counselling (Bensinger, DuPont & Associates 2006; Oregon Department of Human Services 2011). In addition, a proactive stance and an exploration of cultural norms and values in the workplace may also help to reduce negative effects on an organization.

An approachable and flexible employer can also be helpful. Employees working in an environment that fosters open communication may be better able to identify those employees struggling and encourage them to seek help. Toronto's Centre for Addiction and Mental Health has explored factors motivating gamblers to seek help and change their behaviour by examining 19 peer-reviewed articles. The top reasons to seek help included work and legal difficulties, financial problems, relationships with others, and negative emotions (Suurvali, Hodgins, and Cunningham 2010). These explanations help to further clarify the importance of the workplace in identifying those at risk and encouraging treatment sooner rather than later. Problem gamblers often use the workplace to shield or hide their gambling behaviour from their families. For this reason, co-workers are often the first line of defense in detecting and revealing a problem. The workplace could turn out to be critical in saving lives and families while decreasing future costs to society. The following textbox lists some warning signs that may be helpful to managers and co-workers.

Workplace Warning Signs

1. Deterioration of work performance
2. Frequent unexplained absences
3. Motivation to organize and participate in betting opportunities
4. Pay requested in lieu of vacation time and no vacation time taken
5. Excessive use of the Internet and phone (land lines or smartphones)
6. Credit card or loan bills mailed to work
7. False claims made against an expense account
8. Theft of property or merchandise
9. Use of excessive betting language
10. Sport stats or stock information on desk, computer, or phone

Source: Griffiths 2009b; NCPG n.d.

It is rare for individuals to develop gambling problems alone; for example, they are usually influenced by family members, peers, co-workers, celebrities, and creative marketing. They are also influenced by *not* knowing the risks about gambling and by the lack of preventive public health information that exists. Gambling is a community problem with significant community costs. The important message here is not about the liability and protection of organizations per se but rather the social impact of gambling on all areas of life, including family, friends, co-workers, the workplace, and the economy. Problem gambling is financial, emotional, and physical; it affects the bottom line of every aspect of society. For example, employee turnover costs money, bankruptcy costs money, increased health concerns cost money, and broken families cost money. All of these weigh on the social systems and cultural fabric of Canada.

The Government's Role

According to Griffiths (2009b), many employers are reluctant to recognize gambling as a workplace issue. White-collar crimes in general, such as embezzlement and fraud, are often ignored in Canada. We tolerate the current level of gambling because it is billed as creating jobs and revenue for the government. But the reality may be very different.

In Canada, similar to the United States and the United Kingdom, the government has dramatically expanded the extent of legalized gambling in the last few decades (Henriksson 2001). Lotteries and many casinos are owned and operated by the provincial governments which "often see the highly visible proceeds from gambling expansion as an easy out to fund costly programmes such as health care and education for which they are constitutionally responsible" (Henriksson 2001, 115). The government has noticed that people "spend more on legal, government-promoted gambling than on clothing, shoes and medicine combined" (Stevens and Beristain 2004, 320).

Provincial governments continues to put money into creating legalized gambling, anticipating big revenues. But there is a risk here. By promoting gambling as an economic development tool to create jobs (Campbell and Smith 1998), governments ignore the evidence that it closes local businesses (Nieves 1997) and decreases revenue in other areas (Goodman 1995). Furthermore, the National Gambling Impact Study Commission (1999) estimated the annual societal cost of problem gambling at $5 billion in the United States. Although this figure is based on US numbers, it gives us a sense of the potential scale of this problem in Canada. Given these costs associated with an otherwise productive citizen suffering heavy losses, it is troubling how little money and attention is spent on treatment and prevention. Only a small percentage of gambling revenue goes toward treatment (Lesieur 1998; Hall and Scarpelli 2010). After bankruptcies, fraud, unpaid debts, and criminal justice expenses, a single problem gambler costs taxpayers between $13,200 and $52,000 a year (Goodman 1995). To increase revenue in the short term, it seems some provincial governments may be willing to sacrifice addicts, their families, businesses, and taxpayers.

Gambling as the Workplace

Exposure and access to gambling are two risk factors in developing a problem, so it is critical to examine the prevalence of problem gambling among those exposed to gambling every day at work. The importance of this is similar to research in the 1980s on second-hand smoke among employees working in bars and restaurants. Today, research on problem gambling among casino employees is vital; yet, the issue has been somewhat neglected. Two studies provide some important insights.

In 2004, Dangerfield examined job satisfaction, substance use, and gambling behaviour among 123 casino employees from two casinos in Northern Alberta. A second study, funded by the Ontario Problem Gambling Research Centre, explored gambling behaviour and the impact of employment within the gambling industry among 934 Ontario casino employees (Guttentag 2010).

Dangerfield (2004) found that 81 percent of casino employees self-identify as gamblers, consistent with the percentage in the province (82 percent). Lottery, raffle, and instant-win tickets were the top gambling activities among both casino employees and the general Albertan population. Cards and board games with family/friends ranked second among the casino employees (67 percent), while slot machines and VLTs tied for second among the general population (23 percent). The findings were similar in Ontario, with 90 percent of casino employees reporting that they played lottery games within the past year, compared to 52 percent of the general Ontario population (Guttentag 2010). Of those sampled, 55 percent reported that they gambled in a casino and 27 percent took part in other forms of gambling such as betting on sports, playing poker with friends, and investing in stocks (Guttentag 2010).

In Alberta, roughly 19 percent of casino employees were categorized as moderate problem gamblers and 6 percent as severe problem gamblers. These percentages were far above the rates for adults in the area (i.e., 6 percent moderate and 2 percent severe problem gamblers). Problem gambling was prevalent among Ontario casino employees as well but to a lesser extent than those in Alberta. Using the same scale as the previous study (the Problem Gambling Severity Index), respondents were placed into four categories, which revealed that 3 percent were problem gamblers, 9 percent were moderate-risk gamblers, 14 percent were low-risk gamblers, and 74 percent were non-problem gamblers. How does this compare to the general population? Two studies show that about 1 percent of Ontario's adult population are problem gamblers, 3 to 4 percent moderate-risk gamblers, 6 to 8 percent low-risk gamblers, and 88 to 91 percent non-problem gamblers (Guttentag 2010). There is a clear disparity between casino and non-casino employees in problematic gambling behaviour, while the inconsistency in casino employee prevalence may speak to differences in cultural norms around gambling between the provinces.

Among the Ontario casino employees, there was also a clear linear relationship between the amount of money spent per month and problematic gambling behaviour. Research found that a small percentage of casino employees accounted for most of the sample's spending. Specifically, 3 percent of casino employees classified as problem gamblers made up 35 percent of casino employees who gambled $251 or more every month.

What accounts for the high prevalence among casino workers, and does employment in a casino influence an employee's gambling behaviour? Both researchers asked respondents whether their gambling had increased, decreased, or stayed the same since they began working at the casino. In Dangerfield's (2004) study, 29 percent reported that casino employment *decreased* their gambling, 20 percent asserted that casino employment increased their gambling, and the rest believed their gambling frequency had remained the same. Among the Ontario casino employees, 18 percent had decreased their gambling significantly, 10 percent decreased a little, 59 percent remained the same, 9 percent increased a little, and 3 percent increased significantly. What is most striking is that about 40 percent of those classified as moderate-risk or problem gamblers increased their gambling behaviour significantly. The environmental influence of working at the casino may have pushed those already at moderate risk along the continuum toward an addiction and further enabled those already there.

Is it the casino environment that influences the gambler, or are problem gamblers attracted to the environment? Guttentag accounts for changes noted in his study by identifying four workplace influences: exposure to gambling, exposure to the patrons, exposure to the work environment, and training, regulations, and resources. Exposure to gambling had two effects on employees. First, employees no longer considered casinos as entertaining, and employees' knowledge of casino-style games increased as they repeatedly saw the house winning; thus, they decreased their gambling. Second, increased exposure led to the belief that they had an edge in gambling, especially for table games.

Exposure to patrons reminded employees of how problem gambling can affect lives, decreasing employees' interest in it. Exposure to the work environment can be stressful and lead some employees to gambling. While not all employees who gamble cite stress as an influence, those who did were four times more likely to be problem gamblers in the study. Thus, environment may indeed influence those already at risk of developing a problem.

Some of Guttentag's conclusions are supported by the earlier work of Hing and Breen (2005), who consulted with 32 gambling counsellors to gather insight into how the workplace influences a casino worker's behaviour. They identified 40 risk factors and 15 protective factors against gambling problems. The main risk factors included close interaction with gamblers, frequent exposure to gambling, effects of shift work on gambling, encouragement to gamble from work colleagues, reluctance to expose a gambling problem and seek help, gambling to cope with difficult aspects of the job, and frequent exposure to gambling marketing and promotions. Close interaction with gamblers is thought to distort views about winning, create excitement, and cause employees to identify with patrons (Hing and Breen 2005). For example, a cashier who is responsible for paying out prize money may come to have a skewed view that winning is more common than not.

Frequent exposure to gambling may increase accessibility, normalize the behaviour, and lead some to believe they have insider knowledge or an investment edge (Hing and Breen 2005). Employees may also turn to gambling to cope with job dissatisfaction, stress, or low pay. Similarly, shift work is responsible for social isolation, encourages solitary leisure, imposes unsocial hours, and sometimes requires workers to kill time between shifts, putting employees at risk of gambling. Frequent exposure to marketing and promotions may further glamorize and normalize the behaviour. Finally, employees may be hesitant to reveal their gambling problem and seek help out of fear of losing their job and because of the stigma associated with having a gambling problem. Employees will often avoid self-exclusion programs because they cannot take part without their co-workers finding out about it.

Hing and Breen found fewer protective factors, but the following themes emerged: exposure to the negative aspects of gambling, support from work colleagues, staff training in responsible gambling, and venue-based responsible gambling policies. Employees might be repulsed by patrons with a problem, be more likely than non-employees to recognize that the odds of winning are poor, and experience a general loss of interest in playing. Also, policies that ban staff from gambling and staff training in responsible gambling may prevent some problems and encourage others to seek help (Hing and Breen 2005).

It seems the social environment does have some influence on gambling behaviour and employees were exposed to fewer protective factors than risk factors. Dangerfield (2004) concluded that casino employment and the workplace cannot fully explain increases in one's susceptibility to problem gambling as workers who suffer from problem gambling may seek out employment in casinos. This provides important prevention information and suggests that some screening in the hiring process may be useful to protect potential employees from further developing a problem and to protect the casino from any liability. Gambling screening would not be different from screening tests for drug or alcohol abuse and could be used to detect those at risk and to offer them help. Further, services such as awareness programs and access to counselling could be strongly encouraged, or even mandated, as a safeguard during their employment at the casinos. The problem is casinos have yet to recognize that problem gambling is more of a social issue than an individual one and thus have not taken full responsibility in helping to combat the environmental influences on their employees.

So what is being done to protect casinos and their employees? Policies and awareness training are preventive measures currently in place for casino employees across the country. However, policies about employee gambling in workplace casinos vary greatly between jurisdictions. Casino employees in Alberta are legally prohibited from gambling in their casino of employment. The rules are more nuanced in Ontario. Nonsupervisory employees at regular OLG facilities are free to use only resort casinos, and supervisory employees at OLG facilities are strictly forbidden from gambling in any Ontario facility (Guttentag 2010). In contrast, employees of resort casinos are free to gamble anywhere aside from their workplace (Guttentag 2010). Nova Scotia's Gaming Control Act bans casino operators from allowing "officers, directors or partners of the casino operator" and "gaming assistants, casino key employees, casino employees or casino clerks of the casino operator" from playing on their operator's premises (Nova Scotia Legislature 2010). Here, the definition of casino employee includes almost everyone from dealers to groundskeepers.

Do workplace gambling policies even work? The effectiveness of these prevention efforts depend largely on how far the employee needs to travel before they can gamble. However, examining some international data, we see that prohibition on where an employee may gamble does seem to affect employee behaviour. This is obvious in the studies from Macau and Las Vegas. In both cities, gaming accounts for much of their economic activity, and the industry is more or less able to influence government policy and regulate it. For example, in 2007 there were 26 casinos in Macau, a city with a population of 544,600 and an area of 29.5 square kilometres. Further, casino employees are free to patronize any casino they wish (Wu and Wong 2007). Similarly, casinos in Las Vegas are at liberty to decide their own responsible gambling policies (Duquette 1999). Thus, "gambling by casino employees is permitted and even encouraged by casinos through various incentives, such as paycheck cashing drawings and free drink tickets" (Duquette 1999, 33). These policies may account for Las Vegas' 20 percent rate of pathological gambling and Macau's conservatively measured rate of 7 percent for disordered gambling among casino employees. Both of these are higher than rates reported in Alberta or Ontario.

Since 2006, the OLG has provided all existing employees and new hires with training programs that increase awareness of gambling-related problems and best practices in responsible gaming (Guttentag 2010). Some evidence suggests that the training is successful; however, its main flaw is that it focuses more on the patrons than on employee well-being. Employees learn how to spot problems in patrons but not in themselves or co-workers (Guttentag 2010). A 2008 Quebec study explored casino training and found that 89 percent of participants were either very or entirely satisfied with the training session. As well, 77 percent found it very/entirely relevant and useful for their jobs (Giroux et al. 2008).

A follow-up questionnaire, six months later, revealed that partici-pants maintained a good understanding of the notion of chance and randomness; however, some changes in workers' recall and opinions were found. For example, employees forgot when to offer gamblers help, and failed to remember procedures for helping gamblers. Generally, they were less convinced about the value of helping a gambler in crisis and doubted that the self-exclusionary programs were enough to help dis-tressed gamblers (Giroux et al. 2008).

Three important messages come out of these studies. First, more awareness training is needed on employee well-being, specifically about identifying a gambling problem in co-workers and employees them-selves. Second, training needs to occur often throughout the year to help with recall on procedures and to combat complacency in helping

Self-Exclusion Programs

A preventive measure focused more on patrons is the self-exclusionary pro-gram. Casinos in eight Canadian provinces have a voluntary self-exclusion pro-gram in place to help patrons control their gambling. These programs have several common features, but how long the ban can last differs greatly. It ranges from as little as three months in Quebec to a lifetime in Nova Scotia and Ontario. Therefore, problem gamblers can choose to ban themselves from casinos any-where from three months, one to five years, or a lifetime, depending on the province. Typically, individuals that self-exclude are given materials about avail-able counselling services. To help problem gamblers in Quebec, individuals that choose a heightened self-exclusion option also have mandated counselling and support as part of the program.

There are usually no legal implications for individuals trying to gamble at the casino where they have chosen to self-exclude; generally, they are escorted out of the facility without any fuss. However, in Alberta, individuals can be charged with a general offence with a maximum penalty of $10,000 or six months in prison. In most provinces, individuals are not given a chance to reinstate gaming privileges early; however, in Nova Scotia and Ontario, they can petition to be removed from the self-exclusion program after six months of enrolment (NCRG 2010).

Quebec researcher Robert Ladouceur and his colleagues (2007) were one of the first to rigorously investigate the benefits of self-exclusion programs for gamblers. They found a positive impact for most gamblers within six months of enrolment, including a decreased urge to gamble, an increased perception of control over their gambling, and fewer negative effects of gambling on daily ac-tivity, social life, and work. As one might expect, there was also an overall decline in DSM-IV and SOGS measures of problem gambling. However, these effects diminished and, gradually, the program's effect declined for some participants; roughly 40 percent had returned to the casino at least once by the time of their six-month follow-up.

those in need. Finally, more research and awareness is needed on how casino environments may affect employees' gambling behaviour with other forms of gambling such as at-home poker or Internet gaming.

An Employee Assistance Program does exist for many casinos in the country. Over 75 percent of Ontario's casino employees were aware of the program's existence and 52 percent of the respondents showed they would make use of it if necessary. Employees' views on the EAP were mixed, and while the program is confidential, some employees suspected that using it might harm their position at work. A vast majority of the respondents also believed that their direct supervisor would show them where to seek help and not end their contracts if they self-disclosed a gambling problem (Guttentag 2010). Given the increased prevalence of gambling problems among casino employees, it seems that building a supportive environment and more awareness about the meaning of confidentiality and the impact on their job security may be necessary steps in aiding employees to seek help.

So, as one might expect, gambling venues pose especially difficult problems for employees, since they are workplaces with high risks of problem gambling. Overall, evidence points to organizations developing ways to limit and monitor gambling among workers, as well as create employee well-being programs that can address gambling as a health and safety concern.

Closing Remarks

Certain groups recognize the dangers of gambling. But in other circles the existence of this disorder's far-reaching social effects are poorly known or conveniently ignored. Gambling has taken place in the workplace for centuries, but increased access has made this problem more pervasive.

The financial effect of problem gambling appears in the workplace in various forms: absenteeism, lateness, lower productivity, theft/fraud, and turnover. All of these outcomes are costly to both the employees and employers. There is a strong link between regular gambling and lower productivity, which burdens other employees and affects the overall system and work environment (Henriksson 2001). There is, moreover, controversy about the political will within government to address the problem. Currently, the best ways to fight the battle that our own government helps to promote is to make employers aware of this occupational issue, to put pressure on provinces to fund treatment programs, and to reduce the opportunities that "allow" gamblers to deplete their finances in the workplace.

In addition, organizations must look at their corporate culture and the explicit or implicit messages they send about workplace gambling before infringing on people's rights and privacy. The Alberta Workplace study revealed that one-quarter of employees (23 percent) and one-third of employers (35 percent) agreed that gambling was a socially acceptable activity in their workplace. It is much easier and more convenient to blame individuals than to look at the full complexity of the problem in which both governmental promotion and workplace cultures play a part.

Chapter 6

Sports Wagering

Gambling includes a range of activities, in various settings and formats that attracts a mix of people from different ages, classes, and cultures. This is especially true with sports wagering, where there is a multitude of events and ways to wager.

Sports are a popular pastime in North America, and we are flooded with messages about wagering on these events. Sports betting behaviour is often learned from parents, peers, and coaches, and reinforced by the active promotion of sports lotteries and fantasy sport leagues, as well as celebrities who openly wager on sporting events (e.g., Charles Barkley).

Sports wagering is also often in the news, surrounded by scandal and controversy. For instance, in 2010, there were several major stories, including the Memphis Grizzlies basketball players' fist fight over an unpaid personal gambling debt and the investigation into the New York Mets' long-time clubhouse manager for betting on baseball and providing inside information as part of an organized gambling ring.

The connections among betting, media, and sports are tightly woven together by big money. The Canadian Gaming Association (CGA) posts media articles on its website that specifically comment on the positive aspects of gambling, including its entertainment and economic value to our society. The industry seeks to increase its financial outcomes by normalizing the excitement of sport wagering as part of the fan experience: the greater the hype, the larger the audience, the bigger the dollar signs. This relationship is witnessed every year during the Super Bowl, which has the largest viewership and the most expensive commercial space, and generates more wagers than any other sporting event in North America.

It is through this pattern of escalating degrees that sport wagering has become well entrenched in the sporting experience for athletes, fans, and corporations alike, causing concern among scholars. This chapter explores overall trends associated with sport wagering, as well as its financial dimension, its impact on youth and college-age students, and the controversy surrounding regulatory issues.

An Overview of Sports Wagering

Sports wagering existed long before Europeans arrived in Canada. In fact, First Nation peoples wagered on personal games of skill such as tobogganing, canoe races, archery, spear throwing, and running events (Belanger 2006). Sports remain an important part of Canadian life, and while wagering in the distant past provided entertainment and an opportunity to hone survival skills, sport wagering today serves a different purpose: to entertain as well as to generate profit. Legal and illegal sports wagering is a multi-billion-dollar industry in North America (Stevens and Soebbing 2009). In 2009, it was estimated that between one and eight billion dollars was wagered on the Super Bowl, with only a fraction of that done legally (CTV News 2009). In fact, Las Vegas profits were roughly $95 million; it is suspected that the rest was wagered illegally through bookies, offshore sports books, office and Internet betting pools, and person-to-person betting (Stevens and Soebbing 2009). Similarly, the Federal Bureau of Investigation (FBI) estimates that more than $2.5 billion is illegally wagered on the NCAA March Madness Basketball Tournament each year, an amount which towers over the $80 to $90 million that is legally wagered (Simon 2010).

The National Gambling Impact Study conducted in 1999 suggested that illegal US sports wagering amounts to roughly $380 billion per year (Schwabish 2005). This amount is likely to be lower in Canada, given differences in population and the forms of illegal betting in each country. Nonetheless, this figure provides an idea of the value of sports wagering: it is a big-time business on the streets and in bricks-and-mortar establishments.

A heated topic in the media today is whether Canada should legalize sports betting on single event outcomes and acquire the riches that Las Vegas and illegal avenues are snatching up. The major benefits of legalization include revenue from taxes of legally collected wagers, a decrease in illegal gambling, and an increase in tourism (Burns 2010). In contrast, anti-legalists believe that further legalization of sports wagering will cause an increase in addiction and the social problems associated with problem gambling will dramatically decrease the integrity of sporting events and will put pressure on legal bookmakers to maintain a consistent profit (Stevens 2006).

These points lead to a subsequent question: Do enough Canadians wager on sports to even warrant this debate? A national study conducted in 2007 provides some specific numbers. In the year before the survey was conducted,16 percent of Canadians wagered on games of skill (i.e., pool, darts, basketball), while 8 percent bet on sports events, and 5 percent wagered on horse races. Further, 2 to 3 percent (about a million people) bet on sports events and games of skill each week (Wood and Williams 2009).

In general, all sport wagering options have a lower participation rate in Canada than more popular gambling activities, such as traditional lotteries and instant-win scratch tickets. However, individuals who engage in sports wagering (especially those who bet with a bookie) do so more often and spend more money than those who engage in other forms of gambling (Wynne 2002; Holtgraves 2009). In addition, those who report wagering online in the last year bet about three times more often on sports than gamblers who do not bet online (Wood and Williams 2009).

Studies in Canada, the United States, and Australia show that sports gamblers tend to be young adult males between the ages of 19 and 34 who have never been married (Wynne 2002). Some underlying common denominators for this group include risk-taking, free time, and disposable income. Given this profile, it is no surprise that sport wagering is most popular among college/university students and adolescents. Statistics show that 30 percent of adolescents and college/university students take part in sports wagering, compared to only about 15 percent of adults (Korn and Murray 2005).

The Ways to Wager

Sports wagering can occur privately between two friends, within groups (sport pools), in sports lotteries, at the horse track, in Las Vegas, over the Internet, or with a sports bookie. In Canada, only three of these avenues are legal: horse and dog racing (live or off the track), person-to-person betting that does not involve a third-party transaction fee, and government-owned sports lotteries. Privately run sports books, card rooms, and unlicensed games or lotteries are illegal.

Horse races

Until the early 1970s, the only form of legal betting in Canada was horse racing and friendly wagers between friends (Smith 2009). In 2010, 9 percent of Canadians reported wagering on horse races at the track and 6 percent at off-track betting facilities in the last year (Ipsos Reid and CGA 2010). A synthesis of provincial gambling surveys between 2001 and 2009 revealed some important comparisons between provinces.

The highest participation rates for horse racing were in Manitoba and Prince Edward Island, with about 7 percent of residents taking part in the last year. About 4 percent of citizens in British Columbia, Alberta, and Ontario bet on horses, and only 2 percent in the remaining provinces. In 1999, a study in Prince Edward Island found that horse racing was the most popular sports-related wager placed in the last year (15 percent), compared to sports lotteries (8 percent) and bets on personal games of skill (7 percent; Doiron and Nicki 1999). Sports wagering in Canada tends to be affected by seasonal conditions and the availability of venues. The former is especially relevant with horse and dog racing, which experience a decrease in participation throughout the winter months (CPRG 2010).

Personal games of skill and office pools

A private bet between two individuals is likely the simplest and oldest way to wager. Some data are available about the prevalence of betting on personal games of skills, yet little is known about how many people engage in personal bets on college/professional teams or in office pools. In addition, research on the impact of regular wagering between friends and family is scarce. On the one hand, gambling with family or friends may offer some protection from problematic behaviour, because the amount and frequency of the gambling may be monitored. However, on the other hand, it has the potential to create tension. We know that gambling, especially when it involves losing money, affects relationships. Would it be better for families and friends to wager with an objective entity, such as a land-based or virtual casino, that is not intimately involved in their lives? Or would that just remove the age-old purpose of gambling: to share and spread the wealth among those in the community? These questions remain unanswered, but they are important to consider as we continue to explore the social effects of gambling.

What we do know is that many people place bets on personal recreational games of skill, such as golf and basketball. About 7 percent of residents living in Alberta, Saskatchewan, Quebec, and Prince Edward Island take part in this form of wager, while only about 3 percent of those living in Ontario and Newfoundland and 2 percent living in Nova Scotia report such gambling in the last year (CPRG 2010; Doiron and Nicki 1999).

Anecdotally, we know that during March Madness and NHL hockey playoff season office pools spring up between groups of friends and with charities. However, the prevalence of this behaviour has yet to be well documented. In one national survey, 18 percent of Canadians reported engaging in sports pools, while 40 percent of Canadian Internet gamblers reported taking part in the last year (Ipsos Reid and CGA 2010). Two types of sport pools exist: those licensed by provincial governments and run by charities as a fundraiser and those privately organized. Both are legal, but the odds of winning tend to be better for privately run games, which are smaller and have no third party taking a cut from the pool of money (Smith 2009).

Sport Select

The third way to legally wager on sports is through sports lotteries. Provincial lottery corporations offer a sports betting option under the term *Sport Select*—specifically called Mise-o-jeu in Quebec, Pro-Line in Ontario and Atlantic Canada, and Sports Action in British Columbia. The fixed-odds for the events are published each week. Under the Criminal Code of Canada (207.1 4b), wagering on the result of a single sporting event is illegal, so sports lotteries require at least three bets to be placed on two separate sporting events, more commonly known as a parlay (CBC 2010c).

A recent national survey of public gambling views and behaviours revealed that about 5 percent of Canadians gambled on sports lotteries. Among the subsample of Internet gamblers in the study, 17 percent also took part in sports lotteries (Ipsos Reid and CGA 2010). According to data comparing provinces, the highest sports lottery participation is found in Manitoba and Saskatchewan, at 6 percent, followed by Ontario, New Brunswick, and Nova Scotia at 4 percent, and the rest of the provinces at 3 percent (CPRG 2010).

Sports lotteries appeal to a different target group than the traditional lottery ticket buyer, which has provided governments with modest profits over the years (Smith 1992). Sport Select games have mainly focused on North American professional sports leagues, but in recent years, odds have been offered on the English Premier League (soccer), college basketball, and on professional football, tennis, and golf. This expansion has attracted a wider audience. In addition, new games have emerged, such as Over/Under, Point Spread, and Double Play (Smith 2009).

The sports lottery games attract mostly men (83 percent) between the ages of 18 and 44 (Smith 2009). The appeal for sports lotteries is similar to poker in its combination of some skill with some chance. Technically, the word *lotteries* implies that skill and knowledge is not required (Burns 2010). However, gamblers can apply what they know about the teams, players, and game conditions to increase their odds of winning.

Sport Select has come under heavy criticism from Canadian gamblers for its poor odds (Wilkins 2010). The payout percentage—that is, the amount given out in prizes—is critical in discovering the likelihood of beating a game over the long run (Smith 2009). The payout percentage for sports lotteries in Canada is 57 percent. Compare this to the payout rates for horse racing (80 percent), slots (70 percent), and bingo (65 percent). This fact, added to the parlay format in which the gambler must guess several games correctly to win, explains why no amount of skill can consistently beat the government's advantage when they keep 43 percent of the wagered dollar (Smith 2009).

In Nevada, the parlay game is considered the "sucker play" given its poor payout percentages—and the odds in Nevada are even higher than the odds offered in Canada (Smith 2009). It is no wonder then that many Canadian gamblers have turned to the Internet and switched their gambling fix to offshore bookmakers or betting exchanges offering up to 50 percent better odds than an individual match on Sport Select. An additional bonus to these venues is that a wager can be placed on the outcome of a single sporting event, greatly increasing the gambler's odds (Wilkins 2010).

Las Vegas

Las Vegas is the only place in North America where an individual can legally bet on the result of a single sporting event. In 2003, about 18 percent of gamblers from British Columbia travelled to Las Vegas to visit casinos and place sports-related bets (Ipsos Reid Public Affairs and Gemini Research 2008). Though we get a glimpse of our Canadian travels to Sin City in this one study, we do not know how many Canadians across the country visit Las Vegas and how much we contribute to its overall revenue in any given year. However, it is worth noting that airport buses display "Welcome Canadians, We Love You" signs.

According to the American Gaming Association (AGA), more than $2.6 billion was legally wagered in Nevada sports books in 2010, with about two-thirds of the bets placed on professional sporting events (Simon 2010). The top betting events include the Super Bowl, the NFL playoffs, college football bowls, March Madness, the NBA playoffs, the World Series, the Masters tournament, Wimbledon, the Indianapolis and Daytona 500, the Ultimate Fighting Championship and pro boxing, and the Triple Crown horse races (Sheridan, as quoted in McCarthy 2007a). Las Vegas is likely a destination spot for Canadian sports gamblers during these major events. People unable to travel may have street bookies place a bet for them, but the number of people engaging in this type of gambling is unknown.

The percentage of Canadians wagering specifically on sporting events is highest in Manitoba (12 percent), followed by British Columbia (9 percent), and then Alberta, New Brunswick, and Nova Scotia (6 percent), and the rest of the provinces at 4 percent, excluding Quebec at 1 percent (CPRG 2010). It is unclear in the research how individuals actually place their wagers on these events, whether it involves travelling to Las Vegas, using the Internet, making a bet with a friend, or betting with a street bookie (likely a mix of these various betting options is involved).

Bookie wagers

Despite multiple legal avenues for gambling, illegal wagering with sports bookies continues to thrive in Canada (Ferentzy and Turner 2009). This is probably due to increased tolerance for victimless crimes, more favourable payout percentages, and client-friendly services such as credit extension, telephone wagering, and single event sports wagers—services unavailable from government-run sports lotteries (Smith 2009).

The approach to gambling in the first half of the twentieth century was "unofficial tolerance and official condemnation" (Morton 2003, as quoted in Smith 2009). This atmosphere helped the growth of bookmaking operations, which were seen as part of male sporting culture and viewed as a petty crime. Today is no different: with a decrease in funding for law enforcement, illegal gambling has been placed on the low-priority list. It is considered a minor crime compared to misconduct such as child pornography and violent offenses (Smith 2009). Even joint units made up of provincial and municipal police that specialize in illegal gambling enforcement have made little impact in bookmaking operations given the sheer number of operations and the low conviction rate in court cases. It is estimated that more than a thousand bookmaking operations exist in Toronto alone (Smith 2009). Enforcement is also driven by public complaints, so if people do not see this gambling as a problem, or are willing participants in the crime, or if the sports book is run by a friend, they are not likely to report it.

Gambling has historically been connected to organized crime, especially gambling associated with underground casinos, card rooms, and bookmaking, which have been portrayed in movies such as *Goodfellas*, *Casino*, and *The Godfather* (Ferentzy and Turner 2009). Sports bookies offer added services and better odds, but using their services has risks. In particular, gamblers who use bookies have fewer options for collections and are unable to seek bankruptcy protection like those in debt to legal casinos and credit card companies. These added financial pressures can derail those in addiction treatment who return to "quick fixes" such as gambling to pay their debt to organized crime figures (Ferentzy and Turner 2009).

In 2002, betting with a bookie had the lowest rates of participation among those living in Saskatchewan. However, those who did take part did so more often and with higher wagers than other forms of wagering (Wynne 2002). This result was further substantiated by a Canadian study that found those who wager with a bookie bet more frequently and had higher problem gambling scores than those who participate in other forms of gambling (Holtgraves 2009). Bookmaking is a profitable business with few severe penalties, making it a low-risk criminal activity in Canada. Because these businesses will continue, we must consider how vulnerable populations, such as youth and problem gamblers, can be protected from operations which are invisible and seemingly untouchable.

Online sports wagering

Online sports and race books were first introduced in 1996 with about 650 gambling sites. Today, more than 2,500 sites have been created and Canadians spend between $1 and $5 billion on online gambling each year, mainly on poker and sports wagering (CBC 2010c). Yet, the legality of Canadians taking part in offshore sports wagering is murky, given Canada's passive approach to regulation. Nonetheless, offshore websites allow Canadians to wager on single events and on sports from around the world, including cricket, soccer, and rugby, increasing the appeal and accessibility to those who want to gamble on less traditional sports. Essentially, these sites open the door to more betting opportunities, and gambling-related corruption, to sports across the globe.

All forms of sports wagering already discussed in the chapter can also take place over the Internet (except for betting with a bookie). A recent national survey provides some insight on the number of Canadians that wager online. The study revealed that, overall, 5 percent of Canadians wagered on sport-related games online in the last year, while about 2 percent engaged in monthly wagering on each of the following: horse races, sporting events, games of skills (such as backgammon and mahjong), online sport pools, and fantasy contests for money (Ipsos Reid and CGA 2010).

Two important factors have been identified: Internet sport wagerers bet more often and spend more money than people who sports wager offline. In another national report, the activity of Internet gamblers was compared to non-Internet gamblers for three sport wagering games. The results showed that 44 percent of Internet gamblers took part in sports event betting, 73 percent bet on games of skill, and 16 percent bet on horse races, compared to much lower percentages among the non-Internet gamblers reported earlier in the chapter (8 percent, 16 percent, and 5 percent, respectively; Wood and Williams 2009). In addition, Internet gamblers' monthly outlays were about twice as much for horse/dog racing and sports event betting ($77 and $40) than those of non-Internet gamblers ($35 and $26, respectively). This is likely because of the multitude of different payment options and the increased accessibility—gamblers can play as often and long as they want online (Wood and Williams 2009).

Another billion-dollar industry is fantasy sports leagues, which attract some 27 million players from across North America. Essentially, the player acts as an owner, building a virtual team of current professional athletes. League rules apply to the team, and trades occur throughout the season. Fantasy players collect points based on statistical categories of real-life performances of athletes on their team (Finkelstein 2009). Fantasy sports were specifically excluded from the US Internet Gambling Act of 2006, but the legality of taking part under the Canadian law is unclear given several limits in the Criminal Code of Canada (Finkelstein 2009).

Nonetheless, many Canadians do take part in fantasy leagues, and the activity involves a combination of both skill and chance in that an individual's success is based on his or her ability to research the sport and make the best educated guesses on potential outcomes. While participants pay an entry fee, they place no bets or wagers. However, the activity involves many of the same ingredients as gambling and launches behaviour that is easily transferred into the sports wagering world.

The appeal for fantasy leagues is the intellectual challenge, the opportunity to manage a professional sports team and win money, and the social networking opportunities from which significant bonds and friendships can develop. The downside is the initial investment of money and the immense time commitment; numerous hours are dedicated to researching teams and trades and watching games, which can interfere with family, work, and leisure activities (Smith 2009).

Potential Problems

Let's recap some important points: participation rates for sports wagering activities are lower than for other forms of gambling; however, those who do engage in it tend to spend more and play more often (Wynne 2002). This is especially true for people who place bets with bookies;

they tend to have the lowest overall rate of participation but have a very high frequency of wagering behaviour and high problem gambling scores (Wynne 2002; Holtgraves 2009). Similarly, Internet sports gamblers play much more often and wager more than people who make land-based sports wagers (Wood and Williams 2009). These characteristics place many sports gamblers at a greater risk of developing an addiction.

So why do people gamble on sports, especially on games that are outside their own experience and control? Gamblers who wager on sports tend to play for the adrenaline rush from the anticipated outcome rather than to escape problems (a characteristic of those who engage in slots or scratch tickets). Wagering on sports involves a high degree of mental activity before the bet; gamblers examine the odds and figure out the latest injuries on the teams and the game conditions to make the best possible selection. The combination of skill and luck required is attractive for young, active minds, especially those wanting to show dominance within a peer group. In addition, adolescents and young adults (especially males) tend to be more physically involved in sports and sport-related video games, putting them at high risk for early involvement.

The skill-based ingredient involved in sports wagering offers another attractive element to gamblers: gamblers who understand the sport often feel a greater sense of control over their picks (Geffner 2008). This leads to unrealistic expectations about their chances of winning, which in turn leads to problems down the road. Anything can happen on the field at any given moment, from a broken leg, to an off-day for a team or a horse. A recent study revealed that college athletes were nearly twice as likely to be problem gamblers than non-athletes (Korn and Murray 2005), providing some evidence that overconfidence in knowledge of a given sport may contribute to problematic gambling behaviour.

Compulsive checking of game outcomes typically occurs with this type of gambling given the long delay between placing a bet and the outcome (Geffner 2008). Not all sports gamblers watch the games on which they are betting. However, most will track the score in some fashion, either online, over the radio, or in a newspaper's sports pages. This level of information seeking and mental involvement lends itself to increased preoccupation with the activity as the individual moves from social to problematic gambling. Tracking games at family events, at dinner, at the cinema, and even while hiding in the bathroom is common according to therapists who specialize in problem gambling (Geffner 2008). Large wins and losses are possible in a single day, and the rush of picking a group of winning teams can be tremendous. What may seem like a harmless behaviour can easily descend into financial destruction and stress for players and their families.

A study by Wynne (2002) revealed the top five weekly activities of moderate and problem gamblers in Saskatchewan: lottery (39 percent), sport wagering with a bookie (33 percent), bingo (24 percent), sports lotteries/Sport Select (24 percent), and games of skill (23 percent). There is a trend here. Three of the top five activities are sports-related wagering options. Further, an examination of the data across provinces also reveals a correlation between sports wagering involvement and problem gambling. The highest sports wagering participation in the nation (across all formats) are found in Manitoba, Saskatchewan, and Alberta, where the highest prevalence of moderate and severe problem gamblers are also found. On the contrary, the lowest participation in sports wagering and the lowest prevalence of problem gamblers is in Quebec (CPRG 2010). There are likely other factors involved in this correlation, but it is important to recognize the pattern and possible connection.

An interesting study published in 2009 used population-based surveys across Canada from 2001 to 2005 to examine gambling frequency and rates of problem gambling between different gambling activities (Holtgraves 2009). In a sample of about 12,300 gamblers, researchers found that gamblers tended to cluster in one of two groups. Those found in one group tended to partake in Internet gambling and betting on sports and horse races, while those in the second group participated in lotteries, raffles, slots/VTLs, and bingo. Most of those who wagered on sports and the Internet were men (78 percent) and had higher scores on the Canadian Problem Gambling Index (CPGI).

The highest conversion rates were found among those involved in Internet gambling, Sport Select, and placing wagers with a bookie; that is, more people who tried these activities continued to wager more frequently than the people who tried other activities. This finding is especially relevant in the context of the third result: those who played more had higher problem gambling scores (Holtgraves 2009). Taken together, these results suggest that sport wagering is an activity that can become habitual very quickly, increasing the odds that the sports gambler will develop a problem. Lastly, placing bets with a bookie was associated with the highest problem gambling scores in the study, along with slot machine players (Holtgraves 2009).

What signs suggest someone may be addicted to sports wagering? Here are some indications: when the size of the wagers increases over time; when bets involve multiple teams and sports; when aspects of the gambling are hidden from others (e.g., betting on more than one sport); when there are financial problems and bookie debt; when there is excessive sports watching compared to other events; and when gambling becomes seen as an extra source of income. In these cases, there is a strong likelihood that a gambling problem is developing (Geffner 2008).

Canadian Youth and Sports Wagering

Sports wagering varies for different age groups and social groups in Canada. Next, we will discuss this form of wagering for youth, university students, and student athletes.

Youth

Legalized gambling in Canada has experienced rapid growth over the past 10 years. During this time, youth have been exposed to high levels of gambling-positive advertising with little education about gambling's risks. Studies consistently show that adolescents and young adults have a higher inclination for developing a gambling problem than adults (Jacobs 2005; Felsher, Derevensky, and Gupta 2007) and gambling habits picked up in childhood may predispose individuals to more severe problems later in life (Ellenbogen et al. 2008).

Gambling can impede normal adolescent development; it is associated with negative behavioural, psychological, interpersonal, and academic outcomes. These can significantly affect a youth's life trajectory, affecting families and society as a whole (Messerlian, Byrne, and Derevensky 2004). Also, values, attitudes, and character traits learned in adolescence through sports are often transferred into adulthood, placing athletes at an increased risk of gambling addictions (Darden and Rockey 2006).

Some youth begin gambling as early as age 10 or 11, typically with cards or dice, and have more exposure to sports betting as they reach high school (Jacobs 2005). The list of adolescent gambling activities is astonishing. Those specifically related to sports include betting with peers on personal games of skills (e.g., basketball, bowling, video games), sports wagering with friends, wagering at horse and dog tracks or at off-satellite betting parlours, and placing bets with bookies (Jacobs 2005).

Sports are a big part of life for youth, either through physical or virtual participation. Young people are also attracted to the excitement and financial freedom that gambling offers. These characteristics in combination with technology-related interests make land-based and online sports wagering appealing to this age group. Today, many online sites capitalize on these interests, attracting youth with video game software and free wagering choices (Skinner et al. 2004).

Over the last decade, studies by Derevensky and his colleagues from McGill University have painted a picture of youth gambling in Canada. Although discussed in more depth in Chapter 9, some findings related to sports wagering are relevant here. In general, young males tend to gamble on cards, sports pools, sporting events, and games of skill, while young females tend to gamble on cards, lottery tickets, and bingo (Hardoon and Derevensky 2002).

Several older studies provide us with a sense of trends in sport wagering activities among youth over the last decade. In 1998, Adebayo examined the types of gambling played in seventh and eighth grades in Alberta: 37 percent of students reported betting on personal games of skill, 35 percent on sports teams, and 15 percent on Sport Select. In Quebec, sports pools and sports lottery tickets were the most popular forms of gambling, played by 30 to 45 percent of youth in two studies (Gupta and Derevensky 1998; Ladouceur and Mireault 1998). A recurring trend is the increased likelihood that males rather than females wager on sports and other games with a skill-based component (i.e., coin flipping, cards, Sport Select; Adebayo 1998). This finding was further supported in another study which revealed that females were most drawn to draw/scratch tickets, whereas males were most attracted to sporting events and sports lotteries (Gupta and Derevensky 1998).

A more recent study of lottery participation among youth found that 2 percent regularly bought sports tickets and scratch tickets, while 13 percent of the sample occasionally bought sports tickets, and 51 percent played scratch tickets (Felsher, Derevensky, and Gupta 2007). The average age that youth began playing sports lotteries was 11. Although the overall participation was lower, sports betting was played by youth who showed more problematic gambling behaviour.

Clinical work by Gupta and Derevensky (2000) found that sports lotteries were problematic for youth because they reported a higher sense of skill and heightened physiological arousal (thrill) with this form of betting, regardless of whether they won or lost. The increased arousal places youth at higher risk of addiction. In a separate youth study, those who engaged in online sports betting had the highest percentage of probable pathological gambling in the sample (McBride and Derevensky 2009). Given these results, it seems that sports wagering even among youth can be more addictive than other forms of wagering and can become a gateway to further gambling opportunities.

Empirical research is helpful to understand the landscape of youth gambling. The following personal account of two young males' escalation with sports gambling sheds a more personal light on the topic (Doshi 2007). A summary of their story is provided below:

It all started in tenth grade in Trigonometry class when his best friend asked if he wanted to bet $5 on a football game. Within a year, the two of them were betting on everything from college to professional sports, even taking bets from schoolmates. "We felt compelled to bet on everything from cards to sports to video games; we'd even go bowling for hundreds of dollars a game." They took professional bowling lessons to hustle others at the ally, winning over $1000 a night, only to lose it later. "To support our gambling we committed crimes, broke international laws, sacrificed ourselves, lied to our families and pissed off friends." The bets got larger and riskier and the following year, the high school suspected some gambling activity and their small sports booking operation collapsed, leaving them to bet only with each other, once again. However, when they consistently wanted the same sports teams, they decided to turn to blackjack which quickly progressed from playing at home after school to playing in their cars on breaks, in the library and even in class. The instant action produced a "high" not previously experienced. "Our excitement level was constantly mounting and whether we won or lost, it was more the act of gambling that got us off." After a big loss and a significant amount of strain on their friendship, they turned back to sports wagering but this time betting on personal games of skill, specifically tennis and basketball. However, they reported that it was difficult to capture the same level of excitement and high they had experienced with blackjack. Instead they ventured from Detroit over the border to the Windsor Casino with fake IDs. A routine they kept up for some time, sneaking in and out of their homes to spend hours at the casino. A life-changing experience occurred when they spent eight hours at the casino, winning up to $19,000; attracting people from other tables and security to check IDs several times during the winning streak. Ignoring the plea of his best friend to just leave, the bets got riskier and the unstoppable feeling took over. A couple of losing hands took one of them down to $15,000 and when that didn't seem like quite enough, he began chasing his losses and wound up losing it all. "There I was on the cusp of winning a fortune and I couldn't walk away," and had his friend not been there he said he would have gone to the ATM and tried to win it all back again. (Doshi 2007)

This personal account shows the addiction to betting (not the money) and the intensification of gambling from experimentation with sport wagering to casino blackjack, from $5 wagers to risking $19,000, all at the age of 17. This young student was able to reflect on his experience and realize the lack of balance in his life with gambling—but this comprehension may not be possible for all young gamblers.

University students

It is important to examine student sports wagering from both a Canadian and an American perspective to highlight the unique concerns among this vulnerable group. The relationship between university athletics and gambling is strong among students, sports fans, and organized crime (Nelson et al. 2007). The NCAA basketball tournament, also known as March Madness, is the second largest wagering event in North America. During this period, sports pools, personal bets, and wagers with bookies increase dramatically in both Canada and the United States. Many gambling helplines reveal that March is their busiest month, with calls from gamblers themselves as well as from family, friends, employers, law enforcement, and high school/post-secondary teachers, all looking for help and advice (McCarthy 2007b).

A particular concern is the higher prevalence of problem gambling among college students (especially male athletes) who also have higher participation rates with sports wagering (Korn and Murray 2005; LaBrie et al. 2003). Although US colleges do face additional concerns and pressures with high-profile intercollegiate athletic programs in their backyard, the popularity of US college sports does not dissipate at the Canada/US border. In addition, other risk factors important to the prevalence of sport wagering, such as being male and athletic identity, still apply to college-aged Canadians. Furthermore, the increase of college sports on television also increases the likelihood that bets are being placed by Canadians, and these bets may be more prevalent than we realize.

Should parents and universities be more concerned? Yes. We saw earlier that student-age individuals are more likely to wager on sports (if they gamble), and students have higher rates of problem gambling than adult or adolescent populations (Jacobs 2005; Skinner et al. 2004). Mounting evidence suggests that sport wagering can be more problematic than other forms of gambling—clearly an issue when combined with this already at-risk group. Post-secondary students have not been extensively studied in Canada, but research is available from the United States. Of all college students in the United States, 67 percent report betting on sports and between 3 and 11 percent (depending on the study) are problem gamblers (NCRG 2009).

The first national study exploring gambling among athletes, sports fans, and other students in college was published in 2007. It had a couple of important findings. First, higher rates of sports wagering (and other forms of gambling) were found among both college athletes and sports fans than other students on campus (Nelson et al. 2007). No differences were found between athletes and sports fans, suggesting that similar factors influence gambling behaviour within these two groups. Second, the overall campus interest in college sports was related to more sports wagering. Specifically, colleges that placed a greater emphasis on attending college sporting events also had increased gambling on sports, especially placing wagers with a bookie. This result held true even after adjusting for differences in the number of fans and athletes at any given college (Nelson et al. 2007).

It is logical to think that Canadian universities are at lower risk of sports-related gambling since fewer students attend collegiate events. However, risks likely still exist for athletes and sports fans enthused by US college athletics. Also, time spent as a sports fan or athlete exposes individuals to sports gambling opportunities as part of the peer culture (Markle 2003). Thus, students who are part of physical education programs or athletics or who are just avid sports fans may view sports wagering as a normal part of life within their peer group.

We know many young adults in Canada have gambled or been exposed to gambling before university. However, the new-found freedoms of post-secondary life may make it more conducive for first-time gamblers to begin or for current gamblers to play more often. It is not uncommon for young sports gamblers to have relationships with illegal bookmakers by the time they attend university (CCGNJ 2007). It is suspected that millions of dollars are being illegally bet on college sports, and the sheer popularity of this gambling activity is worrisome. With few legal ways to wager on single events, it opens the door for college-age bookies with connections to organized crime.

One interesting study examined how and why post-secondary students become involved and continue to engage in illegal sports gambling. Interviews revealed that students were initially introduced to betting on sports by their fathers or male friends, typically prior to college or university. Their early involvement was through more socially acceptable forms, such as NCAA tournament brackets and Super Bowl squares, but over time their gambling progressed to wagering online or with a bookie. Students disclosed that social acceptability of the activity was the main reason for their participation. Other motivations included a chance to make money, the excitement of the wager, an opportunity to use sports knowledge, and a chance to bond with other gamblers. Also, students reported using campus equipment and facilities to wager and did not recall being exposed to any anti-gambling educational programs, and campus policies/federal laws were not enforced (Otteman 2008).

In this same study, students reported that, over time, the number and amount of their wagers increased and a large part of their day was spent collecting gambling information and watching games—all of which produced negative consequences for them financially, academically, and socially (Otteman 2008). Another interesting finding was that many of the students perceived that their wagering would decrease after college, where unlimited time and disposable money would no longer be a luxury as they moved into the work world. Similar views about smoking behaviour have been reported by social smokers in college; yet, one study revealed that the amount students smoke in college was predictive of their smoking behaviour four years later (Moran, Wechsler, and Rigotti 2004). If this example can be used as a guide, misperceptions among students about the long-term addictive quality of sports wagering may be prevalent.

College students are also targeted with provocative advertising and flashy Internet sites, such as Bet365.com and SportsBooks.com, which use attractive female models to advertise their product. Sports, sex, and a chance to win quick money are an alluring combination for this age group. Young people are also encouraged to become involved with minimal risk. For example, QuarterBets.com featured seven sports (NFL, NBA, MLB, NHL, tennis, and NCAA basketball and football), reaching players in the United States and Canada and targeting college- and university-age students. Players on this site (now out of business) were never required to deposit money to the site and instead were given 25 cents to start wagering, with the option of cashing out once they reached winnings of $20. One of the owners, Grayson Ediger, said, "It's a very fun feeling watching a sports game with money on the line" (as quoted in Samson 2009). The message that sports are more enjoyable with a wager is promoted widely, even when there is little money or risk at stake.

Wagering can be entertaining, but it can also lead to stress, guilt, interpersonal conflict, poor job or school performance, suicide, and criminal behaviour. In 2006, a 23-year-old student (and the son of a police chief) with no previous criminal history was arrested for running an illegal booking operation. He took bets on college and professional teams from students at two local high schools. Some of the students had generated as much as $27,000 in debt and, when they were threatened with collections, they ran to the police (McCarthy 2007c).

In a more serious instance, Wu, a first-year student at the University of Wisconsin from a wealthy Taiwanese family, became involved with sports wagering and lost close to $15,000 (McCarthy 2007c). When he was confronted by his parents about gambling away his tuition and expense money, he became violent, murdering his bookie and two other innocent students (McCarthy 2007c). In custody, Wu admitted his gambling addiction. Although this addiction had likely started before college, the freedom provided by time, money, and decreased parental control may have created an environment that fuelled it further.

What makes this story even more devastating is that the money itself was a drop in the bucket for Wu's family. It was shame and embarrassment that pushed Wu over the edge. Unfortunately, the story does not end there. Wu committed suicide in prison, and a victim's brother was so grief stricken over losing his older brother that he took his own life a year later (McCarthy 2007c). Five deaths and four families were destroyed by sports wagering, gambling addiction, and the allure of a glamorous lifestyle.

This story is one of the worst post-secondary gambling accounts recorded in North America. What will it take before people and institutions recognize the dangers of gambling?

Few universities in the United States have adopted a gambling prevention program or policy to help protect students. In fact, only 22 percent of colleges and universities have any sort of gambling policy, although 100 percent have a policy on alcohol (Shaffer et al. 2005). Efforts have been made to rectify this with the creation of a national task force in 2008, composed of professionals from across the country and chaired by Howard Shaffer, a prominent researcher in addiction from Harvard University. The national report was released in 2009 and addressed gambling behaviour and policy concerns for universities and colleges; yet, little movement has come from the report. University leadership and administrators do not tend to see students gambling or understand the risk of gambling as much as they do with issues such as alcohol, drugs, or sexual violence. This lack of awareness, along with few noticeable warning signs, puts gambling at the back of the bus as an organizational and student health issue for many universities. Despite a less developed intercollegiate athletic system, Canada is leaps and bounds ahead of the United States in terms of prevention strategies for post-secondary students; programs such as kts2 and websites such as www.friends4friends.ca target this group.

Throughout this book, the following important risk factors for a gambling addiction have been identified: being a male between the ages of 18 and 34 and having a competitive nature, a family history of any addiction, early first gambling experiences, and access to gambling and money. Further characteristics specifically related to sports wagering include being an athlete or avid sports fan and engaging in sports wagering or online gambling. Two risk factors (sports wagering and being an athlete) are explored in more depth in the next section.

Student athletes

Student athletes are an extremely vulnerable subgroup of an already at-risk population. Post-secondary school athletes are more likely to gamble than nonsports fans (Nelson et al. 2007) and are twice as likely as non-student athletes to be problem gamblers (Oster and Knapp 1998). Specifically, the NCAA study surveyed just under 20,000 athletes in 2004 and again in 2008, revealing the following important findings:

- Playing cards was reported as the most common first point of entry into wagering, with 26 percent of male athletes reporting they first gambled prior to high school and 66 percent first gambled in high school.
- The top gambling activities were playing cards, betting on games of skill and sporting events, and playing the stock market.
- Overall past-year gambling rates were higher among male athletes (62 percent) than female athletes (43 percent), and male athletes had higher rates of problem gambling. The data revealed that about 4 percent of all male athletes across the United States experience moderate to severe problem gambling symptoms—that's about 9,300 male athletes.
- About 30 percent of the male athletes reported wagering on sports in the past year despite NCAA regulations prohibiting it, and about 9 percent of Division I level athletes across 11 different sports reported wagering on sports at least once a month.
- The highest rate of monthly sports wagering was found among male golfers at the Division I level, at 20 percent. About 10 percent of male soccer, football, and golf players at the Division II level reported wagering, and more than 10 percent of all male athletes at the Division III level wagered on sports (NCAA 2008).

This information raises an important question: What is the connection among men, athleticism, and sports wagering? A 2003 analysis of gender by Markle highlighted three major motivations for sports gambling involvement: culture, social structure, and personal identity. A person's self-concept and identity are developed through social roles. Behavioural patterns are culture-based, and even today, different values and norms are indicated for males and females in North America. Young females are encouraged to be caretakers and play games of co-operation, while young males tend to play games that involve dares and competitions. In fact, "males are more likely than females to [develop] role-identities with risk-management as a salient component of their self-concepts" (Markle 2003, 37).

For instance, young male athletes have both a sports role identity and a risk-manager role identity, which makes them highly susceptible to developing competitive attitudes. These identities increase the likelihood that they will seek out activities such as gambling to experience the excitement and thrill associated with risk, producing a higher prevalence of sports gambling among males than females (Markle 2003). The belief that a daring attitude is desirable for males is internalized from a range of media and peer interaction. Sports wagering serves as a form of both entertainment and self-presentation: a way for males to prove to others that they are confident risk-takers (Markle 2003).

Family and friends help to shape these identities. If a person's social network participates in sports gambling, it normalizes and reinforces the behaviour, increasing the odds that an individual will also engage in gambling. Essentially, peers and family members can glamorize gambling, creating interest and excitement to get involved. This interest can open opportunities that were unknown or unavailable to the person before (Markle 2003). Another theory suggests that gambling among members of team sports is common because it creates a unique bond, one characterized by friendly competition, risk-taking, and boastfulness (Ellenbogen et al. 2008). Athletes who are eager to be accepted by their teammates are vulnerable to group demands and behaviour. In this same regard, coaches can serve as gatekeepers, either promoting or preventing gambling among the team (Wanner and Paskus 2010).

Curry and Jiobu (1995) were among the first to theorize that athletes are at increased risk for gambling problems given the competitive spirit fostered in their main social environment. They believe that the socialization of athletes includes adapting to a competitive atmosphere and being encouraged to seek additional activities that involve risk (Ellenbogen et al. 2008). If we accept this theory, student athletes in the most competitive environments would likely be at a greater risk for developing gambling problems. This was supported by Nelson et al. (2007) in a study that found gambling participation increased on campuses that emphasize attending sporting events.

At first glance, this theory may be a sigh of relief for Canadian athletic programs that do not have the same sport structure, school spirit, money, and attention as American college sports. In fact, a study by Korn and Murray in 2005 found that gambling by student athletes on intercollegiate athletics was generally not perceived to be problematic in Canada. A survey of 80 athletic directors and coaches revealed that for the majority of respondents, awareness of gambling-related problems among student athletes and within intercollegiate athletics in Canada was low. Some knowledge of informal betting and recreational gambling among teammates, friends, and/or family existed, but it was not perceived to be problematic (Korn and Murray 2005).

In Canada, there are no betting lines on intercollegiate sports like in the United States. This fact has led some to conclude that gambling on university games by student athletes and fans is non-existent in Canada. In 2003, the director of athletics at Dalhousie University reported never having heard of sports wagering being a problem on his campus or elsewhere in Canadian university sport. Likewise, the director of athletics at the University of Regina says, "We have no evidence to indicate that this is a concern. I've never heard about it anecdotally or in our conversations at many levels" (Sklar 2007).

While these comments may not seem surprising, it is worth noting that they are strikingly similar to those made by senior university administrators across the United States. Most athletic directors, coaches, professors, and student life professionals have the same reaction and attitude, whether they are associated with Division I athletic programs (with considerable athletic money, school spirit, and attention) or Division III programs, which are most comparable in size, facilities, and budgets to Canadian programs (Wanner 2010). However, as noted, the data suggests otherwise for college students and student athletes in the United States. In fact, the NCAA's gambling behaviour studies (2004 and 2008) show that athletes at Division III schools have the highest participation in sport wagering. It is probably short-sighted to believe that Canadian athletes and college- and university-age sports fans are not betting on intercollegiate sports in Canada and the United States.

This point is further reflected in statements made by Dr. Jeffrey Derevensky, director of the International Centre for Youth Gambling Problems and High-Risk Behaviours at McGill University: "We know gambling activities of all kinds are very popular among young people in this age group. So why is it assumed that they aren't wagering on University games?" (as quoted in Sklar 2007). Derevensky suggests that the difference between the Canadian Interuniversity Sport (CIS) and the NCAA "is that US college students know wagering is against their code of conduct. But it's not even mentioned in the books here" (as quoted in Sklar 2007). The current lack of awareness about gambling as a health issue among Canadian and American university administrators speaks directly to the hidden nature of problem gambling. Further research is

Warning Signs of Problem Gambling Behaviours for Athletes*

1. Athlete hides the extent of his or her gambling involvement from family members, teammates, and coaches.
2. Athlete jeopardizes significant relationships, athletic opportunities, or career opportunities.
3. Athlete frequently misses class or team practice for unexplained reasons.
4. Athlete suffers from decreased concentration, motivation, and athletic performance in practice, and appears lethargic from loss of sleep.
5. Equipment goes missing and athlete has increased conflicts with teammates.

*These are in addition to other signs common to all people struggling with this issue.
Source: Adapted from Darden and Rockey 2006

needed on Canadian campuses to clarify the current reality of students and gambling.

Coach's corner

Gambling is not on the radar for many coaches as either a health or performance issue. Korn and Murray (2005) found that Canadian coaches believed that student athletes would gamble less than other students because of lack of time and money, as well as greater knowledge about sports. In addition, they believed that if athletes did gamble, it occurred mainly in the form of informal sports pools that were not problematic. Gambling may look harmless, but most research suggests a progression of gambling behaviours that start at the recreational or social level and escalates to higher stakes (Darden and Rockey 2006).

The Canadian national coaching standards strongly encourage coaches to adopt an athlete-centred philosophy, which means promoting behaviours that lead to the positive development of young athletes in preparation for adult life (Darden and Rockey 2006). A lack of awareness and attention to athletes' gambling conflicts directly with this philosophy, given what we know about the potential consequences for development.

Another reason coaches should be concerned about gambling is the negative impact it can have on individual and team athletic performance, just as it affects people at work. Preoccupation and lack of sleep affect focus, motivation, and engagement with the task at hand, which in turn influences performance and increases the risk of injury (Buddy 2003; Griffiths 2009b; Wanner and Paskus 2010). In addition, gambling has the potential to create interpersonal conflicts among teammates from borrowed money, missing athletic gear, and gambling debts.

A few media stories reveal the potential effect of gambling on team dynamics. A basketball player on the Memphis Grizzlies was left with significant injuries after a fist fight with a teammate over an unpaid gambling debt; the player subsequently missed the Grizzlies' next game. (This event resulted in a ban on gambling during team flights.) In 2010, Charles Oakley (then playing for the Toronto Raptors) hit Philadelphia 76er Tyrone Hill in the head with a basketball over nonpayment of a reported $54,000 gambling debt, and Jerry Stackhouse of the Detroit Pistons slugged teammate Christian Laettner over similar circumstances (Berger 2011).

In a 2008 NCAA study, 70 percent of athletes believed their teammates would be aware if a particular athlete was gambling on sports; yet, only 30 percent of athletes believed that coaches would be aware of gambling or gambling problems within their team (NCAA 2008). This scenario could place an increased burden on teammates to keep secrets, creating stress and conflict in an environment where all sports wagering is prohibited.

Any professional involved in the development of adolescents and especially those connected to sports (e.g., physical health teachers, coaches, athletic directors, parents) require more knowledge and resources to help prevent and detect gambling problems. Most at-risk behaviours reported in university usually begin in high school, so coaches and physical education teachers could likely have the greatest impact on preventing young athletes from gambling (Darden and Rockey 2006). In fact, colligate athletes reported that coaches were the most effective method of communicating behavioural expectations and information about gambling, followed by personal values and teammates (NCAA 2008).

Coaches, then, should be attuned to gambling language and behaviour in order to detect concerns early on. Furthermore, sport psychologists could screen for gambling when addressing other concerns such as stress, anxiety, financial issues, team conflict, and decreased levels of performance (Wanner and Paskus 2010). In addition to awareness and prevention, everyday citizens need to think critically about the direction of legalized gambling.

Intercollegiate Athletics in the United States

Some specific environmental concerns for athletes in US programs are relevant to this discussion because more and more Canadian athletes are seeking athletic scholarships south of the border. From a systematic

Four-Step Approach to Preventing Problem Gambling among Athletes

1. **Increase Education among Your Players**
   Include gambling in other conversations about ethical or at-risk behaviours such as drug use, eating disorders, cheating, and sportsmanship.

2. **Communicate with Other School Personnel**
   Athletes are skilled at hiding behaviours from people. Make school personnel aware of this issue. If gambling is becoming a problem for an athlete, someone else in school likely knows about it.

3. **Revisit Team Policies**
   Review current team rules and conduct policies to ensure that they address team expectations with regard to gambling behaviours.

4. **Review Mission of Team and School**
   Review current school policies with respect to gambling and fundraising to assure that they support the school and team's mission and values. Forms of gambling such as raffles are commonly used to raise money for sporting teams. This fundraising method may send mixed signals.

Source: Adapted from Darden and Rockey 2006

perspective, gambling among student athletes poses other problems beside the well-being of the team. One of the NCAA's main concerns is protecting the integrity of the game. The perception of athletes betting on other college teams and even professional teams threatens the whole system, as gamblers will not bet if they perceive the game to be fixed, decreasing revenue for sports in many ways.

To help decrease college sport gambling within athletic departments, the NCAA introduced bylaw 10.3, which forbids student athletes and staff members from soliciting or placing a bet on college or professional sports through a bookmaker, a parlay card, or any method employed by organized gambling. In addition, they are prohibited from providing any information concerning intercollegiate athletic competition to individuals involved in organized gambling activities.

In recent years, the NCAA has stepped up its educational and awareness efforts and built stronger relationships with the FBI, athletic governing bodies, professional sports leagues, and gaming regulatory officials, and conducts investigations related to violations of NCAA rules (Saum 1999). Educational efforts have been made, but the NCAA's gambling policy is generally punitive. The punishment for sports wagering is severe, and those caught wagering on professional or amateur sports receive a minimum one-year suspension, and those betting on a contest involving their own institution are subject to a lifetime ban (Ellenbogen et al. 2008).

Fear is one way to govern and it has shown to be effective with gambling rates dropping in Division I programs for many sports from the 2004 to the 2008 NCAA gambling surveys. However, policies driven by fear leave little room for those with addictions to actually seek help. Even athletes who may be struggling with gambling that is not regulated or prohibited by the NCAA, such as poker or scratch tickets, may not talk to coaches or other players out of fear of losing their scholarships. Athletes indicated that they would be most receptive to hearing messages about gambling from their coaches; yet, coaches are not required by the NCAA to educate themselves on warning signs, nor are they required to set team rules about playing cards or dice for money on team trips. It seems, then, that the NCAA regulations and educational efforts are in place to protect both the game and the system but not necessarily to protect athletes from developing a problem, despite the known risks of gambling addictions for this population.

A second major concern with athletes gambling is that they can incur significant losses and develop associations with other gamblers, coming under pressure to share information concerning collegiate events or alter their performance to influence the outcomes of games (Ellenbogen et al. 2008). The most problematic consequence is point shaving, which typically occurs when one or more players try to ensure that the team wins by less than the point spread (the number of points by which gambling houses expect the favoured team to beat the underdog). The team still plays to win, just by fewer points than the betting line; this can be achieved by slacking off on defense, missing free throws, or committing fouls.

Dr. Justin Wolfers analyzed 44,120 NCAA Division I men's basketball games from 1989 to 2005 and concluded that 1 percent (about 500 games) involved gambling-related corruption (McCarthy 2011). The nature of college basketball makes it especially susceptible to point shaving for several reasons: (1) It is a high-scoring game with a wide differential, making it easier to affect the point spread without throwing the whole game. (2) It has a large number of regular season games, which reduces the scrutiny of any one game. (3) In comparison to the large revenues that high-profile sports generate, college athletes are not compensated for their efforts beyond scholarships and limited aid. (4) College basketball players are often less prepared for college than other students and graduate at lower rates than their classmates (Leeds and Diemer 2010). For some players, as time goes by, their dreams of "going pro" begin to dwindle and the lack of time to work and build a resumé has likely not been part of their college experience. This makes opportunities for quick money appealing.

Michael Franzese, a former mob boss with the Colombo crime family, walked away from this lifestyle and now speaks across North America about the dangers of gambling, and specifically of sport wagering. He shares first-hand knowledge about gambling schemes, including point shaving, which he facilitated during his 17 years in the mob. He reports that it is easy for "fixers" to bribe those who have little or no money, making students and student athletes easy targets for professional gamblers. In particular, nonstar players are easier to lure in to exchange inside information for money, especially if they are not going to the professional leagues (McCarthy 2007c).

This scenario echoes that of Harvey McDougle, a University of Toledo football player. In 2005, investigations followed some suspicious betting patterns on Toledo football games. Eventually, McDougle admitted to accepting cash, a car, a phone, and other valuables to share inside information and introduce an organized crime associate to other Toledo football and basketball players interested in similar arrangements (McCarthy 2011).

Conflict theory suggests that violators of rules are often exploited victims portrayed as deviants by those in power. In this way, athletes can be seen as victims of a profit-driven system in which the success they can achieve in the here and now is the only salient concern. In many ways, the system itself opens the door for athletes to seek out financial experiences to help them compensate for being unprepared for the real world. However, the shame associated with college scandals is enormous and is propagated by the system that pathologizes the individual as a deviant without examining the context in which these events occur.

Players are ostracized much like those banished from a kingdom in medieval times. An athletic trainer on staff during a Northwestern University basketball scandal in 1998 shared her experience in a personal presentation at the NCAA sport wagering in-service in 2010. The trainer commented that to that day—13 years after the scandal—former teammates and the sport community at Northwestern will not speak to the four players involved in the point shaving scandal, and they are unwelcome at reunions or other university events. The sport community (at several universities) shuns these rule violators with more vehemence than other students who have committed physical or sexual violence. Does the punishment really fit the crime?

While many discussions centre on players as the source of point shaving, players are not the only possible causes. For example, a coach can affect the scoring by putting a less-skilled player in the game, which has the same result as a player who intentionally does not play up to his ability. Moreover, a referee can unjustifiably call fouls, which has the same impact as a player who unjustifiably commits a foul (Frey 1992). The Black Sox Scandal, the imprisonment of NBA referee Tim Donaghy and many point shaving scandals in college basketball reflect the impact and criticism faced by these sport professionals. Preserving the integrity of the game is one of the most important aspects of the sport system, as it is a direct line to money, demonstrating once again the power of the fans and sports wagerers.

The Great Debate

Arguments for and against the legalization of sports wagering have occurred for decades and can be grouped into three main categories: (1) purely revenue focused; (2) a socio-economic perspective including costs and benefits; and (3) moral/ethical issues in sport.

Legalizing sports betting is an appealing revenue-raising method for governments in the current economic environment. The major economic benefits of sports gambling are greater choice of leisure and entertainment alternatives, the creation of new tourism and hospitality jobs, higher government revenues from controlled gambling, and infrastructure improvements (Stevens 2006). In addition, those in favour of legalization point out that there is currently no legal way for Canadians to bet on the outcomes of single sports events, encouraging them to turn to street bookies, organized crime, or offshore operators which are neither regulated nor taxed (Burns 2010).

The argument is purely revenue-driven and leadership from the CGA (namely, William Rutsey and Paul Burns) has commented on the potential revenue currently flowing to offshore casinos and Las Vegas. A national survey with 400 respondents working in the Canadian gaming industry revealed that 86 percent of respondents were in support of wagering on single sporting events and 50 percent felt that the government should deliver the services (Hall and Scarpelli 2010).

There is no debate that sports books have a small profit margin of about 5 percent, so the net tax revenue is relatively low. This is especially true for single sporting events, where bettors have a high chance of winning and operators have a high chance of losing (Frey 1992). However, these relevant concerns are countered by highlighting the point that it is not the sport wagering itself that will bring in the largest revenue but rather the increase in tourism to areas such as Niagara Falls and Windsor. As mentioned, Las Vegas casinos made $95 million on bets from the Super Bowl in 2009, and even more compelling is that the Super Bowl drew 200,000 visitors to that city, resulting in more than

$100 million spent on hotels, food, and entertainment over the course of a single weekend (Burns 2010).

Dollar signs tend to cloud people's eyes. Nevada pays the price of widespread gambling with a host of problems such as low educational achievement and high addiction rates. Nonetheless, increasing tourism by attracting Americans to cross the Canadian border are enticing arguments for legalizing sports betting. Some supporters have even suggested that provinces should move quickly and establish themselves as a Vegas-style tourist spot before other US states, such as Delaware, capitalize on it (Perkins 2009).

Over the last few decades, three major opponents to legalized sports betting have been racetrack owners, sports leagues, and illegal bookmakers. Horse track owners tend to be against legalization of sports betting because of the potential loss of revenue from their tracks (Frey 1992). Professional sports leagues and college regulatory agencies have worked to restrict further venues for gambling on sports, as they consider betting to be linked to organized crime. Additional ways through which to bet on sports would increase the potential for fixed outcomes, undermining the public's confidence in the sport and affecting sales and the current revenue from gamblers (Smith 1992; NCAA 2008).

The integrity of the game remains important to bettors, operators, and leagues, but some concerns may have shifted in recent years. First, it has been argued that more regulated sports wagering would help to reduce game tampering and decrease fixing or point shaving schemes (Smith 1992). Second, the increase in technology, surveillance, communication, and rules and regulations by the leagues decreases the odds that games can be fixed. Third, the recent collaboration among the NCAA, professional leagues, the FBI, and Las Vegas shows a strong force against fixing. The NCAA is now notified if there are irregularities in the betting line by top professional bookmakers, and most of the leagues have an investigative team dedicated to gambling violations.

Further evidence that times are changing comes from NBA commissioner David Stern, who has stated that it may be time to rethink the NBA's position and reconsider the self-imposed ban from the Ontario sport lottery (Burns 2010). Professional sports could not thrive as they do today without money from sports gamblers, which in turn drives viewership and television contracts. So leagues must be mindful not to exclude these important stakeholders in their decision-making. This is perhaps a good demonstration of the increased hold the gaming industry has on all the major players of the sport industry.

Those opposed to legalizing sports wagering from a socio-economic viewpoint highlight the major costs of gambling to society: its impact on the criminal justice system; the increased strain it puts on the health-care system; the conflicts and severed social ties in causes among gamblers, their friends, and their families; as well as the displacement of local retail, entertainment, and food-service businesses (Stevens 2006). Legalizing sports betting will likely attract people who were previously hesitant to wager through illegal avenues.

Given that sports wagering has been linked to problem gambling, increased availability could open the door to higher rates of addiction, lower productivity among workers, loss of employment, bankruptcy, further impact on youth, and exploitation of at-risk gamblers (Buddy 2003; Griffiths 2009b; Stevens 2006). As such, the trade-off between increased income and retaining the integrity of the sport (not to mention the socio-economic costs) may come out against legalized gambling.

From a moral/ethical standpoint, legalizing sport gambling undermines the fundamental values of sport itself, which is built on sportsmanship, teamwork, and character development (Frey 1992). Especially in Canada, with its athlete-centred philosophy, sport is perceived to have an important ethical purpose: it teaches valuable life skills that are transferable to adulthood. The goal of gambling—a philosophy of money for nothing—conflicts with the hard work and other ideals required in sport. Opponents of sports wagering argue that gambling erodes the natural interest inherently developed when fans watch superb athletes perform to their potential. Instead of appreciating the achievements of great athletes, the audience's focus turns to whether the team will cover the spread (Frey 1992). Recovering pathological gamblers who were addicted to sports wagering report that sporting events often hold little to no interest for them now; their main interest was the stimulus of a bet (Smith 1992).

Those who disagree with the "purity of sport" perspective argue that elite sport already consists of cheating, drug use, violence, and exorbitant salary structures, so gambling fits right into the mix (Frey 1992). Dave Perkins, a sport columnist for the *Toronto Star*, suggests that it is strictly an economics issue—the moral horse left long ago (Perkins 2009).

To help contemplate the various perspectives, Garry Smith has raised the following critical questions about sport lotteries: How much revenue will it create? What are the social implications? Will it breed negative publicity from professional sports interests? Will it change our value structure and will we view sports differently? (1992, 334). The legalization of sports wagering is a direct result of the government's view of the trade-offs. We know that many provinces did opt to support sports lotteries, but it remains unclear how well these issues were explored before they did so. The question remains if governments will review these questions more thoroughly before further legalizing gambling options.

Concluding Remarks

Sports wagering includes many different activities, such as sports lotteries, bets on sporting events, wagers on games of skill (e.g., golf), and bets on horse and dog racing, as well as Internet sports gambling. Those who take part in these activities tend to be young, single adult males. Overall, sports wagering involvement is influenced by many factors, including role identities, social values, the media, as well as family, peers, and coaches—all a product of socialization. A predominately male pastime, sports wagering is an activity where "valued masculine traits such as decision making, boldness and coolness can be displayed" as a test of character among a peer group (Smith 2009, 106).

The freedom of the post-secondary school environment may influence young adults to become more open and enthusiastic about different gambling opportunities and avenues, potentially leading them into dangerous territory with very few safety nets. Gambling behaviour among college and university students in Canada (athletes and/or sports fans) has received little scholarly consideration. Canadian governments and post-secondary schools ought to pay close attention to the impact of sports gambling within colleges in the United States, as cultural influences are likely to spill over into Canada.

Media and gambling industries have promoted sporting events as more enjoyable and exciting when money is on the line, normalizing betting as part of the fan experience, while simultaneously undermining the inherent beauty of the sport. Originally promoted to help generate excitement, sports wagering has become a powerful force, driving decisions about athletes and the sport itself, and connecting average people with organized crime associates.

While participation rates for sports wagering are much lower compared to other forms gambling, we have seen how those who do engage in it tend to spend more money and play more often. This is especially true for sports gamblers who bet with bookies and those who place wagers on the Internet; these two forms of wagering have been linked to greater problematic gambling behaviour.

Chapter 7

Internet Gambling

The evolution of technology has changed humankind in many ways over the last century. Within the gaming industry, Internet gambling is arguably the largest cultural shift in the last decade. Gambling has entered the home, becoming more accessible, convenient, and socially acceptable than ever before. Internet gambling has transformed the way people gamble and changed the practice and regulation of gambling in Canada and around the world. As a result, many countries are wrestling with issues of regulation, profit, and consumer protection.

This change has raised many new questions, in addition to those related to legalization: How do we protect minors and other vulnerable populations? What are the implications of 24-hour gambling accessibility for individuals, families, and other social institutions? There is much debate around these issues, but limited empirical research provides only partial answers to our many questions. This chapter will shed light on the various issues, addressing current trends, prevalence rates, and key arguments about regulation in Canada.

The Basics

There is speculation that Internet gambling participation is growing, that it is more addictive than other forms of gambling, and that there are too few safety regulations to protect consumers.

Internet gambling refers to any form of wagering that occurs over the Internet (Orme, Northey, and Townshend 2010), whereas mobile or remote gambling includes any form of gambling in which the person is not physically present (e.g., via the Internet, a cellphone, or an interactive television; Orme, Northey, and Townshend 2010). Online casinos attempt to replicate land-based ones by using flashy lights and colours as well as familiar games such as bingo, slot machines, roulette, and card games (e.g., poker and blackjack). Furthermore, today's gambling sites incorporate stimulating visuals, video game technology, and other inter-active features to capture consumer attention (Wilson 2003).

The first Internet bingo site (IBingo.com) offered cash prizes in 1998, and the first Internet poker room (PlanetPoker.com) went online the same year. However, it was not until 2003 that there was a major increase in online poker participation, with estimated revenue of roughly $365 million. This number had increased to $2.4 billion in 2006. Not surprising, this boost coincided with the popularity of the World Series of Poker on ESPN where top players qualified from online poker tournaments (Pelisek 2005). In 2010, the well-known site PokerStars.com dealt its 40-billionth hand of poker, resulting in a tournament that attracted more than 36,000 entrants and produced $7 million in prizes (4OnlineGambling.com 2010). In the United Kingdom, online poker and online betting exchanges are among the fastest growing forms of online gambling (Griffiths 2008). In Canada, casino-style games are projected to produce the greatest growth in revenue, while online poker remained steady between 2007 and 2012 (Hall and Scarpelli 2010). In 2007, the most popular online gambling activity for Canadians who played weekly was the lottery, games of skill (e.g., poker), and instant-win tickets (Wood and Williams 2009). In 2009, the top games for those who identified as Internet gamblers were poker, sport wagering, and bingo (Ipsos Reid and CGA 2010).

Over the last several years, between 2,500 and 3,000 online gambling websites have been identified around the globe (Picard 2011), with revenue reaching close to $27 billion in 2009 (Hall and Scarpelli 2010). Today, gambling continues to be the fastest growing form of Internet commerce in the world and it is estimated to grow 42 percent by 2012 when it will reach revenues close to $36 billion (Hall and Scarpelli 2010). Further, Merrill Lynch—the stock broking firm—projects that Internet gambling will produce revenue close to $528 billion worldwide by 2015 (Hartman 2006). Although this prediction may be overzealous, it calls to our attention the dollar signs that dangle in front of corporations and governments seeking entry into the business.

From a corporate perspective, virtual casinos are much more cost-effective than land-based ones in the long run; they are able to reach a global market with relatively low start-up and maintenance costs. It is estimated that, compared to land-based casinos, online casinos are capable of receiving 10 million more spins a month on their slot machines, given their ability to host an unlimited number of people. This, in turn, also enhances player loyalty (Rex and Jackson 2008).

The mechanics of an online gambling site include three major factors: (1) a domain name, site identity, and server to house the site; (2)

gambling software to power the site; and (3) facilities for financial transactions (Wilson 2003). Payment typically occurs in US currency with advance deposits from credit cards or electronic transfer of funds from banks or online financial services (winnings are transferred in the same way). Canadians report that credit cards (35 percent), e-wallet (18 percent), and electronic fund transfers (17 percent) are the most common methods of depositing money to gamble (Ipsos Reid and CGA 2010).

To play online, participants are asked to open an account with their name, address, and date of birth. Usually, the player must be at least 18 or 19 years old to access the service, but few sites verify their users' ages. This lack of authentication allows youth to participate by simply inserting a different year of birth.

There are four models of online gambling. The first is "legalized online gambling," which occurs in countries that have legalized the practice, such as the United Kingdom. The second model, labelled "directory" or "forwarding," is based on sites that direct a consumer toward a pay-to-play online gambling site (Wilson 2003). In Canada, it is illegal to advertise online gaming services for an exchange of money. However, many free sites serve as directories that forward visitors to sites hosted in other countries—a practice that is legal but tends to promote unregulated gambling (Wilson 2003). In addition, there is no clear law banning Canadians from playing on foreign sites, and only a few offshore casinos refuse players from Canada. Even fewer sites check visitors' IP addresses to verify their country of origin.

The third model, labelled as "special cases," is historically the most prevalent in Canada. So-called special cases are a result of "unique local conditions [that] allow gambling in a country where it would otherwise be illegal" (Wilson 2003, 1250). First Nation territories and reserves in Canada are able to set up gambling on their lands and host online sites by providing server space to companies based in other countries. The flexibility of the World Wide Web allows domains to be registered in one country and the server to be housed in another. The Kahnawake Mohawk Nation in Quebec is reported as being the third largest host of online gambling websites in the world (Perkins 2006). Questions have been raised about the legality of this, but little action has resulted (Rex and Jackson 2008). The final model for online gambling is "ambiguous legal climates," which is common in countries that have not legislated online gambling behaviour. This model may best represent where Canada falls today.

Legal issues and decisions related to online gaming vary worldwide. Roughly 90 jurisdictions around the world have legalized Internet gambling or tolerate it in some form (CanWest News 2008).

The United Kingdom, for example, has taken a clear regulation and taxation approach. The Gambling Act of 2005 (effective September 2007) allows all forms of Internet gambling on UK soil as long as the gambling is regulated and licensed. The United States has taken the opposite stance, banning all Internet gambling. The Unlawful Internet Gambling Enforcement Act (UIGEA) of 2006 focuses on payment systems, forbidding the transfer of money from US bank accounts or credit cards to online gambling sites (Orme, Northey, and Townshend 2010). This law was not created to protect the consumer or prevent future gambling-related harm but rather to prevent revenue from leaving the country. Australia upholds strict control of online gambling under its federal law. The Australian Interactive Gambling Act (2001) allows online casinos to run legally in Australia. However, it is illegal to actively advertise (electronically or otherwise) or allow those physically present in Australia to gamble online. This law was passed to prevent gambling problems from increasing in the country. After some pushback, the Australian government has since permitted online sports wagering and lotteries (Humphrey 2008).

By contrast, the legal situation in Canada is less clear. The framework for gambling falls under the Federal Criminal Code. However, the only guidance for online gambling involves laws that apply to traditional gambling. Prior to 1969, all gambling was banned except for some activities for charity and parimutuel betting on horses (Rex and Jackson 2008).

In 1969, a Criminal Code amendment allowed provincial and federal governments to use lotteries to make profit for the country's services and activities. An amendment in 1985 (section 207 in the Criminal Code) gave provincial governments exclusive control of gambling within their own borders and legalized computer, video, and slot devices. Under this amendment, it is legal for governments to conduct and manage lottery schemes and games of chance over the Internet, but it remains a crime for any other organization to do so (Kyer and Hough 2002). A few provinces have already jumped into online gambling, while others continue to consider its legalization. Still others oppose it entirely because of the perceived dangers and future consequences.

In 2009, five provinces offered online lotteries, and in 2010, the first online casino was available in British Columbia. A poll examining gambling behaviours and beliefs revealed that 71 percent of Canadians thought gambling (not including online lottery services) was legal over the Internet, and about 50 percent believed it was government-regulated (Ipsos Reid and CGA 2010).

Who Is Gambling Online?

Legal or not, online betting has been taking place around the globe for over a decade. It is estimated that between 14 and 23 million people worldwide use the Internet to gamble (Orme, Northey, and Townshend 2010). Although rising in popularity, online wagering is the least common form of gambling among Canadians (Wood and Williams 2009). Canada's participation rate is higher than New Zealand's and Iceland's (2 percent) and similar to the United States', Singapore's, and Australia's (4 percent). However, the Canadian participation rate is lower than those of Hong Kong and European countries such as Sweden, Norway, and Finland (7 to 14 percent; Orme, Northey, and Townshend 2010).

An important national study by Wood and Williams conducted in 2007 gives more insight. The study involved a systematic approach whereby researchers interviewed about 8,500 adults by phone across all 10 provinces. They found the overall adult gambling participation rate was 71 percent, including all forms of gambling. Approximately 3.5 percent of respondents indicated that they gambled online, including those who bought and sold high-risk stocks. In 2008, other surveys indicated that 5 percent of Ontario adults gambled online (Rex and Jackson 2008), compared to 3 percent of B.C. residents (Ipsos Reid Public Affairs and Gemini Research 2008). Even more recently, the CGA revealed that 16 percent of Canadians wagered online in the last year (Hall and Scarpelli 2010). However, most gamblers still prefer land-based venues, and over 80 percent of the general population reported being unlikely to play online. The top reasons for this were concerns about the legitimacy of the websites, credit card safety, and professional players/sharks. Another 42 percent of respondents mentioned concerns about developing an addiction (Ipsos Reid and CGA 2010).

The low online gambling participation rate may also be related to Internet gambling's relative novelty among the adult and aging population. Most of the Internet gamblers (78 percent) surveyed in the 2007 study reported gambling online for the first time between the years of 2003 and 2006 (Wood and Williams 2009). In addition, online gambling lacks the human interaction that accompanies traditional forms of wagering. Land-based gambling may satisfy the need to socialize and/ or provide a rationalization for the activity as a way of spending quality time with friends (Griffiths and Parke 2002). Yet, new Internet gambling subscribers seem to adapt quickly to betting online (LaPlante et al. 2008). With several government-owned casinos now offering their own online system, loyal customers may soon be dabbling in the new and more accessible home version.

Researchers have investigated the possibility that distinct characteristics differentiate online gamblers from traditional gamblers. The national telephone study mentioned above compared these two groups, revealing some socio-demographic differences. Most Internet gamblers were male (82 percent), compared to a roughly equal gender spilt among non-Internet gamblers. About 50 percent of Internet gamblers identified themselves as being between the ages of 20 and 29, compared to only 16 percent of non-Internet gamblers. The majority in each group was of European ancestry; however, those claiming Aboriginal ancestry were about four times more likely to be represented (Wood and Williams 2009).

Internet gamblers are more likely to be male, single, students, and well-educated, and also more likely to enjoy a higher household income, engage in illicit drug use, and have higher problematic gambling scores than non-Internet gamblers (Wood and Williams 2009). Similar results were found in a national comparison study with more than 9,000 adults in Britain (Griffiths et al. 2009), adding some validity to the profile of current Internet gamblers, which is useful in understanding future trends and developing prevention strategies.

Appeal and Potential Danger of Internet Gambling

Internet gambling is a socially isolating activity that lacks the protective factors of friends, family, and trained employees. Internet gambling does, however, offer anonymity, convenience, and interactivity—a tempting combination for both frequent and first-time gamblers. Specifically, sophisticated video game software with increased realism, live remote wagering, and inter-competition may attract the eyes of youth, young adults, and "gamers" (Griffiths 2008). Gambling site developers continue to use tantalizing teasers such as misleading and provocative ads, endorsements by celebrities, reward and loyalty programs, free games and trials, and initial deposit bonuses (Derevensky 2010).

In the national telephone study, Canadians reported that the 24-hour availability and convenience of home were the top advantages of online gambling, followed by a better gaming experience, more physical comfort, anonymity, and better payout rates (Wood and Williams 2009). In 2010, similar results were found in Canada, with a few additional reasons reported, such as the ability to play and learn for free as well as incentives and bonuses (Ipsos Reid and CGA 2010). For those who may be uncomfortable stepping up to a casino table, Internet gambling offers an embarrassment-free way to learn and master skills. This feature may entice people that would not otherwise play.

Internet gambling sites may also satisfy a psychological need for acknowledgement and self-esteem in a different way than land-based ones. When an individual experiences a moderate-to-big win, the rest of the gambling site is informed, reaching more people than those sitting at one poker table or next to a slot machine. The broadcast-like experience can fulfill an online gambler's need for confidence and self-worth (Griffiths and Parke 2002). Furthermore, online gambling allows people to escape from their real lives, fulfilling the needs of the pseudo identity (username) rather than their true self.

Online gamblers may also differ from conventional gamblers in their view of money (Griffiths and Parke 2002). This difference may be diminishing, given that most physical casinos have started to use electronic cash similar to what Internet-based casinos use. Casino chips have always been used to psychologically distance players from their money: a strategic tactic that creates the illusion that they are not losing "real money." This separation is likely even more pronounced for online gamblers, who never have to go to an ATM or exchange money for chips or an electronic playing card.

In addition, online gamblers may experience a larger loss because of the perception that online gambling sites have higher payout rates than land-based venues. This view does not arise by chance; it is planted and reinforced by sites that inflate their payout rates during free or learning sessions (Wood and Williams 2007). In Canada, running a gambling website and advertising games for money is prohibited. However, it is legal to promote free game-play websites (OMAC 2010), and about 76 percent of Canadian Internet gamblers report playing free Internet games before playing for real money (Ipsos Reid and CGA 2010). These sites help new online players become familiar with gambling terminology and game rules. They also help to develop patterns and behaviours that can become automatic by the time individuals reach the cash-based gambling environment.

What is dangerous is that these free sites manipulate the odds, creating an illusion that winning is easy and reinforcing the thrill. The new gamblers transfer their expectations to the pay-to-play sites. When they do not win as often, it can lead them to bet larger amounts or play more frequently to recreate that same excitement (Zacharias n.d.). Further problems, such as chasing losses, financial troubles, or intense feelings of anxiety and stress, can emerge.

Researchers believe that online gambling does lead to an increase in frequency of play, contributing to a larger number of problem gamblers

(Azmier 2000; Wood and Williams 2007). This view is supported by the findings of the Responsible Gambling Council (RGC). Although only 1.7 percent of Ontario respondents gambled online, these online gamblers had the highest rate of daily play. About 50 percent gambled online daily, and another 25 percent reported gambling at least once a week (Wiebe, Mun, and Kauffman 2006). In addition, a University of Western Ontario study found that gamblers who played virtually gambled for longer and more often than gamblers in land-based casinos (CanWest News 2008). Even more striking is a result reported in the national telephone study. Among Canadian gamblers, the prevalence of problem gambling was three to four times higher for Internet gamblers (Wood and Williams 2009). More specifically, 17 percent of Internet gamblers were moderate or severe problem gamblers compared to 4 percent of non-Internet gamblers.

Not all studies have found that online gaming leads to more gambling problems. A study that analyzed the real-time sports wagering behaviour of 47,000 bettors in Austria over a two-year period revealed that when players won, they played more, and when they lost, they played less (LaBrie et al. 2008). They were able to moderate their behaviour, and the online format did not appear to encourage excessive gambling. In addition, only 18 percent of sports bettors in the sample tried casino-style games; when they did try this form of gambling, they bet higher amounts but played less frequently (LaBrie et al. 2008). This may reflect a cross-cultural difference. However, other international studies show increased problems. In an international sample, 17 percent of online gamblers reported being either moderate or severe problem gamblers, compared to only 6 percent who played at land-based venues (Wood and Williams 2009). Likewise, problem gambling prevalence rates were significantly higher among Internet gamblers (5 percent) than non-Internet gamblers (0.5 percent) in a British sample, and gambling preoccupation and escapism were the most common symptoms among those who played online (Griffiths et al. 2009). Two other international studies report similar findings (Wardle et al. 2007; Griffiths and Barnes 2008).

Given the evidence, it seems that either Internet gambling is more addictive or players already experiencing problematic behaviours gravitate toward this new and accessible format, thereby increasing problems. Several risk factors have been identified. Online gamblers are more likely to have a problem when they gamble using several gambling formats, have higher gambling expenditures, and report other mental health problems (Wood and Williams 2009). People who suffer from depression tend to be more vulnerable to addiction in general (McDonald 2000). One sign of an alcohol problem is frequently drinking alone.

Likewise, the tendency to gamble alone at home for extended periods may be a warning sign of a problem and thus cause for concern.

According to Evra (2010), "Many consider online casinos the industry equivalent to crack cocaine because of their 24-hour, at-home availability and virtual feel." Online gamblers can play as long as they want with little or no supervision and have higher spending limits. British Columbia's site PlayNow.com recently began to offer a weekly transfer-in limit of $10,000, up from $120 (after only a year in business), providing an opportunity for an individual to gamble away $500,000 a year on its site (Evra 2010). In fact, it is estimated that problem gamblers produce close to 40 percent of provincial gambling revenues across the country (Williams and Wood 2007), and Canadian Internet players have identified online poker and slots as contributing to the bulk of their problem, followed by roulette, VLTs, and lotteries (Wood and Williams 2009).

Researchers and prevention professionals have voiced concern about how this new form of gambling will affect vulnerable populations, including current problem gamblers, youth, and senior citizens. For example, gambling researchers have found that the prevalence of gambling problems among youth is higher than in adult populations. It is also documented that young people use the Internet regularly (Liau, Khoo, and Ang 2008) and thus tend to encounter more advertisements and enticements to visit online gambling sites (Derevensky 2010). Youth are being targeted in many ways, including tactics such as one proposed by the British Columbia Lottery Corporation to provide free music downloads to online gamblers (Armstrong 2008). Furthermore, the commonalities between gambling and gaming continue to increase today, with more free gaming sites offering rewards in the form of tokens or points. The free trials may create future gamblers by encouraging children and youth to play (Derevensky 2010); we discuss this point further in Chapter 9.

Senior citizens are at risk as well, particularly given that their income is often fixed. The 2002 Senior Survey in New Brunswick measured the prevalence of participation in each type of gambling activity available in the province. Results showed a majority of seniors (56 percent) engaged in at least one gambling activity in the last month, and nearly half gambled on one or more activities on a regular monthly basis (or more) during the previous year. Only 4 percent had ever tried Internet gambling: 2 percent had played in the last year, and less than 1 percent participated regularly (Schellink et al. 2002). According to this study, senior citizens were less likely to wager online than engage in other forms of gambling. However, this percentage has likely changed since 2002 and will continue to do so as a more computer-savvy population comes of age.

Those in favour of Internet gambling argue that technology is not solely to blame for any increase in addiction. Rather, the problem arises from the way online habits interact with a given individual's unique makeup. Although personal makeup may be one piece of the pie, several factors outside of the person make online gambling very appealing. These include flashy colours, video game features, incentives, and other advertising tactics. For example, the B.C. government–run site offered a free $10 token to anyone signing up and a one-time gift of $100 in tokens to anyone who deposited at least the same amount (Evra 2010).

The allure and potential danger of online gambling is real. As the availability of online gambling continues to increase, it is vital to examine its impact on vulnerable populations, especially those who have been exposed to legal gambling their entire lives.

Regulation: For and Against

The debate around the regulation of Internet gambling is a heated one, and legitimate arguments exist for both prohibition and legislation in Canada.

There are two main arguments in favour of legalization: money and consumer safety. The basic premise is that it is impossible to effectively prohibit online gambling, so it is preferable for it to be managed by the province to ensure gambler protection and keep funds inside our borders.

Over the last 12 years, online gambling has become a $34 billion industry (Hall and Scarpelli 2010). Canadian citizens spend roughly $1 billion a year on gambling sites that are not regulated (Canadian Press 2010a). In addition, licensed gambling businesses are also affected by unregulated sites. David Wilmot, CEO of Woodbine Entertainment Group, discovered that 130 unknown sites were betting on his horses without giving a share of the money to his business. The loss was estimated to be about $100 million over three years. Horse betting is allowed under Canadian law and the government takes about 1 percent on every wager. From this standpoint, legitimate businesses as well as the government are suffering from offshore sites (Rex and Jackson 2008).

Online casinos would provide a way for struggling governments with deficits to recuperate millions of dollars. The relatively low overhead costs and constant stream of cash makes running an online casino an appealing option. In July 2010, British Columbia became the first Canadian province to develop an online casino (PlayNow.com). The government hopes it will generate some $100 million in profit each year and has promised to use it for public services such as health care and education (Stueck 2010). However, the government has already encountered problems, including a public protest that occurred when the 33 percent of proceeds allocated for community projects, social agencies, and other programs was cut to 10 percent (Stueck 2010). In addition, hours after opening the online gambling site, it experienced a security breach that exposed players' sensitive information and funds. This breach hindered operations for more than a month, and losses amounted to more than $5 million (Canadian Press 2010a).

Regulating and monitoring online gambling is a difficult task with many variables, such as protecting vulnerable populations (including minors), protecting consumers, maintaining the integrity of the game, and policing fraudulent behaviour and those attempting to launder money (Orme, Northey, and Townshend 2010). The issue of integrity is one of the most important elements in online betting according to Canadian gamblers (Ipsos Reid and CGA 2010). Given the security breach in British Columbia, are provincial governments ready to address all of these variables to ensure Canadian safety both as consumers and tax payers?

Further expansion is thought to help Canadians view online gambling sites as "safer and more socially acceptable" (Evra 2010). A survey revealed that only 39 percent of Canadians felt online gambling was an acceptable form of entertainment (Ipsos Reid and CGA 2010). Cotte reports from a qualitative study of 30 frequent gamblers that gamblers prefer to use trusted, reputable websites (quoted in CanWest News 2008). She argues that creating "reputable suppliers" is preferable to trying "to shut [online gambling] down" (quoted in CanWest News 2008). Cotte's opinion leads to the second main argument in favour of regulation: trusted and regulated sites offer consumer protection. To help evaluate this argument, the risks associated with offshore casinos are presented below:

- The integrity of the game cannot be ensured in an offshore online casino. For example, in a virtual poker game, a gambler could be playing against one player with four accounts or a computer-generated program.
- The odds of winning may not be listed on an offshore site and if they do appear, there is no guarantee they are accurate. In addition, the odds could be changed at any time based on betting behaviour without informing the consumer.
- Internet gambling sites typically collect information about player habits and personal information that can be sold to other companies or used to manipulate the game.

- There is no guarantee that offshore gambling sites will transfer winnings into players' bank accounts, and there are no legal protections for Canadians if they are not (Zacharias n.d).

Given these risks, in 2003, Keith Furlong of the Interactive Gaming Council supported British Columbia's legalization of online gambling. He believed it would provide a safer alternative for players and that the money raised from regulation could be put toward programs for problem gamblers (CBC 2003b). However, many of these risks still exist with government-owned sites; they are simply reduced. So are these arguments just fear tactics to encourage people to accept Canadian-owned online casinos?

In further exploring these issues, Wiebe and Lipton (2008) suggest two overarching approaches of regulating online gambling: consumer restriction and social responsibility measures.

Customer restriction can be achieved in several ways. One option is to ask participants to fill out a form indicating where they are from; however, this method is usually unreliable. Another option is to verify where someone is logging in, by using the billing address of the credit card used (Kelley, Todosichuk, and Azmier 2001). A third and very expensive option is to use the Global Positioning System (GPS) to track where customers are located (Falcone and Ader 2001). This satellite-based technology may be the best way "to establish a regulatory environment that ensures that only those who are permitted to place bets online are doing so" (Kelley, Todosichuk, and Azmier 2001, 15).

A province could consider using blocking technology that keeps non-provincially-run Internet gambling sites inaccessible to provincial residents; however, the expense of blocking 2,500 to 3,000 sites could be high. Another alternative, used in Australia, involves blocking access to nationally owned online casinos to residents living within a state or country in order to help reduce gambling problems in that area. The first option protects consumers and the second protects society from future problems.

Those in favour of regulation in Canada encourage responsible gaming strategies as well as the use of blocking technology. Cotte supports built-in safety nets, such as the ability to monitor losses and inform players of how long they have been playing (quoted in CanWest News 2008). This viewpoint sparks other important questions about responsible gambling measures: Are they effective in helping people control their gambling? Moreover, are they in place in Canada?

Responsible gambling measures include having online players set weekly deposit limits and making gamblers aware of both the time and the money they spend per gambling session. For instance, a graphic instrument at the corner of the user's screen could reveal how much money and time remains in that session (Orme, Northey, and Townshend 2010). In addition, reality checks involving pop-up messages are another preventive measure that encourage informed choices.

Some experts believe that those at-risk of a problem begin to develop irrational beliefs about the expectancy of winning, leading to less control over their wagering behaviour (Monaghan 2008). Pop-up messages might disrupt this thinking. However, there is insufficient research on the effectiveness of virtual prevention. How often, for example, would a pop-up message need to appear to counteract a given site's ability to encourage a player to continue? Preventive measures may not be as effective as the propaganda suggests (Evra 2010).

One study investigated pop-up blockers on electronic gaming machines (EGMs) in Nova Scotia, which stopped play for 15 seconds and indicated how long the gamblers had been playing, at 60-, 90-, and 120-minute intervals. The study found that exposure to the 60-minute pop-up message for high-risk gamblers resulted in a small reduction in session length, and decreased expenditures; but the 90- and 120-minute messages had no effect. More than half of the participants reported they did not read the message before continuing to play (Schellink and Schrans 2002). In another study, researchers tested gamblers' exposure to a pop-up message every three to six spins that reminded players that roulette is chance-based and cannot be influenced and that continued play would likely result in losses. This pop-up intervention did result in fewer irrational beliefs and more controlled behaviour (Floyd, Whelan, and Meyers 2006).

Whether online casinos could be persuaded to display these messages is debatable. What may be effective may not be profitable for operators. Another issue is that many of these types of studies take place in a controlled or experimental setting, so little is known about how people would perceive and respond to breaks and pop-up messages in a true gambling environment (Monaghan 2008).

A recent study provides some insight. Bwin Interactive Entertainment both has corporate deposit limits and allows players to set personal limits. A study examined the real-time betting behaviour of those who were self-limiting. They found that people who used the service placed more bets, bet on more days, and gambled on a variety of games (Nelson et al. 2008). While monitoring the gamblers who self-limit could help to identify problem gamblers, the self-limiting option has had little influence on gamblers' actual behaviour, resulting in low effectiveness.

Player-tracking technology software does offer a unique opportunity to study betting behaviour, identify people at risk of developing a problem, and intervene. However, it also gives operators the ability to collect data and build a customer profile to better evaluate the best reward system for that player (e.g., providing vouchers and complimentary amounts to entice him or her to keep playing). It may be risky to give operators this level of control without an outside source monitoring their responsible use of the information.

The overall message is that online casinos *could* offer some protection, and preventive measures may be more easily developed and distributed for online casino players than for land-based gamblers. However, do these measures offset the accessibility and convenience of online casinos?

In Canada, PlayNow.com offers some responsible gambling measures by warning customers when they have played more than 50 games and by offering a temporary self-exclusion option (Evra 2010). On Quebec's casino site, patrons cannot open an Espacejeux account if they have self-excluded from any of Quebec's gaming halls or casinos. The Quebec government also has many other responsible gaming strategies available on its gambling site. These include tips for responsible gaming, signs that a gambler might have a problem, the ability to establish pop-up messages with time spent and money played, and the ability to set limits on deposits, money, and time spent per session. However, these features must be activated, leaving their usage up to the player.

Certainly, keeping money in the country and protecting the consumer from unregulated sites are legitimate arguments for legalization. However, as part of this argument, it is a slippery slope to suggest that regulated sites *could* offer players protection from developing a gambling problem. More research is needed on the effectiveness of responsible gaming strategies to verify this argument.

Risks of Regulation

Risks related to online gambling and regulation have been sprinkled throughout the chapter; however, it is now important to briefly review the main arguments against legalization and regulation of Internet gambling in Canada.

First, by implicitly labelling gambling as "safe and available," the potential for addiction problems increases. Easy access, anonymity, and the convenience of playing at home may lead to increased comfort and a perceived sense of control, encouraging more risk-taking. In addition, free games teach people how to play games that many would not otherwise learn in a more traditional setting.

The Internet in general offers a way to escape, and online gambling takes place quickly, with few breaks and little social context to remind people of other commitments. These characteristics can lead to other life problems, such as being late for work or failing to pick up children from school. In addition, electronic cash diminishes the value of hard-earned money and the credit system may make it easier for people to wager more than they can afford to lose. Any gambler, high-risk or not, can experience losses that greatly affect his or her life in the short and long term. All these risks exist in addition to provocative marketing and sophisticated gaming software that attract youth and other potentially vulnerable populations.

Many political figures in provinces across Canada have expressed concerns over online gambling. For instance, Wesley Sheridan, PEI's minister of finance and municipal affairs, believes Internet gambling is not the right solution for the province at this time (CBC 2010a). Darrell Dexter, the premier of Nova Scotia, has made the same decision, arguing that a provincially run casino would conflict with the public health goal of reducing harm from existing gambling venues and that the government is not capable of monitoring online casinos (Jackson 2010). Dexter's finance minister, Graham Steele, was initially in favour of permitting Internet betting; after discussion with experts, however, his view changed (Jackson 2010).

The problem of provincial regulation can be challenging, a factor that has made Ken Cheveldayoff, the minister responsible for the Saskatchewan Gaming Corporation, avoid committing to legalization: "It's harder to police, it's harder to monitor, you don't know who's on the other end . . . we want to make sure it's those that are above 18 years old and those that are responsible gamers that are taking advantage of it" (CBC 2010b). Given the difficulties mentioned by Cheveldayoff, the provinces of Newfoundland, Prince Edward Island, Manitoba, and Nova Scotia have declined participation in Internet gambling.

Despite risks, Quebec's online lottery, Loto-Québec, was permitted to open a site (Espacejeux.com) in December 2010, and it plans to capture 40 percent of the total gaming revenues in the province (Burton 2010). This move was depicted as a way to eliminate unregulated operations and increase revenue for the province (Burton 2010). Similarly, Paul Godfrey, the chairperson of OLG, supports Internet gambling and opposes the idea of potential revenue going to other provinces or outside of Canada (Canadian Press 2010b). Ontario's site is set to open in 2012, and it is projected to generate $400 million a year in revenue (Benzie 2010).

The second main argument against legalization and regulation of Internet gambling in Canada involves the lack of public health awareness and prevention initiatives to protect citizens and counter the promotion of online gambling. Although Canada allots more money to problem gambling than other countries do, funding for treatment is currently insufficient, especially when gambling is considered (Hall and Scarpelli 2010). In 2010, Canada brought in $15 billion in revenue from gambling operations nationwide, with $9 billion in gross revenues; yet only 74 million was allocated to problem gambling treatment and research, as well as awareness and responsible gambling initiatives (Hall and Scarpelli 2010). There is a lack of research on the effectiveness of virtual responsible gambling strategies and the ones currently offered by government-owned online casinos are available at the request of the consumer, rather than being mandatory. Overall, there is no substantial evidence that legitimizing online gambling, even with a significant amount of money put into prevention and treatment, will offset the harm.

Third, and perhaps the most concerning issue, is that more than one-third of the government's gambling revenue comes from problem gamblers (Priest 2009; Wood and Williams 2009). It does not seem socially responsible or even ethical that a disproportionate amount of revenue is generated from a vulnerable group. Essentially, the government is gathering money through the gambling industry in order to redistribute it for the physical and mental health costs related to or exacerbated by gambling, including unemployment, disability, bankruptcy, and social services for issues such as child neglect.

Gambling critic Sol Boxenbaum notes, "They're creating the problem, and then they're giving two percent of the revenue to fight the problem that wouldn't be there, if they hadn't created it in the first place" (CBC 2003a). A recent survey found that 40 percent of Canadians felt the government should provide more onsite responsible gambling initiatives, 33 percent felt more public service announcements to reduce problem gambling were needed, and 57 percent felt more funding for research was needed (Hall and Scarpelli 2010).

Fourth, and yet another problem with provinces legalizing Internet gambling, is they will not be able to match the existing online sites' odds and payout rates (Williams and Wood 2007; Wilkins 2010). Illegal sites are able to set their odds and change their pay-out rates much more easily than legal sites. Thus, new online gamblers may start with safe province-based sites only to switch to more "player-friendly" ones after they are comfortable with the online process. The overall business case and proposed profit margins for Canadian sites may not reflect this likely trend.

Lastly, the government is a role model for citizen behaviour, and endorsing gambling as a healthy form of entertainment is a mixed message at best. The government would be reinforcing the illusion of quick riches rather than the importance of a strong work ethic and lifelong savings. The explicit and implicit messages it sends for our governments to promote gambling may be more harmful than beneficial in creating a financially responsible and stable country.

Concluding Remarks

Internet gambling continues to be the least common form of gambling among Canadians; however, participation has increased over the last decade. Its attractive features include accessibility, affordability, anonymity, and increased social acceptability, which may entice first-timers, youth, problem gamblers, and other vulnerable populations.

Many studies have shown a higher prevalence of problems among Internet gamblers, and the expansion of Internet gambling has outpaced many of the laws used to regulate it. With the increased use of smartphones, regulations will need to catch up quickly to address many factors associated with mobile or remote gambling.

Online gambling is a huge cash industry for governments and corporations worldwide, making it very enticing for those in power. However, the main social issues related to Internet gambling involve gambling in the home and workplace, unscrupulous online casino operations, the protection of the consumer, marketing tactics, and behavioural tracking. If provincial governments choose to promote online casinos, it is clear they must find ways to protect all consumers by implementing responsible gambling management tools and harm reduction strategies, by providing links to problem gambling organizations, by warning the public about advertising dangers, by finding ways to prevent fraud from other gamblers, and by allocating more funding to treatment for problem gamblers and the families affected by this problem. It is essential to continue an open dialogue on this issue to further examine the potential benefits and harm to our nation.

Chapter 8

Youth Gambling

Over the last century, gambling has shifted from being viewed as "sinful" to a harmless form of entertainment; from being illegal to being legal in many forms; and from being actively prohibited to being actively promoted by communities and governments. Although there is effort to increase the availability of gambling venues to adults, the same level of effort has not been made to enforce age restriction on gambling or protect youth from this increased accessibility. Similar to the tobacco and alcohol industries, gambling is depicted as an activity offering an escape from everyday life, with many rewards and few risks (Derevensky and Gupta 2008).

The glitz and glamour associated with gambling can be particularly alluring to youth, and research indicates that the majority of youth have engaged in some form of wagering/gambling by the time they reach high school (Jacobs 2005). A small but significant percentage of youth gamble excessively, creating many negative life consequences. In fact, problem gambling among youth has also been associated with criminal behaviour and mental health issues such as substance abuse, delinquent behaviours, and suicide (Le et al. 2010).

The prevalence of problem gambling among youth has been the subject of some debate for the last decade. Earlier studies have shown problem gambling rates for youth that were strikingly higher than those of adults, while more recent studies have shown less pronounced differences (Derevensky, Gupta, and Winters 2003; LaBrie et al. 2003). This discrepancy stems from some methodology issues in the earlier years, such as differences in the sampling procedures and the measurement tools used in various studies. As the field further defines protocols and gold standards, more consistent rates across studies will likely emerge. Although an extensive review of the methodological issues is beyond the scope of this chapter, there are two important points to keep in mind: (1) across many studies, the overall prevalence of problem gambling among youth and college/university students has been found to be higher than adults to some degree; and (2) the long-term social impact of our current gambling environment on youth and young adults has yet to be fully realized or quantified.

This chapter will examine current trends in youth gambling, participation and prevalence rates among youth, risk factors that contribute to problem gambling, related mental health concerns, and parental attitudes about youth gambling. A discussion of Internet gambling follows this, as does a consideration of Internet and video game addiction. The chapter concludes with prevention strategies.

Overall Gambling Trends among Youth

A review of research on this topic highlights several trends, including the reasons why young Canadians gamble, types of games played, sources of money, as well as gender and age trends.

Youth participate in gambling for several reasons: to relax, to relieve boredom, to win money, to have fun and experience excitement, as well as to escape from daily problems and depressive feelings (Ellenbogen et al. 2008; Jacobs 2005; Le et al. 2010). Gambling is often promoted as a way to advance socially into the popular crowd, and youth do report gambling to socialize and make friends as well as to deal with loneliness (Gupta and Derevensky 1998; Jacobs 2005). In addition, gambling can seem attractive because it provides a quick-fix solution—a popular concept among youth today who desire and often demand a fast-paced lifestyle, including fast food, money, Internet use, and even relationships. Furthermore, some adolescents view gambling as a rite of passage into adulthood: they plan a trip to buy lottery tickets or visit a casino on their eighteenth or nineteenth birthday (Lin and Yiying 2009).

Overall, we find that the most popular forms of gambling among young people are lottery tickets, and private bets on dice, cards, professional sports, video games, and personal games of skill (e.g., bowling, basketball, or pool; Felsher, Derevensky, and Gupta 2007; Jacobs 2005; Turner et al. 2008). To a lesser extent, youth also wager with bookies and over the Internet (Derevensky and Gupta 2007). A recent study by St-Pierre et al. (2011) examined retailer compliance with lottery laws in and around Montreal. They found that underage youth between 15 and 17 were able to purchase lottery tickets 42 percent of the time without providing any form of identification. This lack of enforcement is likely similar in other places, and this type of access may explain why buying lottery tickets is a top activity among youth today. Society has created many avenues for direct and indirect wagering-like behaviour. Although technically not gambling, even eBay can create a sense of excitement when a purchaser wins a bid after fiercely competing to buy a product (KAAP 2008).

Where do young people acquire the money to gamble? Today, youth have few financial responsibilities but do have access to more disposable money for leisure pursuits than ever before (KAAP 2008). Youth report that their sources of money to gamble come from lunch/bus money, personal savings, selling personal belongings and stolen goods from friends or family, and the use of their parents' credit cards (Jacobs 2005). Some of these money sources were validated among youth Internet gamblers: 63 percent indicated they used personal savings, 30 percent used previous winnings, and 16 percent borrowed money from friends or family to gamble (Derevensky 2010). Parents may unknowingly enable gambling habits when they are not aware of how their child spends money, do not diligently check their financial/credit card records, and do not report theft by their children who steal to gamble (KAAP 2008).

Some important demographic trends among youth gamblers have emerged in the research over the last several decades. Studies show that first gambling experiences occur fairly early, with the median age range between 11 and 13 years old (Jacobs 2005). One study showed that the first gambling experience took place before the age of 10 for 48 percent of problem gamblers between the ages of 13 and 17 (Wynne, Smith, and Jacobs 1996). Older adolescents typically gamble more frequently than younger teens and prefer commercial games such as lotteries, scratch tickets, and gambling machines, while the younger group prefers cards, sports betting, and wagering on personal games of skill (Winters et al. 2002).

A consistent finding in the literature is that a higher percentage of males than females wager on almost all types of gambling activities. There is also a significant gender difference in the types of games preferred, similar to adult trends. Males tend to play more skill/knowledge-based games, such as cards and sports wagering, while females are more drawn to lotteries, scratch tickets, and gambling machines (Winters et al. 2002). Furthermore, studies have found that gender is one of the top predictors of problem gambling. For example, male youth are about six times more likely to have a gambling problem than female youth (Winters et al. 2002). However, the gap may be closing; evidence points to increased female participation, especially among those older than 18 (Welte et al. 2008). This increased participation will likely coincide with more problem gamblers. Another study examined the connection between youth problem gambling and video games, finding that those who reported a higher frequency of gaming were also more likely to be problem gamblers, regardless of gender (Wood et al. 2004).

Prevalence of Youth Gambling

A national survey across 10 provinces found that between 1 and 2 percent of adult Canadians struggle with pathological gambling (Cox et al. 2005). The survey also showed higher rates of problem gambling in provinces with permanent casinos and a high concentration of VTL machines, illustrating that access impacts participation and prevalence in adults. The prevalence rate of youth gambling in Canada also varies slightly across the provinces and territories. Before exploring the specifics, we will consider an overview of these important statistics for North America. Researchers reviewed 10 Canadian studies on adolescent gambling between 1988 and 2001 and discovered that participation rates ranged from 60 to 91 percent (with a median of 67 percent) during this time period (Jacobs 2005). Furthermore, Valentine (2008) provided a more recent literature review on youth gambling in the United Kingdom and North America. He concluded that between 76 and 91 percent of youth have reported gambling at least once in their lifetime, that 5 to 7 percent of youth who gamble are problem gamblers, and that 10 to 15 percent are at risk of developing a gambling problem. Providing additional credibility to those estimates, Winters (2011) reported that the prevalence for adolescents struggling with problem gambling ranges from 1 to 9 percent (with a median of 6 percent). The median prevalence rate of problem gambling among teens being treated for drug or alcohol abuse is 11 percent and the median for adults is just under 1 percent. The consistent findings of these reviews are that many adolescents have gambled underage and suffer from higher rates of problem gambling than adults.

Prevalence of youth gambling in Ontario

In Ontario, gambling seems to be a common leisure activity for nearly half of all adolescents (Cook et al. 2010). An important study was conducted using the Ontario Student Drug Use and Health Survey (OSDUHS) with 9,112 students in grades 7 to 12 across the province (Cook et al. 2010). The researchers found that 43 percent of students reported gambling, with participation increasing with age. Thus, students in grade 12 reported the highest level of participation at 56 percent. If we extrapolate this result to all students across Ontario, it would mean that 452,000 students have gambled on one of ten gambling activities over the past 12 months. The specific types of gambling most commonly practised were cards (20 percent), lottery tickets (16 percent), and sports pools (13 percent). The least common activities engaged in were Internet gambling (3 percent) and gambling at casinos (1 percent). Despite slightly higher rates of Internet gambling among college/university students and adults, this information reveals that underage youth experience some barriers to accessing Internet gambling sites. The results from this province-wide survey indicate that age limit regulations are being enforced at casinos and/or youth are not willing or able to travel to cities where casinos are located.

Overall, this study found that young Ontarian males were more likely to participate in gambling than young females (approximately 51 percent of males compared with 34 percent of females) and were more likely to participate in eight of the eleven gambling activities reported, with the exception of bingo, lottery tickets, and casino gambling. A commonly used measurement scale in. the field—the South-Oaks Gambling Screen: Revised for Adolescents (SOGS-RA)—estimated that approximately 3 percent of youth in Ontario have had a gambling problem, with males displaying more problems than females (4 percent versus 1 percent). While this percentage may not seem high, it equates to approximately 29,000 youth struggling with problem gambling in Ontario (Cook et al. 2010).

Prevalence of youth gambling in the Western provinces

In Alberta, the most recent provincial survey conducted on youth gambling took place in 2005 by The Alberta Youth Experience Survey (TAYES). As in Ontario, the survey was applied to youth in grades 7 through 12. The results indicated that 63 percent of youth reported gambling in the last 12 months, and approximately 4 percent of adolescents could be classified as problem gamblers (also determined by using the SOGS-RA). Similar to general trends, males were more likely to gamble than females. The most common gambling activity among youth in Alberta was playing cards for money (41 percent), a percentage that is more than double that found among adults (20 percent; Elliot-Erickson, Phare, and Lane 2007).

The most recent statistics on youth gambling in British Columbia are derived from the provincial Healthy Youth Development survey conducted in 2003 (May 2004). The results reveal that cards (33 percent) were the number one gambling activity, followed by lottery tickets (26 percent) and sports pools (23 percent). The results are nearly parallel with Alberta's gambling frequency statistics with respect to male/female ratios; the only exception being that a smaller number of youth report gambling (51 percent). While no measure was collected on problem gambling, 6 percent of students reported gambling weekly (May 2004), and given what we know about the relationship between frequency and problems, this group likely represents those at risk or currently experiencing problems.

In Manitoba, according to the 2007 *Student Gambling Report* gambling among youth between grades 7 and 12 is also a popular activity, with more than one in three youth engaging. However, according to the SOGS-RA, only 1 percent of students reported symptoms that would classify them as problem gamblers (AFM 2008).

Lastly, a study conducted in 2005 among youth in Saskatchewan included 1,884 students between 15 and 18 years old. Results revealed similar findings as other provinces on gender differences in participation rates and game choice (Dickinson and Schissel 2005). Overall, 81 percent reported wagering with money on at least one gambling activity, while 18 percent indicated gambling weekly and 8 percent daily. It was also revealed that 20 percent wagred on three or four activities, 18 percent on five or six activities, and 24 percent gambled on 7 or more activities, demonstrating the range and accessibility of the gambling options available to youth. Top gambling activities varied based on frequency. Overall, scratch tickets, games of skill, 50/50 tickets, family games, and private card games were the most frequently played, with 41 to 49 percent of youth reporting involvement. The top activities among those that gambled weekly were games of skill (19 percent), video games (19 percent), and poker (16 percent), and 4 percent reported wagering on games of skill and video games on a daily basis.

An interesting finding emerged when the researcher examined responses about the importance of gambling in youth's lives and their spending habits. Students perceived the importance of gambling to be low; it was ranked last when compared to school, sports, friends, romantic relationships, alcohol, and so on. About 93 percent indicated that gambling was not very important, yet it ranked sixth highest on their monthly reported expenditures, above their purchases of fast food, junk food, video games, DVDs, and CDs. This ranking demonstrates a discrepancy between their perceptions and behaviours with this type of entertainment. Lastly, 9 percent of youth reported knowing someone with a gambling problem, and the majority (at least 75 percent) were able to identify signs of a problem; however, overall, respondents believed that gambling was not a problem among high school students. Given these results, youth do not view gambling as a significant issue, which may reflect a lack of knowledge about gambling and the associated risks among this population.

A measure of problem gambling was not examined in this study, but overall prevalence rates of youth gambling in the Western provinces are comparable to those of youth gambling in Ontario.

Prevalence of youth gambling in Quebec

In 2002, it was estimated that, in Quebec, 0.9 percent of adults were at-risk gamblers and 0.8 percent were probable pathological gamblers (Ladouceur et al. 2005). This pales in comparison to results found in a 2004 study of high school students, which revealed that 6 percent were at-risk gamblers and 2.5 percent were probable pathological gamblers (Chevalier et al. 2005). A recent study conducted by Brunelle and her colleagues (2010) found similar results, with gambling problems among young francophones being more common than those found in adult populations. This study also sheds light on the prevalence of Internet gambling among Quebecois youth, which is reported later in the chapter.

Prevalence of youth gambling in the Atlantic provinces

The prevalence of gambling and problem gambling among youth in Newfoundland and Labrador, Nova Scotia, New Brunswick, and Prince Edward Island is reported in the 2007 *Student Drug Use Survey in the Atlantic Provinces* (SDUSAP). The results of the survey reveal many similarities to youth gambling prevalence in other provinces. About 59 percent of students played at least one of nine gambling activities for money (Poulin and Elliot 2007). Gender differences in the prevalence of gambling and the type of gambling activities played are comparable to other provinces, with males more likely to play cards for money and to bet on sport activities and sport lotteries. The major difference between youth gambling in the Atlantic provinces and those in other provinces is that the most common gambling activity was scratch tabs (35 percent) rather than cards. Among the Atlantic provinces, 3 percent of students met the definition of at-risk gambling and about 1 percent met the criteria for problem gambling. Overall, youth from Nova Scotia reported the highest rate of problem gambling in the region at 1.8 percent, while New Brunswick youth reported the least amount at 0.8 percent (Poulin and Elliot 2007).

Summary of Canadian youth gambling prevalence rates

To help pull all these numbers together, one final overview is worth mentioning. A national study of 5,666 youth, including both adolescent and young adults from 15 to 24 years of age, found that 61 percent gambled in the past 12 months and the national prevalence of moderate-risk or problem gambling was just over 2 percent (3 percent of males versus 1 percent of females). Regional prevalence estimates of youth with moderate-risk or problem gambling were 1.4 percent in British Columbia, 2.2 percent in the Prairie provinces, 2.8 percent in Ontario, 2.1 percent in Quebec, and 1.7 percent in the Atlantic provinces (Huang and Boyer 2007). These rates were calculated using the Canadian Problem Gambling Index Scale (a measurement more commonly used in recent years) and closely matches prevalence rates found in the individual province surveys. These results give some additional credibility to existing prevalence studies, regardless of researcher and measurement tools. In other words, there is some reliability in these numbers.

Across studies, the percentage of adolescents gambling is approaching that reported by adults. In addition, problem gambling rates do appear to be somewhat higher for youth than for adults. However, it is important to note that, generally, adolescent problem gamblers do not suffer to the same extent as adults in terms of job loss, amount of money and equity lost, and the number of relationships strained. In addition, some academics argue that many young problem gamblers may "mature out" of problem gambling as they do other high-risk behaviours such as binge drinking, unsafe sex, and drunk driving (Slutske, Jackson, and Sher 2003).

Youth gambling in other countries

How does gambling among Canadian youth compare with that of youth internationally? Overall, the percentage of youth with gambling problems in Australia appears similar to those in Canada; however, the exact statistical comparison is unknown given differences in measurements among respective studies. Although no national rates are available, research within Australia suggests that youth gambling is common, begins at a young age, and is more prevalent among males than females (Spelvins et al. 2010). A study found that the current rate of problem gambling among youth in Sydney was about 7 percent, a much higher estimate than in other states, where the rate is closer to 3 percent. The specific types of gambling activities played on a weekly or daily basis in this sample were coin tossing, card playing, and lottery ticket buying. Interestingly, coin tossing is the most popular gambling activity played among youth in Australia; Canadian youth do not practise this activity nearly as much.

In England and Wales, rates of problem gambling among youth are nearly parallel to those in Canada as well. The national prevalence survey reveals that about 6 percent of British youth are problem gamblers, 3 percent of whom most frequently play slot (fruit) machines (Fisher 1999). In fact, playing fruit machines is the most common gambling activity among British youth, more common than playing the National Lottery (Fisher 1999). A more recent study conducted on youth gambling in Scotland revealed that fruit machines are the most popular gambling activity there as well and 9 percent of youth are problem gamblers (Moodie and Finnigan 2005).

In the United States, a recent national survey of youth and young adults between the ages of 14 and 21 revealed that some 70 percent had gambled in the last year (Welte et al. 2008). Furthermore, a study in Georgia found that more than 247,000 students (57 percent) between grades 9 and 12 had gambled, and more than 69,000 (16 percent) did so on a regular basis. Also, an important finding revealed that female participation had increased from 33 percent in 2003 to 42 percent in 2005. The most common activities among these youth were cards, sports wagering, and the lottery, similar to those prevalent among Canadian youth.

Risk Factors

Gambling behaviour can be examined along a spectrum, from no gambling, to social gambling, to problem and pathological gambling. Understanding the factors that push individuals along this continuum toward addictive behaviour is critical.

Researchers have identified factors that contribute to youth's gambling participation and have found social and psychological characteristics that lead to the development and maintenance of a gambling problem (Le et al. 2010). Family influences, peer activities, availability of resources (i.e., lottery tickets and the Internet), lack of enforcement on underage gambling, active promotion, and other mental health concerns have been identified as contributing to youth gambling (Hardoon and Derevensky 2002; Messerlian, Byrne, and Derevensky 2004; Winters 2011). Many of the factors are sociological, and even those considered more psychological in nature likely have an environmental component. Youth learn from observing others in their social circle and certain behavioural patterns can be developed as a consequence of their surroundings.

Family and community

Social factors that influence males in our society were discussed in Chapter 7; however, it is worth noting that one of the largest risk factors for developing a gambling problem is gender. Parental gambling is also a significant risk factor (Korn and Tepperman 2005; Winters et al. 2002). Evidence that social learning affects gambling behaviour was found in a study that used qualitative and quantitative approaches and included 360 participants from several ethnocultural groups in Canada (Korn and Tepperman 2005). The main finding revealed that participants who reported seeing their parents gamble or who heard about their parents' gambling were more likely to be serious gamblers in adulthood (Korn and Tepperman 2005). Youth are typically introduced to gambling by watching their parents, who model both explicit and implicit messages about gambling's acceptability. The saying "Do as I say, not as I do" does not always translate perfectly from one generation to the other.

An earlier study by Winters and colleagues (2002) found that parental problem gambling was the most significant predictor of youth problem gambling. In fact, youth who reported that one or both of their parents were problem gamblers were 11 times more likely to also have a problem with gambling. Although a genetic component may be involved, the family environment likely plays an equal or even larger role than biology. The gambling behaviour of other family members (i.e., grandparents or siblings) and a family history of alcohol or drug abuse are also risk factors. Poverty and cultural influences have been found to contribute to rates of gambling as well. The idea of luck, glamour, and family fun can be embedded in cultural messages within a family, culture, or community, influencing gambling behaviour among the most vulnerable groups in society (Korn and Tepperman 2005).

A family's overemphasis on money and competition, and a lack of financial knowledge, are also risk factors for gambling (HFM Prevention Council n.d.). Children who do not learn the value of money may have more difficulty understanding the odds of a game; when this is combined with poor debt management skills, these youth are more prone to chase their losses.

There are, of course, community-based influences as well. Griffiths and Wood (2000) have argued that advertising introduces children and teens to the principles of gambling in a social context where wagering is typically viewed as an exciting yet harmless form of entertainment. Adolescents perceive the central message to be that gambling leads to "easy money" and is fun and enjoyable (Derevensky et al. 2007).

Data from a national population study in the United States suggested that childhood exposure to gambling increased the likelihood of gambling in adulthood (Kallick-Kaufman 1979). Similar to what has been found in studies of alcohol advertising, gambling commercials appear to significantly affect youth. A study revealed that 42 percent of youth report that gambling advertisements make them want to try gambling, and 61 percent imagine or dream about what they could buy with their winnings (Derevensky et al. 2007). Another study found that 39 percent of adolescents would be more likely to purchase a lottery ticket after viewing an advertisement (Felsher, Derevensky, and Gupta 2004).

Social learning theory suggests that individuals learn and model behaviours through observing others in their environment; children and adolescents, then, are likely to model behaviour demonstrated by significant others, people they personally value. In addition to family and friends, these people may be popular celebrities playing televised poker, actors in films about gambling, or celebrities or role models who promote Internet gambling sites. New York Yankees star Alex Rodriguez was recently in the news when under investigation for participating in high-end illegal poker games (Barzilai 2011). Although Rodriguez's activities are not a direct promotion for any particular gambling site, some youth may see his involvement with underground games as cool and wish to emulate his behaviour.

Recent trends in reality television depict gambling problems largely by extremes, concluding with the loss of one's home, career, marriage, and entire net worth. As a result, youth fail to recognize other less noticeable signs of problem gambling, such as disrupted relationships, less time spent with friends, slipping academic performance, and irritable behaviour. They may conclude that problems associated with gambling do not apply to them because they do not own a home or have a job or marriage to lose. Some studies suggest that while youth are aware of the potential risks and issues associated with problem gambling, their belief that problems will arise much later in their life acts to psychologically distance them from any immediate consequences (Gillespie, Derevensky, and Gupta 2007b). Taken together, these findings support the argument that children's exposure to gambling should be regulated. The next section of this chapter provides a brief biological description of early exposure and explores why adolescents may not easily perceive the consequences of their actions.

Brain development

Why so much concern about youth placing a few bets here and there? One thing we know is that early gambling experiences do predict gambling problems later in life (Skinner et al. 2004). We also have evidence that the brain does not fully develop until age 25 (Winters 2011). The adolescent brain has a strong preference for physical activity, high excitement, reward activities, and novel stimuli, all of which can trigger dopamine (a chemical associated with pleasure) to be released in the brain. In fact, these activities trigger greater amounts of dopamine during this life stage than any other (Winters 2011). Essentially, the adolescent brain is somewhat neurologically imbalanced, making it more susceptible to addiction (Le et al. 2010). Youth, then, may be especially vulnerable to the effects of gambling, given that rewards often dominate over consequences in decision-making during this time (Winters 2011). Accessibility to gambling opportunities and the industry's ability to capitalize on novelty and excitement enhances the odds that youth are attracted to gambling. In this way, they are placed at increased risk of developing problems later on in life.

Early involvement in gambling produces excitement or activation of neurological pathways associated with the reward and pleasure centres of the brain. The earlier these neurons fire in a person's life, the greater the likelihood of addiction and impulse control issues later in life. Imagine building a road through a forest. At first, there is no path or perhaps a winding one with many trees and rocks in the way. As you dig and excavate the area, travelling from point A to point B becomes easier and quicker. When gravel is laid down or the road is paved, traffic can increase. At this point, it becomes possible to speed through the forest at 100 kilometres an hour with little thought or concern about hitting a rock or trees to derail the trip. Essentially, this is what happens in the brain over time when an activity is repeated; the more frequently certain neurons are stimulated, the more developed their pathways become, causing structural changes in the brain. In turn, these changes allow signals to travel more quickly and frequently, producing an urge and strongly encouraging individuals to engage in certain behaviours (e.g., gambling, drinking alcohol) to create a chemical release ("a high") that provides a sense of pleasure or relief (Winters 2011). This view of the process is only introductory, but it provides a basic framework for understanding why we may not want youth to engage in behaviours that encourage these types of pathways to develop.

A study by Kessle et al. (quoted in Winters 2011) examined lifetime symptoms of gamblers by asking individuals to identify the age of their first gambling experience and the age when they experienced their first problem gambling symptom (e.g., tolerance, preoccupation). The researchers found that those with five symptoms (and thus considered pathological gamblers by clinical standards) began gambling at about age 16; those experiencing some problems (three to four symptoms) began around age 18; and those with no symptoms began when they were about 24 years old (as quoted in Winters 2011). Certainly this study provides further evidence of the link between age of onset and the severity of gambling problems. However, this study's unique contribution is the information that all groups experienced their first symptom around age 24, regardless of the age at which they started gambling. Although protecting our youth from addiction in their teen years is important, the real message from this research is that true addiction may begin later on in life, and limiting behavioural patterns and the activation of neural pathways during adolescence may be critical in decreasing those risks.

It can be difficult for some to imagine that behavioural activities—those not requiring the ingestion of a substance—could affect brain chemistry in the same way as substances do. However, neuroimaging techniques (e.g., functional magnetic resonance imaging) have revealed that monetary rewards from a gambling experience can produce brain activation in problem gamblers that is similar to a cocaine addict who receives a dose of cocaine (Breiter et al. 2001; Hewig et al. 2010).

What researchers are beginning to understand about addiction is that the object of addiction may be less important than the underlying cause(s) related to structural changes and signals in the brain. Addiction experts at Harvard University have proposed that addiction is a syndrome (a cluster of signs and symptoms) that can manifest or be expressed in various ways (such as through an opium, tobacco, alcohol, or gambling dependency; Odegaard, Peller, and Shaffer 2005). Rather than being separate illnesses, these addictions may actually stem from the same underlying cause(s). The key point here is that youth are more likely to gamble at a younger age than they are to do drugs, drink alcohol, or use tobacco. This early experience may begin to stimulate neural pathways and trigger the underlying cause(s) for an addiction, which could be later expressed as a gambling or drug addiction, depending on the person. Shaffer et al. (2004) have suggested that the risk for developing an addiction stems from three main factors: personal vulnerabilities (i.e., genetics, social learning), exposure to an object (i.e., access), and individual experiences with the object of addiction (i.e., desirability). Essentially, gambling could be an early priming agent for a heightened experience with another substance. So it is important to keep in mind that although gambling may not appear as risky as other behaviours (such as drug use or drunk driving), it is addictive itself and might lay the foundation for the brain to become addicted to something else.

Mental health comorbidity

For many people, problem gambling does not occur in isolation. It is often comorbid with other mental health concerns. However, it is not always clear whether gambling is a symptom of these problems or a contributor to them. For example, does feeling depressed cause an individual to seek the thrill of gambling as a way to feel better, or do consequences of excessive gambling contribute to the depression? In most cases, the directionality is unclear, and the most we can presume is that they co-occur and likely influence each other.

One well-documented connection is the relationship between ADHD and addiction. Compared to people without ADHD, individuals with ADHD are two to five times more likely to suffer from substance abuse and have higher rates of problem gambling during their adolescence and young adult years (Winters 2011). In a sample of adolescents that did not gamble, only 6 percent reported having ADHD, while 34 percent of a sample of pathological gamblers reported struggling with it (Derevensky et al. 2007). One proposed explanation for this is that people with ADHD have a strong preference for short-term over long-term rewards and consequences. This preference coincides with gambling activity, where delayed gratification is not usually part of the game.

Youth who are problem gamblers also more frequently engage in delinquent and criminal behaviour and have higher school truancy and dropout rates (Hardoon and Derevensky 2002). Furthermore, national research in Canada showed that problem gambling among youth is associated with higher rates of depression and anxiety, poor general health, increased risk of alcohol and substance abuse, as well as suicidal thoughts and attempts (Derevensky, Gupta, and Messerlian 2005). In fact, the early onset of gambling behaviour has been found to increase the lifetime risk of suicide (Kaminer, Burleson, and Jadamec 2002).

Nower et al. (2004) examined the connections among mental health, suicide, and youth gambling behaviour by analyzing survey results from three groups of high school students, two from Quebec (1996, 2000) and one from Ontario (2001). Results showed that adolescents with gambling problems were at a greater risk for both reported suicide ideation and attempts, independent of grade or gender. In all three studies, percentages of suicide ideation were double that of nonproblem and social gamblers.

In addition, some important results on gambling and mental health concerns were revealed in the Ontario youth study (Cook et al. 2010) mentioned earlier (see pages 139–40). After controlling for sex and grade, the provincial survey revealed that 61 percent of young problem gamblers experienced elevated levels of psychological distress compared to 15 percent of youth who were not problem gamblers. In addition, students struggling with problem gambling were four times more likely than nonproblem gamblers to report seriously considering committing suicide and 18 times more likely to report a suicide attempt. Although the number of youth struggling with problem gambling in Ontario was low (2.8 percent), this group of 29,000 students is nevertheless a concern given the increased mental health concerns and suicide risks that they experience as a result of or in combination with their gambling behaviour (Cook et al. 2010).

Parental Attitudes about Youth Gambling

What perceptions and beliefs do Canadian parents hold about youth gambling? How well do they understand the risks? A major Canadian study called Parents as Partners was the first in the world to address these important questions with parents of teenagers (DECODE 2009). The research included both quantitative and qualitative components, and a total of 2,700 Canadians participated in the survey; a further 190 were involved in focus groups. There were several important findings. First, only about 13 percent of parents indicated that their child had participated in any gambling for money. This percentage is far lower than the participation rates reported earlier, where rates were between four and six times higher than these parents' perceptions. In the study, similar beliefs were held by both mothers and fathers, but parents with a son did report a higher perceived participation rate (18 percent) than those with a daughter (7 percent). Second, parents were asked to indicate the seriousness of several health-related issues for teens today. Underage gambling was ranked last, with only 40 percent of parents listing it as a concern. The issue rated second lowest was depression, at 60 percent. Interestingly, the top issues were other addictive substances (alcohol and drugs), followed by drunk driving. These findings demonstrate a large gap in parents' awareness about youth gambling participation and the associated health risks for teens (DECODE 2009).

In addition, several discrepancies between parental attitudes and behaviours emerged in the study. The majority of the parents were aware that gambling *could* lead to addiction, poor academic performance, relationship problems, and even criminal behaviour. However, parents were the primary source of lottery tickets for underage youth (many did not view lottery tickets as gambling) and the majority were not concerned about their child's involvement in poker games with friends (DECODE 2009). To highlight the discrepancy further, two-thirds of parents felt gambling was not an appropriate activity for teens because of the risks, yet 66 percent reported rarely or never discussing gambling with their teen. Most parents reported that a conversation was warranted only if they knew their child was participating or felt pressured to gamble. About 57 percent of parents did report concerns about Internet gambling (for free or with money), yet only 9 percent installed antigambling software on their home computers (DECODE 2009). These results further illuminate the lack of awareness about gambling among Canadian parents and the hidden nature of this addiction.

Similar results have been found in the United States. One study reported that between 40 and 68 percent of youth gamble with family members, and 77 percent of adolescents reported that parents bought lottery tickets for them (Harrison 2003). It was also revealed that 80 to 90 percent of parents did not know their child was gambling for money or did not object to it (Harrison 2003). As noted previously, parental gambling is a risk factor for youth, and modelling gambling behaviour may communicate tolerance of, the excitement of, and encouragement for the activity (Korn and Tepperman 2005). This is especially true if parental expectations about gambling and the associated risks are not communicated through regular conversations. Overall, these studies show that parents do not recognize the growing trend of youth gambling.

Furthermore, when Canadian parents were asked to indicate who they felt was responsible for preventing teen gambling, the two top choices endorsed were parents (95 percent) and the teens themselves (79 percent; DECODE 2009). This finding brings up two important points. First, parents claim to be responsible for prevention and are knowledgeable about the risks, yet take few active steps to prevent youth gambling. Second, parents ranked government, the gambling industry, and police much lower on the responsibility scale for preventing youth gambling, highlighting the individualistic perspective that is dominant in our society. It seems parents also minimize the impact of social influences, such as active gambling promotion, unregulated ads, increased accessibility, and tolerance for illegal bookmaking and offshore gaming, on their impressionable teens. This brings us to other important topics related to youth: online gambling, gaming, and Internet use. These are explored briefly in the next section.

Internet Gambling

Today's youth have grown up in an era when having a computer is a normal household necessity for many families. An estimated 99 percent of Canadian children between the ages of 9 and 17 have used the Internet; 94 percent report having Internet access in their homes; and 61 percent have high-speed access (as quoted in Derevensky 2010). Because of regular Internet use, youth are more likely than adults to encounter advertisements for online gambling sites (Derevensky and Gupta 2008) that offer a variety of games identical to land-based casinos, including blackjack, roulette, slot machines, poker, and sports wagering (Messerlian, Byrne, and Derevensky 2004). Furthermore, with options to wager on everything from political outcomes and reality television shows to celebrity adoptions and arrests, betting may be even more appealing with pop culture thrown into the mix.

In an independent research report conducted by the Nova Scotia Gaming Foundation, researchers found that younger respondents revealed higher Internet gambling usage than their older counterparts. For instance, while 12 percent of 19 to 20 year olds indicated gambling online for real or fake money, 15 percent of 18 year olds and 19 percent of 15 to 17 year olds reported gambling online (Meerkamper 2006). Furthermore, the study found that youth between the ages of 15 and 17 were three times more likely to have played online poker in the last year for money than the general population (6 percent versus 2 percent). In Saskatchewan, it was found that 6 percent of youth gambled online for money and 18 percent wagered online on video games (Dickinson and Schissel 2005). These provincial studies, along with others in Canada, reveal that youth gambling and Internet usage are interconnected, and that the age at which adolescents begin to experiment with online gambling may be decreasing.

Adult Internet gamblers report more problems with gambling than land-based gamblers (Wood and Williams 2007). Similar results have been found among adolescents in Quebec (Brunelle et al. 2010; McBride, Derevensky, and Gupta 2007). A study conducted in 2007 found that 9 percent of high school students in Montreal and 6 percent of post-secondary school students from the United States and Canada had gambled online for money in their lifetime. Of those, 70 percent reported gambling weekly, and of those, 28 percent were identified as problem gamblers. This proportion is a much higher sample percentage than what has been documented among land-based youth gamblers. In addition, about half of the sample reported playing on practice sites, mostly playing poker or blackjack (McBride, Derevensky, and Gupta 2007).

A more recent study indicated that 8 percent of students aged 14 to 18 placed Internet bets for money in the last year, while 35 percent reported playing on demo/practice sites (Brunelle et al. 2010). In the entire sample of 825 participants, close to 8 percent were at risk, while 3 percent were probable pathological gamblers; these numbers corresponded to 20 percent and 10 percent, respectively, when the Internet gamblers (137 participants) were isolated in their own group. Those numbers are roughly three times higher than those for non-Internet gamblers. Another study revealed similar percentages of youth playing online for free and for money (Derevensky 2010). A unique aspect of this study was that youth were asked what they learned from using demo/practice sites. The top responses were to "manage risk," to learn how to play casino and card games "better," and to "feel more confident playing for money" (as quoted in Derevensky 2010). It seems evident that practice sites are being used as a stepping stone to real online gambling.

In several of the studies mentioned above, researchers were interested in both those who gambled with money and those who did not. This focus likely stems from some important yet concerning results found in 2004 (Derevensky, Felsher, and Gupta 2004). The researchers of the 2004 study revealed that the majority of pathological gamblers (or, 72 participants) identified in the sample began gambling online with these practice sites between the ages of 10 and 13. Of these pathological gamblers, 80 percent had gambled online without money in the past year and 35 percent had gambled with money. This finding has several important implications. First, it suggests that demo sites are likely involved in the initiation of gambling behaviour, and early onset is a factor in problematic behaviour. Second, the majority of problem gamblers still engage in playing on demo sites, so either these sites are addictive in their own right or they help maintain the addiction by providing "a high" in between real wagering opportunities. Additionally, popular social websites where youth spend a great deal of time, such as Facebook, also offer applications whereby youth can play online games and receive free tokens by inviting other friends to play. These applications have recently been under scrutiny by the FBI and other organizations. Parents should be aware that there are risks involved in online gambling (whether or not money is involved) and that youth playing on practice sites could have a problem with online gambling or other gambling activities.

Internet addiction

Adolescent problem gambling shares risk factors and consequences with both excessive video game playing and Internet use. Thus, it is worth noting some important issues and facts about Internet and video game behaviour.

Dr. Kimberly Young, director for the Center for Internet Addiction Recovery in the United States, dedicates her time to the research and treatment of Internet addiction. She presented the first paper on the topic at the American Psychological Association conference held in Toronto in 1996. Since then, studies reporting Internet addiction have emerged in countries around the world, including Italy, Germany, India, the United Kingdom, and France, with more epidemic numbers of youth addicts in China and South Korea (Fackler 2007; Wu and Zhu 2004). The first military-style treatment facility for Internet addiction was developed in Beijing in 2006; it treats people addicted to online games,

Internet pornography, cybersex, and chat rooms. In 2009, a residential treatment centre for "pathological computer use" opened near Seattle, Washington (Geranios 2009).

Warning signs of a problem include failed attempts to stay offline, neglecting friends and family, engaging in the activity at the expense of sleep and other obligations, maladaptive cognitions and rationalizations (e.g., "I'm not as bad as others"), and increased anxiety when unable to be online. The majority of individuals who seek treatment for Internet addiction also report involvement in online sexual activity such as pornography or explicit sexual conversations (Young 2009). This finding is especially relevant in the context of a new and increasingly popular trend among youth today called sexting: texting explicit pictures or words from mobile devices.

Some of the documented consequences for Internet addiction include social isolation, academic and physical problems, relationship issues, poor productivity, and job loss (Young 2009). Although there is substantial evidence that Internet addiction can cause disruption in people's lives, debate arises around its classification as a true addiction by clinical standards. Some argue that Internet addiction disorder meets criteria established for other substance and behavioural addictions, such as increased tolerance and negative life consequences, while others feel it does not (Block 2008; Byun et al. 2009). Griffiths concluded in 2009 that Internet addiction does meet criteria for addiction in a small number of cases. Furthermore, scientists have found that excessive Internet use is related to structural changes in the brain, impairing short-term memory and decision-making skills similar to other addictions (Yuan et al. 2011). Although some evidence exists, the American Psychiatric Association has requested that more research be done before it determines whether Internet addiction should be included in the DSM-V (Edlund 2011). The alternative public health term being used in the literature is *Internet overuse* (Byun et al. 2009). We will now discuss similar concerns about excessive video and Internet gaming among youth today.

Video games and Internet gaming

Is excessive video game playing really dangerous? Treatment centres have opened around the world, and several deaths have been reported from related behaviour (Young 2009). The first detox centre for video game overuse was opened in the Netherlands. An addiction centre in Richmond, British Columbia, reported that excessive gaming accounts for 80 percent of its youth counsellors' caseloads (Bennett 2006). Furthermore, a national study of 1,178 children and teens between the ages of 8 and 18 in the United States discovered that about 9 percent of young video game players exhibited signs of addiction to gaming (Gentile 2009). The researcher found that excessive video gaming affected school work, interaction with family and friends, and physical health (Gentile 2009).

In Beijing, a 24-year-old gamer died after playing video games for 86 hours straight. In another story, an infant died from neglect in South Korea while a couple played games at an Internet café (Edlund 2011). Although rare, gaming-related deaths are associated with intense sleep deprivation in combination with stimulants (e.g., energy drinks) and lack of food, leading to heart failure. Real dangers can arise when adolescents and young adults are socially isolated and "trapped in a time warp" with constant brain stimulation and caffeine (Edlund 2011).

In 1996, a link was found between video game playing (not online) and gambling in youth aged 9 to 14. Children who frequently played video games were also more regular gamblers and more likely to exhibit risk-taking tendencies compared to low-frequency video game players (Gupta and Derevensky 1996). These results lay the foundation for future concern as video gaming, Internet gaming, and gambling become less distinct activities.

Video game websites have become extremely popular over the last decade. These games can be easily played at home, offering the first taste of online gambling–related behaviour. An example of this sort of video game site is iWin.com, which offers gamers several free and purchasable video games, one of which is penny slots. Although this sort of site offers video games, it is only a click away from online casinos with similar enticing deals, flashy colours, and animations. Many gaming sites offer rewards in the form of tokens. Players start with a certain amount of free credit, which they use to play (i.e., make their initial wager), and they receive payout amounts depending on the player's skill level (Messerlian, Byrne, and Derevensky 2004). Think about the popular kid's establishment Chuck E Cheese's. At this restaurant, game players receive a certain number of tickets based on performance, which can later be exchanged for prizes. This concept is very similar to the operation of many gaming sites, but the sites are available 24 hours a day.

Most of these gaming websites incorporate at least two of the three elements that legally define an activity as gambling. Some consist of a consideration (purchase) to play a game but have no winnings or provide points that can be exchanged for money later. Others have a free membership (no consideration) but people play games of chance and/or skill for cash or prizes. Either way, the sites closely resemble online gambling, and they acquaint many users with the gambling process.

According to Derevensky and colleagues (2007, 2010), gaming sites and free trials are intended to create future gamblers and encourage children to play, increasing future customers, and subsequently resulting in more problem gamblers.

Virgin Gaming (launched in June 2010) has now taken online gambling one step further, offering a new type of legalized wagering in Canada: gambling in the form of video games. The site organizes competitive console gaming for cash, prizes, or points and grows by an estimated 1,000 users a day (Sorensen 2010). The site features popular video games such as *FIFA*, *Madden NFL*, and *Halo*, and unlike some other online gambling, these games are based more on skill than on chance. The site is designed to target young video game players with a minimum age of 18 and a bet limit of $1,000 (Sorensen 2010). This new form of betting most clearly demonstrates the convergence between gaming and gambling.

Preventive Strategies

There is controversy surrounding which risk factors should be addressed in prevention programs. This tension exists because scientific knowledge about the prevention of adolescent problem gambling is rarely translated into science-based prevention initiatives. However, there is a general consensus that preventing youth gambling requires an effective combination of policy initiatives, limiting the availability of gambling, and educational strategies that change knowledge, attitudes, beliefs, and skills in order to prevent risky gambling behaviour (Nation et al. 2003; Stockwell et al. 2005; Williams, West, and Simpson 2007b, 2008). Dickson, Derevensky, and Gupta (2003) proposed a conceptual framework for prevention that applies the common elements of existing tobacco, alcohol, and drug abuse prevention programs. Their program included common risk and protective factors across addictions and proposed a model of youth gambling prevention that involved primary, secondary, and tertiary levels. In addition, Delfabbro, Lahn, and Grabosky (2005) suggested that educational strategies should include role-playing games, youth-focused gambling websites, and helplines designed specifically for youth with gambling problems. A few of these strategies have been widely adopted. Taking a different approach, Messerlian, Derevensky, and Gupta (2005) suggested using social marketing techniques to prevent youth gambling. They suggested that media-based strategies need to appeal emotionally to adolescents by depicting real life and portraying the negative consequences of problem gambling. Additional information about specific gambling prevention programs in Canada are briefly discussed in the appendix. However, a few prevention strategies are listed below for parents, schools, and communities.

Parent involvement

It is important that parents learn the warning signs of a gambling problem. They should check bank and credit card statements frequently; help youth build financial management skills; talk to their children about the risk of gambling; and teach techniques for safer wagering. Increasing children's knowledge about the value of a dollar and practising good financial management at home may help prevent gambling-related losses in the family and future problems with addiction. To protect youth from gambling online, parents can purchase online gambling blocking software, such as GamBlock, which prevents access to all online gambling on personal computers.

School involvement

Gambling shares many of the same risk factors as other addictions and therefore can be easily incorporated into current prevention strategies and conversations about tobacco, alcohol, and other drugs in health classes. It is important that interventions are age and gender specific, as well as developmentally appropriate (Clarkson 2007; KAAP 2008). In addition, peer-to-peer education has shown to be effective in educating youth on risky behaviours such as gambling (Le et al. 2010). A website called friends4friends.ca provides information and warning signs for peers to look out for. Promoting this site and other bystander interventions to engage youth in helping one another may be the best way to catch problems before they really begin. In addition, educating youth on positive coping skills, life skills, and alternative forms of entertainment may be indirect ways to help reduce early participation in gambling behaviour (Le et al. 2010).

A national study revealed that parents would like to receive information about youth gambling from schools (DECODE 2009). However, only 15 percent of parents reported receiving information about the risks of gambling, and only 10 percent reported that their child participated in any gambling-related awareness program at school (DECODE 2009). Given this information, it seems that schools could be an important hub for disseminating information to both parents and youth. Lastly, university policies on gambling will likely help to curb gambling on campuses, as long as the policies are well distributed and consistently enforced.

Community involvement

Gambling is a social and public health issue worthy of further consideration, research, and prevention. Provincial governments must consider the impact of increased accessibility to gambling venues on the quality of life for youth and adults and engage in harm-reduction strategies to minimize health issues and costs (Messerlian, Byrne, and Derevensky 2004; Le et al. 2010). Since no individual prevention method has been proven to be the most effective, a multi-faceted approach is needed in which youth hear preventive messages about gambling from parents, friends, schools, and the government. At the micro level, communities can continue to engage and initiate prevention efforts such as increasing knowledge and awareness about the risks associated with gambling; developing and using a gambling-prevention curriculum for middle schools and high schools; increasing education about screening for gambling problems among physical and mental health professionals; and supporting in-service training for other professionals who work with youth (i.e., camp counsellors, coaches, teachers, mentors; KAAP 2008; Le et al. 2010).

Youth who report stronger attachments to their family, school, and community report lower levels of gambling (Le et al. 2010). Strengthening these ties among youth may be a protective factor against many addictions and risky behaviours. In addition, the development of personal competence, social competence, and self-esteem has been found to protect youth from problem gambling (Dickson et al. 2002; Lussier et al. 2007). These individual factors are often fostered in positive social networks and environments.

Although prevention strategies at the individual level are an important factor, they do not address the societal issues around gambling. Governments, communities, and those developing public health policies must work together to reduce access to gambling products and exposure to one-sided (positive) gambling advertisements and to increase the enforcement of currents laws. Derevensky and Gillespie (2005) have suggested that the enforcement of gambling age regulations is limited; with the exception of accessing casinos, young people can easily circumvent restrictions. Canadian institutions have a duty to protect youth from potentially harmful activities, and this social issue warrants greater critical analysis and discussion, especially with regard to the expansion of gambling, the gambling industry's marketing tactics, and underage gambling.

Closing Remarks

Youth today have grown up in an environment in which gambling is considered legal. The prevalence of youth gambling and problem gambling in Canada differs slightly across provinces. However, national estimates suggest that nearly half of youth engage in some form of gambling activity and roughly 3 to 6 percent are problem gamblers, with slightly more at risk of developing a problem. Youth tend to have higher rates of problem gambling than adults, and card games are the most common gambling activity played among Canadian youth. British youth most commonly gamble on fruit machines, and Australian youth prefer coin tossing.

The following social influences affect the prevalence of youth gambling: video game mania, powerful advertisements, parental modelling, increased social acceptability and accessibility, and lack of prevention and awareness (Derevensky 2010; Derevensky and Gupta 2008; Le et al. 2010). In addition, the use of personal computers, widespread access to the Internet, and the increasingly ambiguous nature of gaming and gambling may be factors in the appeal of gambling among youth (Derevensky and Gupta 2007). Furthermore, in normal brain development, there is an increase in risk-taking, a greater propensity toward high-excitement activities, and an increased sensitivity to novel stimuli during adolescence, which may account in part for youth's attraction to gambling (Winters 2011). The industry certainly capitalizes on this "brain state" with flashy colours, stimulating software, and free trials.

Some commonalties among youth who experience problems with their gambling include being male; a family history of gambling; early gambling experiences; feeling lonely, depressed, or bored; a desire to escape from stressful situations; and an overemphasis of money, competition, and risk-taking in one's social network.

The true impact of our legalized gambling environment on youth and young adults will not be fully seen for several decades. However, it would be ill-advised to wait for this research to take action when enough current evidence suggests more regulation on advertising, greater enforcement of underage gambling, and an increase in prevention and interventions for middle school and high school students. Regardless of whether or not youth gambling can be considered an epidemic today, most problem gamblers begin gambling at an early age. The link between youth gambling and adult problem gambling is very strong. More research, legislative action, and prevention programs from our government, communities, and institutions are needed to protect our youth, families, and society from future increases in problems, crime, and health-care costs related to problem gambling.

Chapter 9

Sources of Information on Gambling

The French philosopher Michel Foucault has explored the link between knowledge and power in society. From what sources does the public gather knowledge about important social issues? Who generates this knowledge, and how do we come to trust it? Consider the issue of smoking and health. Researchers have long known of the link between smoking and compromised health, including the dangers of passive smoking. However, the tobacco industry promoted controversy around this research, stalling attempts to protect the health of many smokers and passive smokers. It is only relatively recently that second-hand smoke is widely accepted to be harmful and that smoking has been banned in public places. The relationship between smoking and ill health has become ingrained as knowledge through government-sponsored campaigns, which help to legitimize the science behind anti-smoking claims. In this context, then, "knowledge" is merely information spoken in the voice of power; information is sometimes just noise with expert credibility.

The history of smoking and public health reveals how knowledge is rarely neutral when profit and revenue are involved. Many voices contribute to our store of knowledge on the subject of gambling and problem gambling; the sheer quantity of "noise" can make it difficult to disentangle the source (and validity) of our understanding of this issue.

A recent study found four specific influences on the public perception of gambling. First, there is government participation: the government actively participates in gambling as both a promoter and a regulator of lotteries, casinos, and raffles. Second, there is the generally accepted thinking about addiction, given an evident association between gambling and wider social problems such as addiction or crime. Third, there is the economic importance of gambling for many community and provincial budgets. Finally, and related, there is the public interest in continuing to reap these revenues; many public goods, including hospitals, cultural institutions, and amateur sport, are funded through gambling (Seelig and Seelig 1998).

The Five Stakeholders of Gambling Knowledge

These influences, in turn, are manipulated—intentionally or otherwise—by at least five groups of stakeholders. We can call these groups the Researchers, the Gamblers, the Regulators, the Promoters, and the Medicalizers. Each of these groups has some influence on the knowledge that circulates in the public sphere. Some of them generate research-based knowledge about gambling; others try to manage how this knowledge is understood by the public; and yet others circulate their own knowledge to one another.

The researchers

This first group consists of academic researchers based at institutions or universities. Researchers arguably have the least impact on public perceptions of gambling, despite the fact that this group is the most important potential source of knowledge about gambling and problem gambling.

Academics who work within the fields of psychology, psychiatry, clinical social work, medicine, and counselling and treatment professions focus on individuals, and sometimes families. Sociologists and public health researchers, meanwhile, are more likely to focus on the social causes and effects of gambling. In turn, research may be used to inform health professionals and organizations; it has also led to the development of measures such as the South Oaks Gambling Screen (SOGS; Lesieur and Blume 1987) and the Canadian Problem Gambling Index (CPGI; Ferris and Wynne 2001).

The gamblers

The informal information that gamblers provide to one another probably has more influence on social behaviour than academic research findings.

But this information is very often biased. This bias, or slant, is most pronounced in problem gamblers. As psychologists point out, problem gambling is a cognitive disorder, marked by an inability to correctly assess the risks associated with gambling behaviour. As a result, problem gamblers have difficulty making use of information that is critical of gambling. The more severe the gambling problem, the less rational the thought processes that accompany it tend to be, especially on topics related to gambling (Emond and Marmurek 2010). This means that the very people who most need new, therapeutic information about problem gambling are the least open to receiving that information and the least able to process it.

Misguided gambling behaviour is also linked to a person's view of himself or herself as a "gambler" or "nongambler." In a survey of under-graduate students, Lange (2001) asked participants to report on their gambling. Despite the fact that half of the respondents said they did not gamble, almost all of the respondents reported taking part in what might reasonably be called gambling activities.

The respondents differed mainly in the frequency and type of gambling activity in which they engaged. Those who labelled themselves as gamblers took part in activities that were not necessarily legal, such as off-track betting, dice games, video poker, dogfights or cockfights, or placing bets with a bookie. By contrast, self-styled nongamblers often took part in games of chance that did not constitute gambling in their view: for example, bingo, local poker games and sports pools, or scratch or lottery tickets. In effect, people can gamble without seeing themselves as doing so.

The regulators

Politicians and policy-makers provide influential, but sometimes con-flicting, information on gambling and problem gambling. They exercise their main influence through legislation that regulates how people may and may not gamble. However, regulators have an obvious conflict of interest.

Ideally, government should play a neutral role, as referees, or even as advocates, for the public interest where matters of health and safety are concerned. This is true both at the provincial level, where gambling is regulated, and also at the federal level, which has an interest in certain types of national health issues. The federal government has by and large chosen to ignore gambling, and the various provincial governments are in a conflict of interest: they may support public health in principle, but they are committed to raising revenues through public gambling.[1]

In Canada, a variety of quasi-governmental bodies play a role in both the regulation and promotion of gambling by overseeing gaming activi-ties, collecting data, funding gaming-related research, and marketing gaming. These bodies include gambling, lottery, and/or gaming com-missions and Crown corporations.

We have seen how legislators have shifted their approach to gambling from one of criminal prohibitions to regulatory administration of gambling as a commercial matter (Seelig and Seelig 1998).[2] This sea change in governmental treatment of gambling has by extension influenced society's attitudes. When lotteries were decriminalized in Canada to raise funds for the 1976 Olympic Games (Cosgrave and Klassen 2001), provincial governments were able to license charity or church lotteries. The control of gambling shifted from the federal government to provincial governments. With an amendment to the Criminal Code in 1985, provincial governments were granted the right to extend their own gambling activities, allowing them to run provincial gambling operations with the help of organizations and agencies licensed to provide gambling services. By the end of the 1990s, legal, widespread gambling had been fully legitimized as a source of governmental and corporate revenue.

With the legalization of gambling, the connection between crime and gambling became less visible. The involvement of government also helped to dispel negative connotations. In effect, when gambling was legalized, it was also normalized and sanitized.

The promoters

Commercial gaming operators are a fourth influence on the construction of knowledge about gambling and problem gambling. This group includes state enterprise officials and members of Aboriginal governments and local bands, as well as private-sector investors such as large casino or bingo hall owner-operators, convenience store owners who provide lottery services, and bar owners who may host VLTs.

Promoters today in Canada and elsewhere promote gambling as a draw for tourism and as a legitimate leisure activity (Duffy 1997; Kang, Long, and Perdue 1996; Nickerson 1995; Sirakaya, Delen, and Choi 2005). Gambling is often presented in ways that glamorize the activity. For example, in a study of the legalization of riverboat casino gambling in Iowa, Duffy (1997) found that gambling promotion used several fantasy themes to portray riverboats as part of Iowa's historical heritage, as family-friendly entertainment, and as a draw for tourism. In Canada, the OLG promotes its large, resort-style casino at Niagara Falls in the same manner. According to the OLG, "No trip to the breathtaking wonders of Niagara Falls would be complete without a visit to one of the most action-packed attractions in Canada—Casino Niagara" (OLG 2008, 1).

The medicalizers

While concern with gambling as a social problem has a long history, it was not seen as a medical problem until the late twentieth century. This perception has opened gambling knowledge to the influence of health authorities and organizations, including medical, psychological, and psychiatric professionals, researchers, and medical associations, such as the Canadian Medical Association and the American Psychiatric Association.

One study has explored how our understanding of problem gambling evolved over time: where once it was seen as a form of deviant behaviour, more recently it has been defined as a medical problem (Rosecrance 1985). In the 1920s, Freud linked the excessive gambling of Russian novelist Fyodor Dostoevsky to his failure to advance properly through the stages of oedipal development (Lesieur and Rosenthal 1991). To Freud and others, this behaviour was *pathological*. Gambling was redefined as a sickness, and, importantly, a treatable one (Rosecrance 1985).

As we saw in the previous chapter, psychoanalyst Edmund Bergler, in his well-known book *The Psychology of Gambling* (1943/1957), described the neurotic gambler as marked by habit, excess, disinterest in nongambling activities, an inability to stop even despite losses, and a constant search for the "thrill" of the game (Bergler [1943/1957], as quoted in Rosecrance 1985). Since loss of money was the most common result of gambling, Bergler assumed that self-punishment is the gambler's unconscious purpose. (Therefore, he might also have believed that lung cancer is the purpose of smoking and weight gain is the purpose of dieting; his views on these topics were not recorded.)

As problem gambling became more medicalized, it was aligned with the "disease model" of alcoholism, which sees alcohol addiction as an illness rather than a moral failure (Rosecrance 1985). The "compulsion model" of problem gambling, which described excessive gambling as a result of ungovernable urges, evolved from here. This model was endorsed by the fledgling organization Gamblers Anonymous (GA). Though not a medical or psychiatric organization, GA leads efforts to treat problem gambling; GA methods emphasize abstinence as key to avoiding the risk of relapse (Browne 1994; Collins 1996). GA also lobbied to secure the legitimacy of a medical definition of problem/pathological gambling, and continues to do so today (Rossol 2001).

The final stage of what Rosecrance sees as the definition of problem gambling in a medical model is the "institutionalization of a medical designation." This occurred when pathological gambling was added to the third edition of the Diagnostic and Statistical Manual (DSM-III).

Pathological gambling has remained in the DSM since this edition; perhaps in part because of its successful inclusion, other "new addictions" have been added or considered for inclusion.

This new view of gambling has influenced behaviour in several ways. First and most obviously, it has removed much of the moral stigma associated with gambling. Second, with the removal of this stigma, problem gamblers are more readily forgiven provided they show willingness to receive treatment—which leads to a greater willingness to seek treatment. Third, new ways of understanding gambling have led the public to "forgive" the providers of gambling opportunities, so long as these providers give people the opportunity to exclude themselves from gambling risks that may make them "sick." This view has facilitated the spread and growth of gambling opportunities.

In short, the medical model of gambling appears to serve everyone's interests: no one is to blame and anyone can be cured, if only he or she follows expert advice. In this blameless new world of consumer pleasures, only excess is a problem—and even the tendency to excess is (potentially) curable.

Public Knowledge

What effect do all these voices have on the public understanding of gambling? Different understandings, and misunderstandings, of just what comprises gambling are widespread. Turner et al. (2005) surveyed Ontarians to learn about their awareness of problem gambling, responsible gambling, and their own gambling behaviours. They found that many Ontarians have only a limited understanding of problem gambling. In Turner's study, about one in three respondents reported knowing someone with a gambling problem; yet these same respondents were unable to identify any signs of pathological gambling beyond financial difficulties. They did not consider the social or psychological effects of excessive gambling to be signs of a problem.

Awareness of public initiatives to reduce problem gambling was limited as well. Almost two-thirds of respondents in Turner's study were unaware of such initiatives. Respondents who gambled in venues where information on problem gambling is available (e.g., casinos) were slightly more aware of programs to help problem gamblers. However, those who were aware of initiatives were most likely to have received their information from television (39.6 percent), in conversation (39.3 percent), and in newspapers (37 percent; Turner et al. 2005).

Peers, family, and the mass media provide information, not only about gambling policies, but also about gambling norms. People usually try to act in a socially acceptable way by conforming to the norms and conventions they learn from sources such as parents, peers, and the media. Moore and Ohtsuka (1999b) studied how people were influenced by the perceived gambling attitudes of their significant others. Not surprisingly, respondents with a positive attitude toward gambling were most likely to think that their significant others shared their view, and these were the people most likely to gamble. In particular, male respondents who viewed gambling as socially acceptable were more likely to gamble than any other group. Gamblers are like drinkers in this way: they adjust their own notions of normality, and their own behaviours, to what they believe are the prevailing norms of their group or community.

Closing Remarks

Our perspectives on gambling and problem gambling have been shaped by different voices, and in particular, five groups—the Researchers, the Gamblers, the Regulators, the Promoters, and the Medicalizers—have dominated the discourse on problem gambling.

This chapter has explored how gambling behaviour is influenced by legislation that controls the extent and type of gambling activities available. In Canada, the legislation of gambling in turn has been heavily influenced by the process of medicalization, which gradually changed how gambling, as well as many other addictions and social problems, have come to be understood.

The trend of medicalization follows a broader trend of increasing reliance on authority figures. People base important decisions on the information that is supplied by these figures and delivered via the pervasive mass media. So whether or not this information is valid and unbiased becomes an important concern.

Experts and decision-makers, including politicians, quasi-governmental bodies such as those of the gambling industry, commercial gaming operators, health authorities and regulators, and academic researchers put together studies to inform other individuals and groups about the nature of gambling in our society. Given the divergent assumptions and motivations of these different authorities and their funders, the constant flow of information about gambling is difficult to examine objectively.

Nowhere is this conflict of interest clearer than in the debate about what constitutes reliable research on the topic of problem gambling. There seem to be no ground rules about what information is to be considered reliable, credible, and worthwhile in drafting policy to curb problem gambling. In the next chapter, we will look at what happens when gambling information is systematically gathered and tested, and what impediments prevent the translation of research into social policy concerning gambling.

Chapter 10

The Great Gambling Debate

As we noted in the previous chapter, information and knowledge about gambling is rarely neutral. Those with a financial stake in the gambling industry have challenged the findings of academic gambling researchers. Evidence of this has been noted by Mark Vandermaas (2008), a doctoral student at the University of Toronto, in unpublished research supported by the OPGRC. However, though familiar in the fields of tobacco and pharmaceutical research, the tactics used by the gambling industry have only recently surfaced in gambling research.

Through the US-based National Center for Responsible Gambling, the gambling industry has funded one-sided research projects on the social costs of problem gambling. These studies by and large endorse one or more of four arguments: (1) that the gains from gambling outweigh the social costs; (2) that individual rights and freedoms should trump other concerns; (3) that current methods of measuring social costs are inadequate and unreliable; and (4) that public opinion and policy is rarely based on unbiased and factual information, and that gambling research fails to meet the prevailing standard for policy-making. This industry-funded research often fails to convince when held up to more rigorous methodology.

How the Public Views Gambling

Many aspects of gambling are part of a large-scale branding effort on the part of government and gambling providers. It is true that gambling generates a great deal of money for governments and communities, as well as for private entrepreneurs, as argued in the "greater good" outlook. It provides public revenue through a heavy tax on gambling profits, through government ownership (in part or full) of certain forms of gambling, and through philanthropic donations by gambling entrepreneurs. This revenue allows the government to spend more on public programs without increasing the rates of income tax or property tax. Those businesses that provide gambling venues often foreground the positive contributions of the revenue they generate.

And so do governments. Beyond the general benefit of lower taxes, provinces often set aside portions of gambling revenue for particular projects. Some provinces even brand projects funded by gambling, as in Alberta:

> The province of Alberta uses all its gambling revenues to specifically fund a number of core government responsibilities (for example, transportation, health, learning, municipal affairs). For example, "Alberta Lottery Fund" symbols appear on projects across the province to remind citizens of the good works gambling supports. (Azmier 2005, 10)

Such advertising promotes the belief that provincially run gambling has concrete benefits for the general population.

This branding strategy may be extended by explicitly linking public revenue to a specific type of gambling activity. Such linking has been used to defend types of gambling shown to be especially addictive, such as VLTs, which were recently brought under public and academic scrutiny given their addictive nature. Yet some provinces justify permitting VLTs on the basis of the revenue they yield. According to a report by Decima Research, VLT revenue accounts for about 75 percent of the Atlantic Lottery Corporation's net revenue in the Maritimes. Any drastic changes to VLT policy would remove this revenue (Eby 2007, 2). ·

Gambling revenue is used in other ways that promote branding in the public eye. Some gambling revenues are reserved for programs that directly address the social costs of gambling, either by helping to treat problem gamblers or by informing the public about the risk involved in gambling. Ontario, for example, devoted $75 million to such treatment and education plans in 2003/2004 (Williams and Wood 2007).

But a quick look at the math shows another side to this apparently beneficial income: $75 million is clearly a lot of money. However, it represents only 1.2 percent of that time period's total gambling revenue. When compared to the revenues estimated to come from problem gamblers alone—nearly 36 percent of total gambling revenue—this seems like a modest amount to spend on treatment (Williams and Wood 2007, 381).

Furthermore, a good deal of this revenue in fact goes back into branding gambling. The gambling industry (i.e., government) spent $248 million to *advertise* gambling in 2003/2004. In other words, the industry/

State spends three times more money seeking to draw in new gamblers than they spend on treating people with gambling problems (Azmier 2005, 11). This may not seem that strange or necessarily suggest anything unusually nefarious in and of itself—for example, tobacco and alcohol companies presumably spend more on advertising than they do on fixing various problems associated with product use. However, it does illustrate the imbalance in firepower between contending sides in this debate. Academic researchers face an uphill battle to place their findings in the public view.

The gambling industry has also raised other arguments that are part of a branding strategy. Proponents argue that the economic benefits of gambling extend even beyond direct revenues. It has been suggested that gambling venues boost local economies.

A report prepared by the United States General Accounting Office, *Impacts of Gambling: Economic Effects More Measurable than Social Effects*, credited the gambling industry with the creation of 300,000 casino-related and 119,000 parimutuel jobs in Atlantic City, New Jersey (US GAO 2000). The report also credited gambling with the declining unemployment rates for Atlantic County, which fell from 12.2 percent in 1976 to 7.8 percent in 1998 (US GAO 2000).

Industry research in perspective

On closer inspection, the research in *Impacts of Gambling* is flawed. The trends in unemployment for Atlantic City follow the same peaks and valleys as national and state averages, suggesting this drop in unemployment is not the result of gambling but rather of broader economic trends. Furthermore, it becomes clear from one of the report's appendices that despite decreases, the unemployment rate of Atlantic City remains above the state and national averages (US GAO 2000). This report, prepared for a member of the United States House of Representatives, is likely to have an impact on forming government policy; however, it is full of misrepresentations and contradictions, perhaps purposely.

The most significant fact about gambling revenue is that it is produced by a service, not a product. Gambling does not create new wealth; it is more accurately a transfer of wealth. With gambling, money is drawn out of a local economy, not invested or exchanged for products that might represent a real economic gain. Williams and Wood (2007, 383) add, "This transfer is not innocuous; it harms a significant minority of people (problem gamblers) in the process, and it tends to generate its revenue through cannibalizing or crowding-out other (privately owned) entertainment industries."

Therefore, these noted economic benefits appear because the gambling industry, specifically in the form of casinos, takes over certain niches, monopolizing the entertainment industry. A shift of money to gambling means a shift of money away from other entertainment, and perhaps away from other purchases. It is in reality a long way from a net inflow of "new" money.

The next argument put forward by the gaming industry points to individuals' rights and freedoms. Here, citizens should be given the freedom to gamble if they so choose, and gambling businesses should have the right to compete in a fair market. In this view, the responsibility for gambling rests with the individual, not the industry, and problem gambling is the result of poor self-control. The gambling industry is portrayed as providing an entertainment service that people may voluntarily use or ignore. Bell (2000), for example, puts forward this view in an article written for the CATO Institute, a libertarian public policy research institute. Bell argues that people who gamble on the Internet or elsewhere risk only their own money and are within their rights to do so.

In Canada, gambling opportunities vary from one province to another. For example, VLTs are less common in British Colombia and Ontario than elsewhere. Yet critics note there is no significant difference in the rates of problem gambling between provinces, suggesting that rates are independent of opportunities (PSGSC 2000, 35). By this logic, increasing gambling opportunities will not increase the proportion of problem gamblers, or the risk of problem gambling. Moreover, if this is true, regulation and control of gambling opportunities is unnecessary, as we will see shortly.

The Canadian Gaming Association (CGA), an industry lobby group, also puts forth this view. A report produced for the CGA by Wiebe and Volberg (2007), two notable researchers in the gambling research field, portrays problem gambling as an individual issue affecting only a small minority. The report goes on to describe the regulation of gambling as an infringement of civil liberties, rather than a response to a social problem. This report is a far cry from Volberg's earlier work—not funded by the CGA—which presents institutionalized gambling in Canada as a form of social domination (Volberg and Wray 2007, 57). Volberg and Wiebe's work for the CGA shows that the gambling industry influences research.

Independent Gambling Research

Outside of industry-sponsored studies, the dominant view in gambling research is different. A common finding in addiction research is that factors such as access, price, and convenience influence the incidence and repetition of addictive behaviours (just as they influence the incidence and repetition of non-addictive behaviours). In short, the more people who gamble, the more problem gamblers there will be. Some infrequent gamblers will become frequent gamblers, and some frequent gamblers will become problem gamblers.

So, for example, John W. Welte, in a 2005 study using a national survey sample conducted at the University at Buffalo's Research Institute on Addictions, found that a casino within 10 miles (16 kilometres) of home is associated with a 90 percent increase in the likelihood that residents will be pathological or problem gamblers. According to Welte, this likely happens because some people who would otherwise not gamble are more apt to develop a gambling pathology when they have easy access to gambling opportunities.

Welte also stressed that while geographic location nearly doubled the risk, "individual traits have a stronger relationship to gambling pathology than geographic factors" (University at Buffalo 2005). Social and environmental influences attract attention "because localities can control the location and density of gambling opportunities, such as casinos or lottery outlets[; so] policy makers have some influence over the rates of problem gambling in our society" (Welte, as quoted in University at Buffalo 2005).

However, research supporters of the gambling industry, most notably the National Center for Responsible Gambling (NCRG), have been quick to adopt the idea that problem gambling, like drug addiction, is a biological phenomenon (Vrecko 2008, 56). The stated goal of the NCRG is to increase the interest in and production of peer-reviewed research on gambling. However, their economic interests incline them to support research that highlights problem gambling as the result of biological processes in the human brain: for example, to use brain imaging and other physiological research strategies to understand problem gambling.

An argument that is perhaps the most commonly used for discrediting gambling research is that social costs are too difficult to measure, and therefore cannot be useful in guiding policy. Measures based on the *economic* aspects of gambling are considered to be preferable because they are easier to gauge. Measuring the effects of gambling in purely monetary terms is often supported by arguments that focus on cause and effect relationships. These simple models suggest that the relationship between gambling and social welfare is straightforward: gamblers lose money to the government, which redirects that money toward worthy projects. This is an instrumental, utilitarian analysis of the problem that chooses to ignore inconvenient and hard-to-measure social impacts.

Connecting gambling to social costs is more difficult, especially because of demands for proof of causation and not merely correlation. The importance of demonstrating causation is highlighted in the report prepared by General Accounting for US Congressman Wolfe (US GAO 2000, 3). In that report, even pathological gambling is dismissed as a clear cause of other social costs:

> NGISC reported that pathological gambling often occurs with other behavioural problems, including substance abuse, mood disorders, and personality disorders—a joint occurrence, which is termed comorbidity. Because of this, even when an individual admits that gambling contributed to a particular family or social problem, it is difficult to decide exactly what caused the problem. (US GAO 2000, 28)

By this argument, proponents of unregulated gambling can ignore any evidence that gambling leads to wider social costs, since other possible factors could also contribute to the social problem in question. Even the testimony of problem gamblers is rendered inadequate by this viewpoint, given that gambling is not seen as the sole, proven cause of their problems.

Critiques of research that examines the social costs of gambling also point to a lack of consensus among researchers about how to measure these costs. They argue that without a standard method, studies cannot be compared and findings are unreliable.

Standardized measurements of social costs would undeniably be useful to researchers. However, demanding standardization can render invalid any or all past or current research. Current information may be less useful than it might ideally be, but it is far from useless. Furthermore, by this standard, no social science research—and almost no research at all—could ever pass the test of truth for policy purposes. Without research as a guide, policy-makers would be forced to turn to mere hunches, prejudices, interests, and ideologies.

Where does the responsibility for proof lie? Should it be the responsibility of gambling researchers to prove that gambling makes some people sick? Or should it be the responsibility of gambling industry officials to prove gambling does not make any people sick? Should gambling researchers have to prove that gambling has hidden societal costs and low societal benefits?

The industry has successfully placed research on the defensive. Some critics point to the variety of methods used to determine the prevalence in rates of problem gambling. Reliable rates are essential given the importance of counting the number of problem gamblers before assessing the size of the social problem and, accordingly, the scale of the necessary policy response. Critics insist that any variation in estimates stems from methods of research that are "imprecise and unreliable" (Walker 2007, 635).

A variation in numbers does suggest that some of the existing studies are imprecise or unreliable. However, this is far from the case for all the studies. Even census counts of the national and local populations of Canada are recognized as being approximate, within a range of error that may be as high as 5 percent for some subgroups. And yet, all kinds of social policies—including legislation, electoral districting, taxation, and tax sharing—are based on these counts.

To correct or at least reduce the problem of multiple methods in gambling research, the different methods of measuring social costs and prevalence rates must be compared and assessed on the basis of their relative strengths and weaknesses. This comparison has for the most part already been done in a recent Canadian report, "The Socio-Economic Impact of Gambling (SEIG) Framework" (Wynne and Shaffer 2003).

The report attempts, first, to propose principles for a meaningful analysis of the socio-economic impacts of gambling and then to review nearly 500 existing studies on this topic. The report concludes that an assessment of gambling's impact will always contain subjective judgments. It is simply not possible to combine all of the social and economic impacts and come up with a single, reliable answer.

With that in mind, the authors suggest that researchers interested in measuring the impact of gambling should steer clear of trying to reduce nonmonetary impacts to dollar figures. Instead, they should examine group and regional geographic impacts at both the macro and micro levels, comparing these impacts with changes in control communities. Wherever possible, they should use longitudinal research to chart the changes in communities affected by gambling.

In general, research finds that the most reliable effect of gambling is an increase in government revenues, public services, and regulatory costs. The most reliable social impact is increased problem gambling—especially right after the introduction of new gambling opportunities. To a small extent, the research also finds an increase in crime, an increase in social and economic inequality, and more negative attitudes toward gambling.

While there are evident difficulties in measuring social costs and benefits that are not present in analyses of economic costs and benefits, this obstacle need not pose a problem for policy-makers who can think in the broader terms of human welfare. For example, research finds a relation between the accessibility of gambling and the prevalence of problem gambling (Lester 1994; NGISC 1999; Productivity Commission 1999; Shaffer, LaBrie, and LaPlante 2004; Welte, Barnes, and Hoffman 2004). At the very least, this should tell policy-makers not to create any new gambling opportunities without increasing the availability of treatment for problem gambling at the same time.

Another criticism of gambling research is that conclusions emerge from irrational feelings, not reasonable and reliable findings. For example, proponents of the gambling industry pointed to potential flaws in the following independent research. In this recent survey, nearly one in three Canadians reported knowing someone personally, or knowing of someone, who has some form of a gambling problem (Eby 2007, 2). The gambling industry questioned the finding, pointing out that other gambling research has shown that less than 5 percent of adults have a gambling problem; this newer research would put that number at 33 percent—a very different number. But this argument by no means discredits the finding. Given that people have social networks that number in the hundreds or even thousands, rudimentary statistics would suggest that one-third of Canadians could be aware of another person with a gambling problem, even if the true prevalence is less than 5 percent.

The gaming industry also explains the occasional unflattering portrayals as the result of misinformation and bias. Researchers, it is argued, seek media attention by making wild claims, misrepresenting information to suggest that problem gambling is a bigger threat than it really is (Eby 2007, 10).

Gambling Policy in Practice

Although gambling regulations vary around the world, gambling policy generally has three purposes: regulating the industry, preventing gambling, and reducing harm.

The goal of public policy is to regulate public goods that cannot be monitored through general interactions in the marketplace for some reason. Food and drug safety legislation is important, for example, because markets cannot be relied on to protect the consumer without such regulation. Sometimes people are unable to determine their own best interests, and sometimes they cannot secure their best interests when they have to act on their own against large corporations.

Regulating the gambling industry

By implication, there may be a role for public policy in respect to gambling. Policy could better ensure the health and well-being of prospective gamblers. Gambling research is important, therefore, because it may have policy implications. On a societal level, policy change may mean a reorganization of social institutions and changes in how social issues are publicly defined. On an individual level, policies have the potential to influence how people view gambling, whether they choose to gamble, and whether they develop gambling problems.

Not surprisingly, gambling policies vary widely around the world. This variation reflects differences in countries' specific situations as well as ideological differences. Bostock (2005), considering gambling policy options for Australia, outlines five approaches to gambling policy around the world. Two of these reflect extremes: the fundamentalist option (a complete ban) and the Monaco option (based on the Principality of Monaco, where tourists are encouraged to gamble and provide a major source of revenue for the country; locals, however, are prohibited). A third approach, the Buthelezi option, named after South African Zulu leader Mangosuthu Buthelezi, designs gambling to redirect disposable income from the richer to the poorer.

In a fourth option, the Tasmanian Green Youth Network/New Zealand Gambling Workshop option, controls are in place to promote healthy gambling. This option, supported by GA, emphasizes both control of access to gambling opportunities for problem gamblers as a short-term solution and education about gambling behaviour to promote healthy gambling in the long term.

Finally, in the so-called survival-of-the-fittest option, gambling is deregulated. Here, responsibility for the costs of gambling is removed from both government, through reduced involvement, and the industry, through reduced regulation. Responsibility is passed instead to those who gamble, with the assumption that "all gamblers are of sound mental health and therefore capable of rational decision-making while remaining fully in control of their impulses" (Bostock 2005, 13). Pathological gambling is seen as evidence of individuals' personal failings, not a symptom of a system that encourages compulsive gambling.

However, as we have noted, the reality is that costs are not borne merely by individual gamblers but by society as a whole. Studies show that deregulation results in related social problems, including homelessness, an increase in crime rates, and addiction. This policy approach is just as impractical or ineffective over the long term as the fundamentalist option, since over time it results in increasing social destruction. Nevertheless, it has remained the option chosen by many governments.

According to research, more than 80 percent of Australian adults are gamblers, thought to be the highest rates in the world. Many complaints have been made against the government for increasing the number of casinos and gaming machines. These increases were made, however, as a result of the government's reliance on gambling revenue, seen as a form of voluntary, almost painless, taxation. However, critics say that the so-called painless taxation mentality exploits the poor by engendering the belief that gambling benefits them. Furthermore, as Bostock (2005, 12) notes, "Many of the taxation contributors are, at the time of making their contribution to taxation, affected by drugs, alcohol, and possibly mental illness."

In Australia, gambling policy is controlled by the states. However, because governments at both the state and federal level are now dependent on gambling revenue, the (federal) Commonwealth has been playing a more active role in regulating the industry. The result is that Australia now has its own federal gambling policy. Its harm minimization measures include information for gamblers, liquidity controls, restricted promotion of gambling, community or counselling services, and technical measures.

In Canada, by contrast, exclusive control of gambling is vested in the provincial and territorial, rather than national, levels (Stevens 2001/2005). While provincial and territorial governments work within the framework of the Criminal Code of Canada, each government reserves the right to make its own decisions about availability, revenue usage, and social implications. These provincial differences influence the overall situation in Canada as a whole.

There is currently some confusion over the regulation of Internet gambling in Canada, for example. On a national level, the Criminal Code of Canada has specified that it is illegal to run an online gambling operation. Meanwhile, under section 207 of the Criminal Code, provincial and territorial governments are permitted to control the various kinds of gambling operations within their borders. Some provinces (such as British Columbia and Ontario) have chosen to permit Internet gambling, while others are still deciding. Still others have rejected Internet gambling outright, leaving the country without a consensus on an Internet gambling policy. Inconsistencies such as this can be found in many areas of gambling-related policy.

That said, in general, Canadian gambling policy has chosen the path of deregulation, which is equivalent to provincial control. In turn, research has found a subsequent rise in the negative effects of gambling;

there are calls for policy-makers to address these matters (Papoff and Norris 2009; Bernhard and Preston 2007; Wynne and Shaffer 2003). Good-quality research is needed both to continually tease out the effects of public policy and to inform emerging policies.

It is already clear from recent research that aggressive marketing by the gambling industry and government has attempted to spread gambling practices. One could argue that governments (in particular) are pushing something on their constituents that they do not seem to want—while this sort of marketing action is common for corporations, governments should not be doing this with taxpayers' money. Leading gambling researchers in Alberta (Smith et al. 2011) analyzed data from the Alberta Leisure, Lifestyle, and Lifecycle Project, a five-year longitudinal study that explored Albertans' gambling patterns and included questions on the scope of respondents' gambling activity; public opinion toward legal gambling; and trends in gambling participation, including recovery from gambling addiction. The project also investigated the biopsychosocial variables that predict a variety of gambling behaviours.

The study found that, outside of young males without a gambling problem, few Albertans show much interest in or support for the extension of gambling activities. On this, the authors write:

> Results also indicate that Albertans are ambivalent about gambling and that gambling and public policy are misaligned to the extent that gambling's harms are thought to outweigh its benefits. Likely reasons for the gap between gambling policy and public opinion are that gambling issues lack the salience of ongoing high-profile topics such as the economy, health care, education, and the environment, and gambling dependent special interest groups can exert considerable influence on gambling policy in ways that may not harmonise with the public interest. (Smith et al. 2011, 57)

Preventing gambling

The Levels-of-Prevention Framework classifies prevention initiatives into three categories. Primary prevention centres on preventing problematic gambling behaviour; secondary prevention looks for potential problems; and tertiary prevention focuses on preventing further harm (Dickson-Gillespie et al. 2008).

This framework has already been applied to problem gambling by the Independent Pricing and Regulatory Tribunal (IPART) of New South Wales, Australia. IPART has formulated a clear policy with goals that include preventing vulnerable individuals from developing gambling problems and reducing negative social and health consequences associated with problem gambling for individuals, their families, and their communities. At the same time, the approach seeks to maintain the freedom of recreational (nonproblem) gamblers and to ensure that the livelihood of those associated with the gaming industry is not compromised unnecessarily. Given this comprehensive approach, the Australian IPART policies seem to be the "most integrated model of prevention and harm minimization yet developed" (Dickson-Gillespie et al. 2008).

Canadian examples of harm minimization policies aimed at preventing or delaying problem gambling include New Brunswick's video lottery program. Among other changes, this program mandates reducing the number of VLT machines and VLT sites, managing VLT access to appropriate age-controlled environments, and introducing annual registration fees and responsible gaming requirements. The so-called responsible gambling approach is also supported by the American Gaming Association's *Code of Conduct for Responsible Gaming* (AGA 2003). This Code contains a set of principles for its companies, employees, the public and patrons, and casino advertising and marketing. Among other recommendations, the Code calls for responsible gambling messages—that is, responsible advertising.

Policies undertaken by government and industry to prevent or lower the risk of problem gambling do not always assume that decreasing gambling availability will also reduce problems. However, many policies recognize the important role played by regulating availability and access. According to Williams, West, and Simpson (2007a), policies relating to availability are divided into three categories: restrictions on the accessibility, controlling who is allowed to gamble, and regulating the process of delivery.

First, restrictions on general availability assume that the use of or dependence on gambling relies on the easy availability of gambling opportunities: abundant availability means greater use. This relationship between use and access has been demonstrated with respect to both alcohol consumption and gun use, and evidence suggests a similar link exists for gambling. Consequently, many jurisdictions around the world limit gambling access.

Access can be reduced by limiting the number of venues. Some countries restrict the number of casino gambling opportunities; this can be seen in the reduction of casinos and gambling houses in Austria, Belgium, Italy, and the United Kingdom. We have already mentioned the VLT program in New Brunswick, which proposes a 50 percent decrease of a number of VLT sites (New Brunswick 2007).

Other jurisdictions place special restrictions on the more harmful types of gambling. These policies respond to claims made by researchers and treatment agencies that the types of gambling opportunities available, not the ease of access to gambling, produce the most problems in Western societies.[1] In particular, VLTs (in some jurisdictions known as electronic gambling machines) have been identified as addictive. In British Columbia, VLT use is one of the most common activities of problem gamblers. Indeed, VLTs have provided a huge revenue yield (e.g., $1,322,123,000 in 2007–8). To reduce the harmful impacts of VLTs, the province established a Responsible Gambling Strategy that includes restricting VLTs to specific gaming areas.

According to Wiebe, Cox, and Falkowski-Ham (2003), Internet gambling is a fundamentally different activity from land-based gambling practices. Because of Internet gambling's highly addictive nature, the United States proscribes some online gambling through the UIGEA of 2006, although this policy may also reflect the likelihood that revenues from Internet gambling may go to offshore entrepreneurs, given the impossibility of regulating a web-based gambling venue.

Meanwhile, another policy approach involves restricting the availability of gambling outside of specific venues. European countries such as Cyprus, France, Greece, and Luxembourg have forbidden VLT gambling outside of allotted legal venues. Other countries such as Lithuania, Latvia, and the Netherlands also have restricted VLTs to bars and restaurants (Sychold 2006).

The location of gambling venues can also be subject to policy restrictions. For instance, casinos in the United States and Europe are often purposely situated in tourist destinations some distance away from city centres, following the logic that casinos are harmful and distracting for ordinary working-class citizens. As well, this placement recognizes that some urban residents are more susceptible than others, particularly in poor neighbourhoods (Welte, Barnes, and Hoffman 2004).

Finally, some jurisdictions limit the hours of operation of gambling venues, intended to reduce the effects of gambling linked to extensive playing. This approach is evident in Nova Scotia's policy of closing down EGMs outside the casinos at midnight, a step that resulted in a reported 18 percent decrease in spending by problem gamblers.

Reducing harm

Generally, policies aimed at preventing gambling are paired with programs that help to minimize gambling harm. Funds for these programs are often derived directly from gambling revenue. One source has estimated that 2 percent of slot machine revenue is directed toward gambling prevention, treatment, and research in Ontario (Sadinsky 2005). Government programs to reduce harm include responsible gambling programs, telephone helplines, and treatment services.

Responsible gambling refers to initiatives designed to encourage clients to gamble in a healthy manner. While such initiatives tend to be promoted by the gambling industry, they are often ineffective. For instance, responsible gambling approaches to the addictive nature of VLTs include a time-out function that prevents prolonged gambling and onscreen tracking of the amount of money wagered. An evaluation of these features, carried out in Nova Scotia, showed an overall *increase* in VLT spending after implementation (James 2003), due to the addictive nature of these game machines.

Other responsible gambling strategies include ensuring the presence of clocks and natural light in gambling venues to allow patrons to sense time passing, posting the odds of winning, and creating self-exclusion programs. Self-exclusion has been implemented in many jurisdictions, including Alberta, where more than 300 people have signed up (James 2003). However, the effectiveness of self-exclusion in controlling problem gambling is questionable, given the widespread availability of gambling opportunities outside of casinos.

Despite the lack of solid evidence supporting this and other responsible gambling tactics, the industry frequently trumpets its commitment to responsible gambling as evidence of social responsibility. In Ontario, the OLG features the slogan "Know your limit, play within it" in promotional materials for casinos and other gaming venues:

> The intent of this message is to constantly remind patrons that they should decide how much they can afford to pay for their gambling entertainment before they commence gambling. The message is also intended to convey that patrons have the responsibility to monitor their own play. (Sadinsky 2005, 130)

Responsible gambling programs are consistent with an individualistic, rather than a societal, outlook on problem gambling.

Meanwhile, telephone helplines are another common government gambling program. They are present in every province in Canada (as well as in every state in the United States). Citizens concerned about their own gambling, or the gambling of a friend or loved one, can call to receive advice and referrals to services. Evaluations of these services (e.g., Moore's 2008 evaluation of Oregon's helpline and other gambling programs) tend to suggest that helplines are effective in enabling gamblers to access treatment.

Finally, governments may choose to fund treatment programs for problem gamblers. They do this most often by channelling funds into existing mental health services. The government of Ontario, for instance, provides funds dedicated to problem gambling treatment to 22 community agencies (Sadinsky 2005). Treatment may also be provided by non-governmental organizations, such as GA, and by private practitioners. (Research on gambling has implications even in the realm of treatment and counselling because it determines the therapeutic approach taken by practitioners.)

Closing Remarks

The gambling industry has attempted to undermine research on social costs of gambling, as well as the resulting policies to address these costs. There are still too few answers to the big questions: how best to measure the prevalence and incidence of problem gambling, or indeed even its main causes. Determining policies in view of these gaps in knowledge is difficult. However, despite industry-funded research institutes, it seems unlikely that the gambling industry is fully invested in finding the answers.

Industries that have compromised public health—for example, pharmaceutical and tobacco companies—have in the past used strategies to discredit research harmful to their interests. The gambling industry is no exception. Although some of the strategies may be different, the goal remains to neutralize criticism of the industry and deflect demands for regulation and change.

The gambling industry and gambling researchers are by nature at odds, and governments are caught between these two opposing influences on policy. The source of the industry's sway over government is clear: gambling revenues are important. In fact, some researchers, such as James Cosgrave, have argued (for good reason) that it is almost impossible to distinguish between the gambling industry and government. If so, government is not caught between two opposing influences at all. It is a key player in the production of problem gamblers.

Researchers must continue to fight to prove the legitimacy of their findings. Until questions about the applicability of research in policy-making are resolved, the conflict among researchers, gaming entrepreneurs, and government policy-makers will continue.

Chapter 11

Unresolved Questions

Just as we set out to review the final version of this book, a new message arrived from William Rutsey, on behalf of the CGA. It contained the most up-to-date information about the social and economic benefits of the gambling industry in Canada. Specifically, the *2010 Economic Impact of the Canadian Gaming Industry* report showcased Canada's continued growth as a major player in the global gaming scene, noting:

> The Canadian gaming industry generates significant benefits and activities across the broader Canadian economy—totalling more than $31-billion in gross output and $14-billion in purchased goods and services. The Study shows that legalized gaming, at $16-billion, has almost tripled since 1995. Among the findings of the Study are that gaming in Canada continues to:
>
> - Be the largest segment of the Canadian entertainment industry;
> - Be a pillar of the broader hospitality industry; and
> - Raise significant non-tax revenues to fund key government and charitable programs and initiatives.
>
> Gaming in Canada directly supports more than 128,000 full-time jobs . . . and generates $8.7-billion annually to fund government and community programs and services . . . [T]he majority of goods and services needed to sustain operations are now produced and/or offered in Canada, and a number in Canadian companies export gaming related products and services internationally.

The news release accompanying this report also notes that the "Gaming industry outpaces the combined revenues generated by magazine and book sales, social establishments, spectators sports, movie theatres and the performing arts" (CGA 2011).

However, as we have seen, there are other issues to consider and some debates yet to be resolved. This chapter, the last in the book, will end with some of these unresolved issues. It is intended to make sure the reader realizes the magnitude of the problem posed by problem gambling. We will end the chapter with a discussion of two particular types of harm: one a present harm and the other a future harm. Specifically, we will talk about the present relationship of problem gambling to suicide and about the growing problem of game addiction. We will argue that we need to solve the problems posed by problem gambling because we want to decrease suicide rates and prevent and prepare for dangerous new forms of addiction that are just around the corner.

The problems discussed in this book will not go away on their own. Concerted action will be needed because both our culture and economy are changing in dangerous ways. Today, we live in a pleasure economy. Fifty years ago, Canada depended mainly on manufacturing and primary industries (e.g., farming, mining, and forestry). Now our economy is largely service-based. Further, those services have been increasingly oriented to providing *pleasure*, including entertainment, professional sports, travel, hospitality, and food. These services include a range of pleasure-related activities that occupy something of a grey zone and have historically been connected with organized crime: the sex trade, pornography, illegal drugs, and gambling.

Leading sociologists such as Gerda Reith in the United Kingdom have noted the importance of this new pleasure economy for the image of gambling and, equally, the need to create an acceptable image of problem gambling in the consumerist context. On this, Reith (2007, 33) wrote:

> Although historically gambling has been criticized for undermining the ethic of production, today the notion of problem gambling is articulated in terms that are oppositional to the ideology of a "consumption ethic" based on the values of self-control, self-actualization, responsibility, and reason. This is related to wide socioeconomic trends whereby the decline of external forms of regulation is matched by rising demands for individual self-control, which is conducted through consumption. In the case of gambling, the liberalization and deregulation of the industry and the simultaneous expectation that individual players govern themselves express the tensions inherent in consumer capitalism and create the conditions for the emergence of the problem gambler as a unique historical type.

Like Reith, many have commented that the dominant style of life in this society is consumerism, promoted by advertising and mass media; we are ever keen to buy new things and new experiences. With this pleasure-oriented consumerism, we have seen the growth of old addictions and the spread of new ones. These new addictions—some would call them mere variants of compulsive behaviour, but others disagree—include addictions to shopping, sex, the Internet, and, of course, gambling. The following question remains: How, as concerned citizens, voters, researchers, and family members, should we respond?

This book has explored the complexities of problem gambling, and the different views held by different actors, from gamblers themselves to researchers and owners of gambling establishments and government officials. This closing chapter will review some of the difficult questions that have been raised, ending with a brief discussion of the broader social implications of reaching a decision based on consensus.

In fact, it could be said that this book is about *tragic choices*, a term coined by legal scholar Guido Calabresi to characterize social and legislative choices that allow no permanent satisfactory solution to any practical or policy-related issue. There is no permanent, universally agreed upon solution simply because, for this issue, there are multiple legitimate principles or points of view.

We can identify three main master questions at the root of these controversies. With some imagination, we can see how these master questions apply well beyond the problem of gambling to other social problems. These are (1) questions of harm, (2) questions of blame, and (3) questions of certainty.

Questions of Harm

We have seen that there is an ongoing, seemingly never-ending debate about the amount of harm done by problem gambling versus the benefit of the revenue it generates either directly through taxes or indirectly through economic development that occurs around casinos and other gambling-related entertainments. How much benefit justifies how much harm? Is the production of a hundred new gambling addicts justified by the funding of (say) a thousand new hospital beds, school classrooms, or recreation programs for elderly Canadians? Stated otherwise, is one year of suffering by a problem gambler and their family justified by 10 years of happiness for an orphan, a shut-in, or a single mother?

These examples demonstrate the classic utilitarian question first asked by nineteenth-century philosophers such as Jeremy Bentham and John Stuart Mill, who wanted to maximize human happiness through social legislation and debated the best means of doing so. Where interests are in conflict, more happiness for some may mean less happiness or even misery for others. How much of the one balances how much of the other, in moral terms? Or, as other philosophers might argue, should we refuse to take a utilitarian stance, arguing that human lives must be viewed as ends in themselves, not instruments to other ends? If so, we might refuse to accept the premise that any amount of social benefit should be sought (and achieved) at the cost of (expected) suffering.

Some observers might say that modern liberal societies have already had this debate. We are all utilitarian today in the sense that we recognize the State's right to collect taxes and make policies that benefit some more than others and harm some more than others. That being so, all we can do now is to ensure that we get the numbers right. But, surely, that cannot be the whole answer.

Without going deeply into philosophical disputes, we can see that a purely utilitarian position is unacceptable for at least two reasons. First, we cannot agree on a metric by which to decide how much harm (to some) is balanced by how much benefit (to others). Should we measure this balance in terms of relative happiness, economic well-being, good health, or otherwise? So far, there has been no debate—much less, agreement—on this matter.

Second, as a society, Canadians have seemingly rejected a purely utilitarian outlook. Otherwise, how can we explain the Charter of Rights and Freedoms that grants everyone certain fundamental protections that are inalienable and non-negotiable? Under a modern rule of law, in a society such as ours which has a constitution and rights that accrue to all citizens, there are clear limits to the degree to which we can use other people as fodder of statecraft.

So while we have tended to discuss the issue of gambling and problem gambling with an emphasis on social benefit, there are clear limits to how far this argument will ever be able to go. In part, that is because pure utilitarianism is inhuman—even totalitarian. As well, a utilitarian focus directs our attention to costs and benefits, but there are disagreements about who should gain what benefits and who should pay what costs. In particular, questions are asked about blame: Who is responsible for paying which costs of their own and other people's lives?

Questions of Blame

In the second set of questions, centred on the issue of blame, we have seen a continuing debate about the causes of problem gambling and the virtues of responsible gambling. What *responsible gambling* means at bottom is that problem gamblers will be held responsible for their addiction. Gamblers will be expected to avoid becoming addicted to gambling, and if they do become addicted, they will be expected to seek and receive treatment.

Under this rubric of blaming the addict, the gaming industry will be ideally responsible for excluding (i.e., forbidding service to) self-declared gambling addicts and providing treatment services if requested. Also, in combination with government, the gaming industry will support and encourage research into the psychological causes of problem gambling and into the effectiveness of proposed treatments for this addiction.

This view, as we have seen, is related to the medicalization of gambling addiction, in the sense that gambling addicts are now viewed as people who occupy the so-called sick role. According to the social rules of this sick role, problem gamblers are permitted to break the social rules if (and only if) they have been diagnosed as sick and willingly undertake expert treatment for their sickness. That is, we agree to remove some of their blameworthiness if they admit the addiction is their personal problem and they agree to seek a personal cure.

Clearly this approach to gambling addiction is at odds with a public health conception of problem gambling—or indeed of any addiction—which focuses on social determinants of the addiction. Examples of such determinants would include factors such as advertising and other media glorification of gambling; widespread access and inducements to gambling; and the organization of gambling in ways that hypnotize, confuse, and excite gamblers so they behave irrationally. By this perspective, problem gambling is a societal problem—not merely a personal problem—that demands the regulation of advertising, gambling inducements, and psychological manipulation at the gambling place.

We have been unable to resolve this question of blame because, in turn, it feeds into an even larger philosophical question—namely, the question of liberty versus protection (the so-called nanny state issue). To understand this debate more clearly, consider three alternative points of view on blame. We will call them the Helen Keller Model, the Smoking and Cancer Model, and the Harm Reduction Model.

We have named the Helen Keller Model after the early twentieth-century prodigy who, admittedly with help from a dedicated teacher, miraculously managed to overcome both blindness and deafness in order to communicate with others. In so doing, she became a role model for all people with disabilities—indeed, a model for all who seek to overcome adversity through sheer force of personal effort. Citing the example of Helen Keller, a proponent of unregulated gambling might argue that people can avoid or escape a gambling addiction if they simply put their minds to it. A failure to do so signals a failure to try hard enough; it warrants blame, not pity.

The Smoking and Cancer Model refers to the long-lasting debate about whether, and how, smoking was related to lung cancer. Here, the tobacco industry tried for decades to deny and obscure any connection between smoking and cancer; but, in the end, the weight of evidence sank Big Tobacco's case. Though people are free to smoke or not smoke, and even to quit smoking if they want to avoid harm, we now recognize that government should play some role in protecting us against our own weaknesses and vices. We no longer permit the sales of cigarettes to minors, nor do we allow the advertising of tobacco products in the mass media.

Finally, the Harm Reduction Model takes a third position. It assumes we need to recognize that people have weaknesses and will need help; that regulation of access, for example, will be inadequate and people will still manage to harm themselves; and that we will collectively need to mitigate the harm. So, for instance, we understand that—despite clear warnings to the contrary—many people will eat themselves into obesity, leaving themselves vulnerable to diabetes, heart disease, mobility problems, and other hardships. Our public health system does not deny obese people equal health treatment because they created their own problem through overeating. In the Harm Reduction Model, they are not blamed for being obese, nor are they urged by restaurants to become "responsible eaters."

There are initiatives afoot to change eating patterns, increase physical activity, and generally lead to more healthy lives; but, meanwhile, we accept a public responsibility to both prevent and reduce harm wherever possible. With regard to addiction, this approach is most obvious in the Insite Safe Injection site in Vancouver, which is strongly opposed by a Conservative federal government. Similar debates are being waged about harm reduction for sex workers, where blame and causation are less immediately important than mitigating danger for participants.

Issues concerning harm reduction tend to be practical. So much of the discussion then shifts to the effectiveness and efficiency of proposed solutions. This, in turn, shifts the discussion invariably to issues of what is known, and how it is known.

We saw in the last chapter that industries under attack (e.g., tobacco, pharmaceuticals, and gambling) counterattack by calling academic research into question, producing industrial science. Science funded by and for industry does not run according to the same rules as traditional science; for example, the findings of corporate research are unlikely to be published and debated in public. Added to this is an attack on academic science—the so-called junk science debate—aimed at making the public doubt whether researchers know much about the causes and consequences of gambling, smoking, or other products and services. We can view this tactic as a cynical effort by the industry to protect its profitability, whatever the cost to its victims and society as a whole. Or, perhaps we can view it more generously as an epistemological problem—a problem of knowing "how to know" and what knowledge to trust.

Questions of Certainty

The third master question has to do with epistemology—the study of knowledge and, more specifically, how we know what we know. The application of scientific research to real-life problems has a built-in problem. The problem, as noted earlier, is that science is never 100 percent certain of anything. Arguably, in fact, certainty is not the job of science; science should remain uncertain and skeptical. By contrast, policy-makers who need to keep the support of the electorate periodically have to account for the spending of public dollars. The policy-makers will have to avoid blame for any unsuccessful programs that failed to produce results and justify any outlays of cash by showing they exercised due diligence in deciding what programs to support.

The question of certainty, then, is reduced to a question of due diligence. How much do decision-makers need to know about the link between problem gambling and, for example, gambling access or advertising to warrant rules that will reduce gambling, gambling profitability, and even tax revenues from gambling? Do they need to be 99.9 percent certain about the link, or is 80 percent certainty good enough for regulatory policy-making? And do policy-makers need to know that $1 million lost in gambling revenues (because of regulation) will be counterbalanced by at least $1 million less money spent on the fallout from problem gambling (on things such as domestic violence, for example)?

Here, we seem to be returning to the issue of benefit and harm; but, in fact, there is another point here, which is that there is no universal agreement in science (or in policy-making) on what kinds of research findings justify what kinds of policy-making and public spending.

We might cynically say that, in the end, policy-makers will do whatever suits them best, funding programs and perks that will gain them the most support in the next election, regardless of social utility. (Recall the public spending in Muskoka during the 2010 G8 meetings.) However, in principle and sometimes in practice, policies do reflect reasoned research and a clear idea of the public interest.

In the area of gambling research, there are disputes about the reliability and value of certain key research findings. Take the famous finding by psychologist Robert Williams and sociologist Rob Wood (2007) that more than one-third of all of Ontario's gambling revenue is generated by that small fraction of gamblers—roughly 5 percent—who have a measurable gambling problem. In effect, Ontario is relying on gambling addiction to fund millions or even billions of dollars in social spending. The gambling industry doubted this finding, arguing that it relies on a sample of gamblers remembering and correctly reporting on how much money they lost in the preceding year.

But it seems likely that Williams and Wood got the numbers right: the figures in the statements about the money lost by gamblers tally up to the total amount of gambling revenue in the same year. However, this example shows the general problem: we do not have a universally agreed upon standard for evaluating the quality of scientific findings and their applicability to policy issues. We need one, for without such a standard, every effort to discuss gambling policy will decline into an improvised shouting match about whether the numbers are reliable enough for policy-making.

Why Should We Care?

If you've read this far in the book, you probably have some reason for wanting to understand problem gambling. You may have a gambling addiction yourself or know someone who does; or you may simply be fascinated by the great increase of interest in gambling and gambling-related social problems in the past 20 years. Most likely, you understand by now that something big is at stake here: something that affects the health, safety, and well-being of thousands of Canadians.

So, in conclusion, let's consider two admittedly extreme cases: people who kill themselves because of gambling addiction and people whose young lives are ruined by an addiction that is eerily like, and probably related to, gambling addiction—namely, gaming addiction.

The current problem of gambling-related suicide

Suicide and problem gambling go together. Researchers have found that suicide attempts are more common among pathological gamblers than those with any other addictive disorder (Canada Safety Council 2005). Between 20 and 30 percent of individuals addicted to gambling have made a suicide attempt (Jones 2009).

When we think about the nature of a gambling addiction, this result is not surprising. Problem gambling produces financial strife faster than any other addiction, typically causing a cascade of other problems, from job loss, to bankruptcy, to homelessness.

A 2006 study investigated suicidal ideation and attempts among a group of problem gamblers with co-occurring issues such as depression or drug abuse. The study found that 7 percent of the entire sample, or 21 percent of those attempting suicide, did so because of their gambling behaviour. Furthermore, the study found that gambling was the last precipitating event before the suicide crisis among many of these individuals (Hodgins, Mansley, and Thygesen 2006). Similar results were found around the globe. In an Australian hospital study, 17 percent of the suicidal patients admitted were problem gamblers (Hagen 2010). Moreover, increased legalized gambling has been found to be associated with higher suicide rates in major gaming communities in the United States (Jones 2009).

The most comprehensive evaluation of the link between suicide and problem gambling comes from a study based on autopsy reports from 1994 to 2000 on suicide completers in Quebec (Bourget, Ward, and Gagné 2003). Two forensic psychiatrists examined 75 cases of completed suicides where problem gambling behaviour was implicated. Co-occurring issues were similar to rates found in other studies, with alcohol abuse (39 percent), depression (33 percent), and previous suicide attempts (26 percent) also evident in the sample. Most victims had suffered many losses as a result of their gambling, such as significant financial loss (56 percent), divorce/separation (7 percent), loss of personal or professional status (1 percent), or a combination of the three (22 percent).

Researchers evaluated the motivation for suicide and found that in about 35 percent of the sample gambling-related issues were the sole contributing factor. About half of the suicides resulted from a combination of gambling and psychiatric problems; some 30 percent resulted from intoxication alongside either gambling or psychiatric disorders. Researchers found several important differences between gamblers who had committed suicide and nongamblers who had committed suicide. Typical protective factors such as employment and marriage were not deterrents in completing suicide for the majority of the sample, and in more than 65 percent of the cases, there was no prior warning or treatment seeking.

This suggests that risks of suicide may be even more difficult to detect among problem gamblers. A recent study with a similar protocol found that problem gamblers who had completed suicide had been less likely to be in contact with mental health providers in the last week, month, or year than nonproblem gamblers who had completed suicide (Séguin et al. 2010).

The increased risk of suicidal ideation and attempts is particularly concerning among post-secondary school students, where suicide is already ranked the second leading cause of death in North America (Jones 2009). In a tragic 2006 event, Joseph Kupchik, age 19, stabbed himself in the chest with a knife and then jumped from the ninth floor of a Cleveland parking garage. The accounting student had lost a considerable amount of money on online gambling. He had transferred $3,500 in tuition money to his checking account and then transferred $3,400 of that money to a website in the Caribbean. In addition, sports betting notes were found scattered throughout his car (McCarthy 2007a).

Moshe Pergament, a 19-year-old community college student in New York, threatened police with a fake gun. They shot him, later finding a note in his car that read, "To the officer who shot me: I'm sorry to get you involved." Pergament had lost $6,000 on the World Series (McCarthy 2007a). For college and university students, sometimes the guilt of gambling away their car, rent, or school tuition (similar to their "life savings") is overwhelming, and suicide seems like the only answer.

In a study of 1,471 Quebec college students, suicide attempts were significantly higher among problem gamblers (27 percent) than those at risk of a problem (8 percent) or students with no gambling problem (7 percent). The results indicated that pathological gambling was also associated with substance use, illegal behaviours, and eating disorders (Ladouceur, Dubé, and Bujold 1994).

Although parents may be more concerned about alcohol, drugs, and drunk driving, problem gambling is also associated with many other mental health problems and is a risk factor for suicide. Thus, we should be acutely aware of the natural progression of gambling behaviours, beginning at middle school and high school ages and moving into young adulthood, when prevention can be the most effective.

The growing problem of online multiplayer gaming

We should also be acutely aware of the links between problem gambling and problem gaming, also beginning at middle school and high school ages and moving into young adulthood.

The issues highlighted in this book are general social issues, extending far beyond the boundaries of problem gambling alone. A recent story about some family friends highlights the interconnections among individual addiction, research, and policy response.

The story may seem puzzling for a moment: it is a story about video game addiction, not gambling addiction. However, addiction researchers see many similarities between Internet gambling and Internet video games: they both involve playing games, they both cost money to play, and they are both highly addictive. They have the same kinds of disruptive effects on people's lives, and they raise the same ethical and policy issues, issues which we have discussed throughout this book. Finally, they both seem to mobilize powerful drives connected with the brain's pleasure centre.

The following example of video game addiction shows that "game addiction" (as we have understood it up to now in traditional forms of gambling) now has an extended reach because its forms are becoming more varied. As we dither about how to solve the problems associated with traditional gambling, we plunge into new, uncharted problems associated with new, equally dangerous game addictions.

Here are the facts you need to know: A short time ago, we learned that Sarah (not her real name), an old friend from work, was having serious family issues. Sarah and her husband, Jake, are both highly educated, well-paid professionals, each successful within their own domain of work. They live with their two children, a son and a daughter, in an upscale house in one of the trendier parts of Toronto. Both children attend private schools, and they seemed to be doing well as they entered adolescence. Then, life changed for their son Matthew. He developed an addiction to video games.

In a short time, without any clear warning or reason, Matthew became completely fixated on playing video games alone in his room. He skipped school, refused to wash or eat regularly, ignored his friends, and acted out against his sister, father, and mother. On several occasions, he stole his father's credit card to finance game playing, after expressly being forbidden to use the card. Depressed, Matthew also began to cut himself and to speak about committing suicide.

Sarah and Jake were understandably alarmed. They sought treatment, only to find there were no treatment programs for children Matthew's age and no expertise in treating this new addiction. They started looking for research literature on the problem, talking about the problem to trusted friends, and seeking desperately for solutions before something even more terrible happened to their otherwise perfect family.

We looked into the literature ourselves to find out the state of knowledge about video game addiction. By doing so, we learned this topic is a rapidly growing field of concern all over the world; but, the scores of research articles—there are not yet hundreds on this topic—only scratch the surface.

In effect, this field of concern is much like problem gambling 30 years ago. Technology has given us a new addiction problem to worry about—online video gaming. Here, in brief, is what researchers know about it, as suggested by a handful of recent journal articles (shortened for reasons of space and clarity):

- A two-year, longitudinal study of elementary and secondary school children in Singapore found that roughly 9 percent reported evidence of pathological gaming—similar to the rate reported in other countries. Measured outcomes of this problem included depression, anxiety, social phobias, and lower school performance (Gentile et al. 2011).
- A panel study of Dutch adolescents found that time spent playing violent games increased physical aggression. In fact, pathological gaming, regardless of the game content, predicted an increase in physical aggression among boys, though not girls (Lemmens, Valkenburg, and Peter 2011).
- A German study of ninth graders found that boys are about 10 times as likely as girls to be diagnosed as addicted to video games. The data also show a clear dividing line between video game addiction and other less problematic gaming practices. The game-addicted adolescents show more psychosocial stress, lower school achievement, increased truancy, reduced sleep time, fewer spare time activities, and increased thoughts of committing suicide (Rehbein, Kleimann, and Mössle 2009).
- Along similar lines, a German study found that 1.5 to 3.5 percent of adolescents show signs of an addictive use of computer and video games. There is evidence the disorder is associated with higher rates of depression and anxiety, as well as lower school achievements. The researchers argue from neurobiological data that the disorder can be viewed as behavioural addiction. However, it may be necessary to train their relatives to help increase the motivation for a behavioural change by the addicted person (Peukert et al. 2010).
- Porter et al. (2010) also discovered that youth who were identified as problem video game users differed significantly from other youth on relevant variables. For example, they played longer than planned and with greater frequency, and more often played even though they did not want to and despite believing that they should refrain. Though they found it easy to meet people online, they had fewer friends in real life, and more often reported excessive caffeine consumption.
- Evidently, the problems start at a young age: a study of fourth and fifth graders found that roughly one-third of respondents admitted to substance use: alcohol use, illegal drug use, smoking/tobacco use, or

sniffing solvents. Such substance use was significantly greater than average among children who devoted three or more hours a day to watching television or playing video games, compared to those who played video games for only one to two hours a day (Armstrong, Bush, and Jones 2010).

- A study by Han et al. (2010) found changes in brain activity after six weeks of Internet video game play, in the direction of what could be considered a new addiction. The increased craving for Internet video games was positively correlated with an increased activity of the anterior cingulate. Such changes in frontal lobe activity following extended video game play may be similar to changes normally witnessed during early stages of other addictions.
- Along similar lines, Weinstein (2010) noted that computer game playing may lead to long-term changes in brain circuitry—specifically, changed dopamine flow and receptivity—that resemble the effects of substance addiction. Research finds that computer game addicts show reduced dopamine response to stimuli associated with their addiction, presumably due to sensitization—meaning they have to play longer than before to get the same amount of pleasure.
- Because gaming addiction shifts brain functioning the same way as other addictions, it responds to similar chemical treatments. Han et al. (2010), for example, found that the antidepressant Bupropion—used to treat substance dependence—also works for people with a gaming addiction. After a six-week period of Bupropion treatment, craving for Internet video game play, total game playtime, and cue-induced brain activity were all decreased in gaming addicts.
- Based on findings such as these, Van Rooij et al. (2010) argue that online video game consumers should be told about addiction risks associated with these games. In fact, game publishers should set up referral services for addicted players, if only to prevent governmental intervention that will limit their revenue.

These studies and others show that the study of video game addiction is at its beginning stage. Nonetheless, it is already raising the kinds of questions we have discussed in respect to problem gambling: issues concerning how to measure the problem, how to distinguish cause from effect, who is to blame, what should be done, and so on. Based on earlier precedents, we can expect that the multi-million-dollar video gaming industry will take all possible steps to discourage regulation that might limit its profitability.

Meanwhile, Sarah and Jake wonder, day after day, whether an answer can be found to help Matthew before he flunks out of school or perhaps even kills himself. And if the research community finds an answer by identifying the causes and effects of this new addiction, will there be a therapist (and suitable therapy) to carry out the research findings on Matthew's behalf? Equally, will the government take note of these findings and look into regulating video games to prevent the addiction of Matthew's younger cousins and schoolmates? If not, are Canadians prepared to accept the consequences of yet another gambling-related addiction?

The recent history of problem gambling in Canada, marked by a rapid increase in gambling risks, suggests Matthew is unlikely to find relief soon. We need more research into addictions, to be sure, but we also need to answer certain key questions about the public role in regulating addictive activities. More governmental attentiveness is required, as well as more industrial responsibility—unless, of course, we think Matthew is to blame and that somehow, through some miraculous effort and after a prolonged period of pain, he will be able to solve his own problem.

Prevention Programs in Canada

Prevention programs for problem gambling for Canadian youth are diverse. These programs typically take a harm-reduction approach rather than one based on abstinence. They increase knowledge about gambling and offer risk-assessment tools. The Problem Gambling Institute of Ontario identifies two main approaches to prevention: (1) reducing "the potential for future harm to youth who choose to gamble" and (2) informing "youth about the resources available if they need help." Prevention programs are often age-specific and take the form of entertainment. A few programs are for elementary school students, but the majority are for high school and post-secondary students.

The International Centre for Youth Gambling Problems and High-Risk Behaviours (based at McGill University) has produced two prevention programs aimed at elementary school children. The first is a workshop titled *Youth Gambling: An Awareness and Prevention Workshop—Level I.* The second is a computer game, *The Amazing Chateau*, for grades 4 through 6. Both programs teach students about the difference between games of skill and luck, gambling myths, how to resist peer pressure, as well as other valuable lessons designed to increase gambling awareness and resiliency (International Centre for Youth Gambling Problems and High-Risk Behaviors n.d.).

Problem gambling prevention resources for adolescents are much more numerous. The Responsible Gambling Council (RGC) has developed two complementary prevention programs for this age group. The first tool is the Flash Fiction Contest, which encourages contestants to write a fictional, informative short story that teaches other high school students about the risks of gambling. Winners are given a scholarship. Some winning entries are then incorporated into the RGC's second prevention tool, a drama presentation for an audience of high school students. The second tool is the Youth Drama Program, which has reached 208,000 students since its creation in 2000.

The Centre for Addiction and Mental Health (CAMH) offers two educational videos on gambling prevention targeted at youth. These can be borrowed from the CAMH Library. *Playing with Fire: Aboriginal Adolescent Gambling* is intended specifically for Aboriginal youth between the ages of 12 and 15 and aims at prevention while simultaneously recognizing that gaming has a traditional place in Aboriginal culture. The second film, *Spare Time, Spare Cash*, aimed at youth between the ages of 12 and 18, increases awareness by questioning certain gambling assumptions.

The International Centre for Youth Gambling Problems and High-Risk Behaviors has developed a large number of prevention tools and programs for high school students. Two of these are a problem gambling prevention workshop and a video game. These tools are similar to the ones created for elementary schools, but they have a higher level of difficulty and more complex concepts. The video game *Hooked City* focuses on the risks and consequences of gambling and challenges players to rethink their conceptions of what constitutes gambling. Another tool for adolescents is a docudrama called *Clean Break*. This film explores gambling risks and consequences. Also available is an interactive game called *Know Limits*, which is played in teams and provides a platform for players to learn their gambling limits in a safe environment. This approach tries to reduce risk and increase resiliency. The Centre has also created two media packages specifically designed for professionals: *Youth Gambling Problems: Practical Information for Professionals in the Criminal Justice System* and *Youth Gambling Problems: Practical Information for Health Practitioners*. All prevention tools may be ordered through the Centre and used by teachers, community centres, and parents.

The YMCA of Greater Toronto has made many positive contributions to the effort to expand problem gambling prevention programs in the Toronto area and beyond. Its harm reduction awareness program currently operates interactive sessions for children and youth, aged 8 to 24. The YMCA Youth Gambling Awareness Program has also developed curriculum support packages for grades 3 to 12, which help teachers to address problem gambling prevention in their classrooms and also to identify students who may be at risk for problem gambling.

The RGC has also introduced a program for problem gambling prevention among college and university students. kts2, which has grown from the original Know the Score program, uses social media such as Facebook, a website, and Bluetooth technology on campus to reach students. kts2 "looks at the real chances of winning and losing, highlights signs of problem gambling, shares local problem gambling services and suggests ways to keep gambling safer" (RGC n.d.). kts2 has reached 107 campuses in various provinces since 2002. More than 260,000 students have been included in this program (RGC n.d.). One of the problem gambling services referred by kts2 is the Problem Gambling Helpline. This confidential helpline is available 24 hours a day in Canada and Australia and is also operational during the day in the United Kingdom (RGC n.d.). In addition, Gam-Anon is a 12-step program for family and friends of problem gamblers; it helps loved ones cope with problems that emerge from being in an enabling or helping role.

A great number of programs in Canada address prevention of problem gambling among youth. Diverse resources, from computer games to docudramas, are being developed in Canada and are available for groups or individuals. It is worth noting that most programs are offered through high school and post-secondary institutions, and are less accessible to others. Offering widespread accessibility to these resources is urgent.

Treatment for problem gambling involves counselling, step-based programs, self-help, peer support, medication, and programs that increase awareness of the risks involved in online gambling. Researchers argue that problem gamblers make less use of professional services available for treating mental illness than those with other issues (Séguin et al. 2010). The low number of problem gamblers who seek help is explained in part by the shame experienced because of their behaviour, alongside the secrecy associated with these problems in general. In addition, no single treatment has been found to be a perfect solution; gambling prevention is always the best use of time and resources over the long term.

Notes

Chapter 1

1. See also, for example, Canadian Gaming Association, *VLT Gaming in Canada* (March 2006), and *Economic Impact of the Canadian Gaming Industry: Key Findings Report* (January 2008). Both reports were prepared by HLT Advisory. Original source on the Reno Model: Blaszczynski, Ladouceur, and Shaffer 2004.

Chapter 4

1. These headings are not intended to be defining categories but rather convenient terms to reflect how our Canadian respondents would best identify their heritage or community.
2. This quotation, along with others in this chapter, is taken from research studies conducted in 2003 and 2005 and published in *Betting Their Lives: The Close Relations of Problem Gamblers* (Tepperman 2009, Oxford University Press).

Chapter 5

1. This quotation, along with others in this chapter, is taken from research studies conducted in 2003 and 2005 and published in *Betting Their Lives: The Close Relations of Problem Gamblers* (Tepperman 2009, Oxford University Press).

Chapter 10

1. This issue is considered in more detail in the recent report *Accountability and Social Responsibility in Ontario's Gambling Regime* (Smith and Rubenstein 2009). Many of the issues we discuss in Chapters 10 and 11 are discussed at greater length in that report.
2. A recent report called *The Social and Economic Impact of Gambling* highlights the enormous significance of gambling for provincial revenue (Williams, Rehm, and Stevens 2011). The report can be found on the Ontario Problem Gambling Research Centre and Alberta Gaming Research Institute websites.

Chapter 11

1. On this, see Dowling, Smith, and Thomas 2005; Smith and Wynne 2002.

References

4OnlineGambling.com. 2010. *Online Casino Industry Development Timeline*. Available online.

Adams, Gerald, Anne-Marie Cantwell, Leo Keating, Keith Horton, Rosanne Menna, and Ann Marie Guilmette. n.d. *Identity Formation of University Students and Gambling Behaviour: Predictions from Identity Theory Regarding Escaping the Self*. Guelph: Ontario Problem Gambling Research Centre.

Addictions Foundation of Manitoba (AFM). 2008. *Student Gambling Report: Manitoba 2007*. Available online.

———. 2010. *Workplace Issues*. Available online.

Adebayo, Bob. 1998. "Gambling Behavior of Students in Grades Seven and Eight in Alberta, Canada." *Journal of School Health* 68 (1): 7–11.

Alberta Alcohol and Drug Abuse Commission (AADAC). 2002. *Substance Use and Gambling in the Alberta Workplace: A Replication Study*. Available online.

———. 2007. *Gambling among Alberta Youth: The Alberta Youth Experience Survey 2005*. Available online.

American Gaming Association (AGA). 2003. *Code of Conduct for Responsible Gaming*. Available online.

Amey, Ben. 2001. *People's Participation in and Attitudes to Gaming, 1985–2000: Final Results of the 2000 Survey*. Wellington: Department of Internal Affairs.

Armstrong, Jane. 2008. "Music Download Offer Hits Sour Note." *Globe and Mail*, 16 October: A3.

Armstrong, Kia E., Heather M. Bush, and Jeff Jones. 2010. "Television and Video Game Viewing and Its Association with Substance Use by Kentucky Elementary School Students, 2006." *Public Health Reports* 125 (3): 433–40.

Associated Press. 2011. "Ex-Fry's Electronics Exec Files for Bankruptcy, Owes $20M to Las Vegas Casinos." *Las Vegas Sun*, 19 August. Available online.

Australian Gaming Council. 2007. *New Directions: Gambling Education and Financial Literacy for Young People*. Melbourne: Australian Gambling Council.

Azmier, Jason J. 2000. *Canadian Gambling Behaviour and Attitudes: Summary Report*. Calgary: Canada West Foundation. Available online.

———. 2005. *Gambling in Canada 2005: Statistics and Context*. Edmonton: Canada West Foundation.

Bailey, S. 2003. "VLT Addicts' Suit Gains Global Notice; Lawyer Lost $150,000 to Lotto-Quebec's VLTs." *Hamilton Spectator*, 25 February: D01.

Barber, M. 2008. "Brandon Crisp Died after Falling from a Tree: Autopsy." Canwest News Service, 8 November. Available online.

Barzilai, Peter. 2011. "MLB Investigating Alex Rodriguez for Poker Play." *USA Today*, 3 August. Available online.

Beck, Ulrich, and Elisabeth Beck-Gernsheim. 2002. *Individualization: Institutionalized Individualism and Its Social and Political Consequences*. London and Thousand Oaks, CA: Sage.

Belanger, Yale D. 2006. *Gambling with the Future: The Evolution of Aboriginal Gaming in Canada*. Saskatoon: Punch Publishing.

Bell, Daniel. 1953. "Crime as an American way of life: The Queer Ladder of Social Mobility." *Antioch Review* 50 (1–2): 109–30; reprinted as Chapter 7 in *The End of Ideology*. New York: The Free Press, 1960.

Bell, Tom W. 2000. *Online-Gambling Foes Lose a Hand.* CATO Institute. Available online.

Bennett, N. 2006. "When the Game Gets Serious." *Richmond News,* 8 December. Available online.

Bensinger, DuPont & Associates. 2006. *Problem Gambling Prevalent in the Workplace.* HR.BLR.com, 26 September. Available online.

Benzie, Robert. 2004. "Lottery Tax a Bad Bet, Sobara Says." *Toronto Star,* 29 April: A08.

———. 2010. "Online Gambling Coming to Ontario." *Toronto Star,* 10 August. Available online.

Berg, Bruce L. 2004. *Qualitative Research Methods for the Social Sciences.* 5th ed. San Francisco: Pearson Education.

Berger, Ken. 2011. "It's Time to Fold on the NBA's Gambling Subculture." CBS Sports, 5 January. Available online.

Bergler, Edmund. 1958. *Psychology of Gambling.* New York: Hill & Wang.

Berman, Linda, and Mary-Ellen Siegel. 2008. "The Dynamics of the Family Business and the Compulsive/Problem Gambling Member." Slide show presented at the 22nd National Conference on Problem Gambling, Long Beach.

Bernhard, Bo J. 2002. "From Sin to Sickness: A Sociological History of the Problem Gambler." PhD diss., Univ. of Nevada at Las Vegas.

———. 2007a. "Sociological Speculations on Treating Problem Gamblers: A Clinical Sociological Imagination via a Bio-psycho-social-sociological Model." *American Behavioral Scientist* 51 (1): 122–38.

———. 2007b. "The Voices of Vices." *American Behavioral Scientist* 51 (1): 8–32.

Bernhard, Bo J., and Frederick W. Preston. 2007. "Sociologies of Problem Gambling." *American Behavioral Scientist* 51 (1): 3–7.

Binde, Per. 2007a. "The Good, the Bad and the Unhappy: The Cultural Meanings of Newspaper Reporting on Jackpot Winners." *International Gambling Studies* 7 (2): 213–32.

———. 2007b. "Selling Dreams—Causing Nightmares?" *Journal of Gambling Issues* 20: 167–92.

———. 2009. "Exploring the Impact of Gambling Advertising: An Interview Study of Problem Gamblers." *International Journal of Mental Health and Addiction* 7 (4): 541–54.

Blackwell, T. 2001. "Gambling Take Up $6b Since '92: Revenues Reach $9-billion: Governments Collect While Debate Rages over Ethics of Betting." *National Post,* 15 June: A01.

Blaszczynski, Alex, Robert Ladouceur, and Howard Shaffer. 2004. "A Science-Based Framework for Responsible Gambling: The Reno Model." *Journal of Gambling Studies* 20 (3): 301–17.

Blaszczynski, Alex, and Lia Nower. 2002. "A Pathway Model of Problem and Pathological Gambling." *Addiction* 97: 487–99.

Block, Jerald. 2008. "Issues for DSM-IV." *American Journal of Psychiatry* 165 (3). Available online.

Bostock, William W. 2005. "Australia's Gambling Policy: Motivations, Implications, and Options." *Journal of Gambling Issues* 13 (March): 1–14.

Bourget, Dominque, Helen Ward, and Pierre Gagné. 2003. "Characteristics of 75 Gambling-Related Suicides in Quebec." *CPA Bulletin* 35 (6): 17–21.

Boxenbaum, S. 2003. "Governments as Gambling Addicts." *Globe and Mail,* 28 February: A13.

Breiter, Hans C., Itzhak Aharon, Daniel Kahneman, Anders Dale, and Peter Shizgal. 2001. "Functional Imaging of Neural Responses to Expectancy and Experience of Monetary Gains and Losses." *Neuron* 30 (2): 619–39.

Broda, Anja, Debi A. LaPlante, Sarah E. Nelson, Richard A. LaBrie, Leslie B. Bosworth, and Howard J. Shaffer. 2008. "Virtual Harm Reduction Efforts for Internet Gambling: Effects of Deposit Limits on Actual Internet Sports Gambling Behavior." *Harm Reduction Journal* 5: 27. Available online.

Browne, Basil R. 1994. "Really Not God: Secularization and Pragmatism in Gamblers Anonymous." *Journal of Gambling Studies* 10 (3): 247–60.

Brunelle, Natacha, Annie Gendron, Magali Dufour, Marie-Marthe Cousineau, and Danielle Leclerc. 2010. "Internet Gambling and Youth in Quebec: A Risky Behaviour for Adolescents?" *Gambling Research Reveals* 9 (2): 3–4.

Buddy, T. 2003. *Substance Abuse in the Workplace: A Dangerous and Expensive Problem.* About.com Guide, 20 November. Available online.

Burns, Paul. 2010. "Sports Betting in Ontario Casinos—It's Time." *Toronto Sun*, 1 February. Available online.

Burton, Earl. 2010. "Quebec to Enter Online Poker Market." *Poker News Daily*, 6 February. Available online.

Bush, Alan, Craig Martin, and Victoria Bush. 2004. "Sports Celebrity Influence on the Behavioral Intentions of Generation Y." *Journal of Advertising Research* 44: 108–18.

Byrne, Andrea M., Laurie Dickson, Jeffrey Derevensky, and Rina Gupta. 2004. *An Examination of Social Marketing Campaigns for the Prevention of Youth Problem Gambling.* Guelph: Ontario Problem Gambling Research Centre.

Byron, Kristin. 2005. "A Meta-Analytic Review of Work–Family Conflict and Its Antecedents." *Journal of Vocational Behavior* 67 (2): 169–98.

Byun, Sookeun, Celestino Ruffini, Juline E. Mills, Alecia C. Douglas, Mamadou Niang, Svetlana Stepchenkova, Seul Ki Lee, et al. 2009. "Internet Addiction: Metasynthesis of 1996–2006 Quantitative Research." *Cyberpsychology & Behavior* 12 (2): 203–7.

Callan, Mitchell J., John H. Ellard, N. Will Shead, and David C. Hodgins. 2008. "Gambling as a Search for Justice: Examining the Role of Personal Relative Deprivation in Gambling Urges and Gambling Behaviour." *Personality and Social Psychology Bulletin* 34 (11): 1514–29.

Campbell, Colin, Jeffrey Derevensky, Eric Meerkamper, and Joanna Cutajar. 2011. "Parents' Perceptions of Adolescent Gambling: A Canadian National Study." *Journal of Gambling Issues* 25: 36–53.

Campbell, Colin S., Timothy F. Hartnagel, and Garry J. Smith. 2005. *The Legalization of Gambling in Canada.* The Law Commission of Canada. Available online.

Campbell, Colin S., and Garry J. Smith. 1998. "Canadian Gambling: Trends and Public Policy Issues." *The Annals of the American Academy* 556: 22–35.

———. 2003. "Gambling in Canada, from Vice to Disease to Responsibility: A Negotiated History". *Canadian Bulletin of Medical History* 20 (1): 121–49.

Canada Safety Council. 2005. *Canadian Roulette: Odds of Suicide.* Available online.

———. 2010. *Gambling Addiction.* Available online.

Canadian Broadcasting Corporation (CBC). 2003a. "Betting the Farm: An Overview of Gambling Addiction." CBC News, 19 November. Available online.

———. 2003b. "Online Gambling." CBC News, 17 November. Available online.

———. 2010a. "Online Casino Gambling Ruled Out for P.E.I." CBC News, 22 October. Available online.

———. 2010b. "Sask. Interested in Online Gambling: Minister." CBC News, 10 August. Available online.

———. 2010c. "Sports Betting Would Save Jobs, says MP." CBC News, 29 January. Available online.

Canadian Centre on Substance Abuse (CCSA). 2011. *Statistics.* Available online.

———. n.d. Working to Reduce Alcohol and Drug-Related Harm: Workplace Overview. Available online.

Canadian Gaming Association (CGA). 2006. *Study Reveals Support for Canadian Gaming Industry.* CGA website, 26 April. Available online.

———. 2011. *Canadian Gaming Industry Matures into One of the Largest Entertainment Industries in the Country, the CGA's Economic Impact Study Finds.* CGA website, 19 October. Available online.

Canadian Gaming Business. 2011. "OLG Achieves $6.7 Billion in Revenues, $2 Billion in Profits." July. Available online.

Canadian Partnership for Responsible Gambling (CPRG). 2007. *Canadian Gambling Digest 2007–2008.* Available online.

———. 2010. *Canadian Gambling Digest 2008–2009.* Available online.

Canadian Press. 2008. "Gambling Employs 267,000 in Canada." *Toronto Star*, 8 April. Available online.

———. 2010a. "Ontario Bets Big on Online Gambling". *Globe and Mail*, 10 August. Available online.

———. 2010b. "Ontario Ponders Joining Other Provinces Allowing Online Gambling." *Toronto Star*, 23 February. Available online.

CanWest News. 2008. "Ontario Prof Calls for Online Gambling Rules." Canada.com, 15 July. Available online.

Castellani, Brian. 2000. *Pathological Gambling: The Making of a Medical Problem.* Albany: SUNY Press.

Centre for Addiction and Mental Health (CAMH). 1999. *Alcohol and Drug Prevention Programs for Youth: What Works?* Toronto: CAMH.

———. 2010. *Library - AV List Subject Heading Index.* Available online.

Chevalier, S., I. Martin, Rina Gupta, and Jeffrey Derevensky. 2005. "Jeux de hasard et d'argent." In *Enquête québécoise sur le tabac, l'alcool, la drogue et le jeu chez les élèves du secondaire, 2004. Quoi de neuf depuis 2002?*, edited by Gaëtane Dubé, 131–46. Quebec: Institut de la statistique du Quebec.

Chhabra, Deepak. 2007. "Ethnicity and Marginality Effects on Casino Gambling Behaviour." *Journal of Vacation Marketing* 13: 3–21.

Clapson, Mark. 1991. "A Bit of a Flutter." *History Today* 41: 38–44.

Clarkson, L.S. 2007. *Epidemiology of Youth Gambling in Georgia.* Georgia Department of Human Resources, Division of Public Health. Available online.

Collins, Alan F. 1996. "The Pathological Gambler and the Government of Gambling." *History of the Human Sciences* 9 (3): 69–100.

Cook, Steven, Nigel Turner, Angela Paglia-Boak, Edward M. Adlaf, and Robert E. Mann. 2010. *Ontario Youth Gambling Report: Data from the 2009 Ontario Student Drug Use and Health Survey.* Toronto: Problem Gambling Institute of Ontario.

Cosgrave, James F. 2010. "Embedded Addiction: The Social Production of Gambling Knowledge and the Development of Gambling Markets." *Canadian Journal of Sociology* 35 (1): 113–34.

Cosgrave, Jim, and Thomas R. Klassen. 2001. "Gambling against the State: The State and the Legitimisation of Gambling." *Current Sociology* 49 (5): 1–15.

Council on Compulsive Gambling of New Jersey (CCGNJ). 2007. *March Madness Betting is Just the Beginning.* Available online.

Cox, Brian J., Nancy Yu, Tracie O. Afifi, and Robert Ladouceur. 2005. "A National Survey of Gambling Problems in Canada." *Canadian Journal of Psychiatry* 50 (4): 213–17.

Cox, K. 2001. "Stakes High in N.B." *Globe and Mail*, 14 May: A7.

CTV News. 2009. *Legalizing Sports Betting* [video file]. 31 January. Available online.

Currie, Shawn R., David C. Hodgins, Jianli Wang, Nady El-Guebaly, Harold Wynne, and Sophie Chen. 2006. "Risk of Harm among Gamblers in the General Population as a Function of Level of Participation in Gambling Activities." *Addiction* 101 (4): 570–80.

Curry, Timothy J., and Robert M. Jiobu. 1995. "Do Motives Matter? Modeling Gambling on Sports among Athletes." *Sociology of Sport Journal* 12 (1): 21–35.

Dangerfield, Lyndsey. 2004. "Job Satisfaction, Substance Use, and Gambling Behaviour of Northern Albertan Casino Employees." PhD diss., University of Lethbridge.

Darden, Gib, and Don Rockey. 2006. "Student-Athlete Gambling: The Invisible Problem." *Coach and Athletic Director* (January). Available online.

Davies, Andrew. 1991. "The Police and the People: Gambling in Salford, 1900–1939." *The Historical Journal* 34 (1): 87–115.

Davis, Reade. 2006. "All or Nothing: Video Lottery Terminal Gambling and Economic Restructuring in Rural Newfoundland." *Identities: Global Studies in Culture and Power* 13 (4): 503–31.

DECODE. 2009. *Parents as Partners: Quantitative National Findings.* Available online.

Delfabbro, Paul, Julie Lahn, and Peter Grabosky. 2005. *Adolescent Gambling in the ACT.* Canberra, Australia: ACT Gambling and Racing Commission. Available online.

Dement, Jeffrey W. 1999. *Going for Broke: The Depiction of Compulsive Gambling in Film.* Lanham, MD: The Scarecrow Press.

Derevensky, Jeffrey. 2010. "Internet Gambling among Youth: Should We Be Considered?" Slide show presented at the annual conference of NCRG, Las Vegas.

Derevensky, Jeffrey, Jennifer Felsher, and Rina Gupta. 2004. "Lottery Playing amongst Youth: Implications for Prevention and Social Policy." *Journal of Gambling Studies* 20 (2). Available online.

Derevensky, Jeffrey, and Meredith Gillespie. 2005. "Keynote Address: Gambling in Canada." *International Journal of Mental Health and Addiction* 3: 3–14.

Derevensky, Jeffrey, and Rina Gupta. 1996. "The Relationship Between Gambling and Video-Game Playing Behavior in Children and Adolescents." *Journal of Gambling Studies* 12 (4): 375–94.

———. 2007. "Internet Gambling among Adolescents: A Growing Concern." *International Journal of Mental Health Addiction* 5 (2): 93–101.

———. 2008. "The Impact of Gambling Advertisements on Adolescent Gambling Behaviors." Slide show presented for National Council on Problem Gambling, Long Beach, California.

Derevensky, Jeffrey, Rina Gupta, and Carmen Messerlian. 2005. "Youth Gambling Problems: A Public Health Perspective." *Health Promotion International* 20(1): 69–79.

Derevensky, Jeffrey, Rina Gupta, and Ken Winters. 2003. "Prevalence Rates of Youth Gambling Problems: Are the Current Rates Inflated?" *Journal of Gambling Studies* 19 (4): 405–25.

Derevensky, Jeffrey, A. Sklar, Rina Gupta, and Carmen Messerlian. 2010. "An Empirical Study Examining the Impact of Gambling Advertisements on Adolescent Gambling Attitudes and Behaviors." *International Journal of Mental Health and Addiction* 8 (1): 21–34.

Derevensky, Jeffrey, A. Sklar, Rina Gupta, Carmen Messerlian, M. Laroche, and S. Mansour. 2007. *The Effects of Gambling Advertisements on Child and Adolescent Gambling Attitudes and Behaviors.* Fonds québécois de la recherche sur la société et la culture.

Di Nicola, Marco, Daniela Tedeschi, Marianna Mazza, Giovanni Martinotti, Desiree Harnic, Valeria Catalano, Angelo Bruschi, et al. 2010. "Behavioural Addictions in

Bipolar Disorder Patients: Role of Impulsivity and Personality Dimensions." *Journal of Affective Disorders* 125 (1): 82–88.

Dickinson, Harley, and Bernard Schissel. 2005. "Youth Gambling in Saskatchewan: Perceptions, Behaviours, and Youth Culture." Saskatchewan: Saskatchewan Ministry of Health.

Dickson, Laurie, Jeffrey Derevensky, and Rina Gupta. 2003. *Youth Gambling Problems: The Identification of Risk and Protective Factors.* Guelph: Ontario Problem Gambling Research Centre.

———. 2002. "The Prevention of Youth Gambling Problems: A Conceptual Model." *Journal of Gambling Studies* 18: 97–159.

Dickson-Gillespie, Laurie, Lori Rugle, Richard Rosenthal, and Timothy Fong. 2008. "Preventing the Incidence and Harm of Gambling Problems." *Journal of Primary Prevention* 29 (1): 37–55. Available online.

Doiron, Jason, and Richard Nicki. 1999. *The Prevalence of Problem Gambling in Prince Edward Island.* Available online.

Doshi, Atish. 2007. "The Rush of Losing $19,000." *The Booze News Magazine.*

Dowling, Nicki, David Smith, and Trang Thomas. 2005. "Electronic Gaming Machines: Are They the 'Crack-Cocaine' of Gambling?" *Addiction* 100: 33–45.

Duffy, Margaret. 1997. "High Stakes: A Fantasy Theme Analysis of the Selling of Riverboat Gambling in Iowa." *Southern Communication Journal* 62 (2): 117–32.

Duquette, Karen B. 1999. "Casino Employee Gambling Behavior." PhD diss., University of Nevada, Las Vegas.

Eby, Kurt. 2007. "Watchdogs Take New EGMs." *Gaming Market Insights* 1 (March): 4–5. Availble online.

Edlund, Matthew. 2011. "Internet Gambing: The Latest Addiction." *Huffpost Health,* 11 March. Available online.

Ellenbogen, Stephen, Durand Jacobs, Jeffrey Derevensky, Rina Gupta, and Tom Paskus. 2008. "Gambling Behavior among College Student-Athletes." *Journal of Applied Sports Psychology* 20 (3): 349–62. Available online.

Elliot-Erickson, Sara Stephanie Phare, and Jodi Lane. 2007. *Gambling among Alberta Youth: The Alberta Youth Experience Survey 2005.* Edmonton: Alberta Health Services.

Emond, Melissa S., and Harvey H.C. Marmurek. 2010. "Gambling Related Cognitons Mediate the Association between Thinking Style and Problem Gambling Severity." *Journal of Gambling Studies* 26: 257–67.

Evra, Jennifer Van. 2010. "British Columbia's High Stakes Bet on Online Gambling." *Globe and Mail,* 3 September. Available online.

Fackler, Martin. 2007. "In Korea, a Boot Camp Cure for Web Obsession." *New York Times,* 18 November. Available online.

Falcone, Marc J., and Jason N. Ader. 2001. *Gaming Industry: E-Gaming Revisited at Odds with the World.* New York: Bear Stearns Equity Research.

Felsher, Jennifer R., Jeffrey Derevensky, and Rina Gupta. 2004. "Lottery Playing amongst Youth: Implications for Prevention and Social Policy." *Journal of Gambling Studies* 20 (2): 127–53.

———. 2007. "Lottery Participation by Youth with Gambling Problems: Are Lottery Tickets a Gateway to Other Gambling Venues?" *International Gambling Studies* 4 (2): 109–25.

———. 2009. "Gambling and Organized Crime: A Review of the Literature." *Journal of Gambling Studies* 23: 111–56.

Ferris, Jackie, and Harold J. Wynne. 2001. *The Canadian Problem Gambling Index: Final Report.* Ottawa: Canadian Centre on Substance Abuse.

Fifield, R. 2010. "Questioning the Ethics and Economics of Government Owned and Operated Gambling." Slide show. Spectrum Security Services (owner).

Finkelstein, Chad. 2009. "Living in a Fantasy: The Legality of Fantasy Sports Leagues in Canada." *Canadian Gaming Lawyer Magazine* 4 (May). Available online.

Fisher, Susan. 1999. "A Prevalence Study of Gambling and Problem Gambling in British Adolescents." *Addiction Research* 76: 509–38.

Floyd, Kim, James P. Whelan, and Andrew W. Meyers. 2006. "Use of Warning Messages to Modify Gambling Beliefs and Behavior in a Laboratory Investigation." *Psychology of Addictive Behaviors* 20 (1): 69–74.

Fox, Mark, Larry Phillips, and Ganesan Vaidyanathan. 2003. "Managing Internet Gambling in the Workplace." *First Monday* 8 (4). Available online.

Fragomeni, C. 2004. "Charity Bingos Plead for Slots; About 200 of the City's Cash-Strapped Groups Say They're Losing Customers to Casinos." *Hamilton Spectator*, 20 October: A08.

Francis, D. 2006. "Regulate Gambling or Lose the Income: Online Betting Is a Grey Area of Law with Huge Profits." *National Post*, 7 October: FP2.

Freud, Sigmund. 1928. "Dostoevsky and Parricide." In Vol. 21, *The Standard Edition of the Complete Psychological Works of Sigmund Freud*. New York: Vintage, 1999.

Frey, James H. 1992. "Gambling on Sport: Policy Issues." *Journal of Gambling Studies* 8 (4): 351–60.

Gainsbury, Sally. 2010. "Internet-Based Treatment Options for Problem Gambling: A Review of Existing Evidence and Models." Presented at the Alberta Gaming Research Institute's 9th annual conference, Banff.

Game Planit Interactive. 2006. *Workshops for Business*. Available online.

Gazso, Amber, and Lorne Tepperman, with the assistance of Katherine Osterlund and Sarah Fox. 2008. *Media Discourse, Public Attitudes, and Gambling Practices*. Guelph: Ontario Problem Gambling Research Centre.

Geffner, Eric. 2008. "Sports Betting." StopGamblingNow.com. Available online.

Geist, Michael. 2002. "Computer and E-mail Workplace Surveillance in Canada: The Shift from Reasonable Expectation of Privacy to Reasonable Surveillance." *Canadian Judicial Council* 15: 2–38.

Gentile, Douglas. 2009. *Pathological Video-Game Use among Youth Ages 8 to 18*. Association for Psychological Science. Available online.

Gentile, Douglas, Hyekyung Choo, Albert Liau, Timothy Sim, Dongdong Li, Daniel Fung, and Angeline Khoo. 2011. "Pathological Video Game Use among Youths: A Two-Year Longitudinal Study." *Pediatrics* 127 (2).

Geranios, Nicholas K. 2009. "Internet Addiction Center Opens in US." Associated Press, 3 September. Available online.

Gillespie, Meredith, Jeffrey Derevensky, and Rina Gupta. 2007a. "Adolescent Problem Gambling: Developing a Gambling Expectancy Instrument." *Journal of Gambling Issues* 19. Available online.

———. 2007b. "The Utility of Outcome Expectancies in the Prediction of Adolescent Gambling Behaviour." *Journal of Gambling Issues* 19: 69–85.

Giroux, Isabelle, Claude Boutin, Robert Ladouceur, Stella Lachance, and Magouli Dufour. 2008. "Awareness Training Program on Responsible Gambling for Casino Employees." *International Journal of Mental Health and Addiction* 6 (4): 594–601.

Glickman, Gail E. 1979. "Our Gaming Laws: Conditions Dicey, to Say the Least." *Canadian Lawyer* 3 (5): 10–12.

Glionna, J.M. 2006. "Gambling, Addiction and Asian Culture." In *Asian-Nation: Asian American History, Demographies and Issues.* Available online.

Godot, David. 2010. "Cultural Factors in Problem Gambling among the Chinese." Cultural Psychology Community Blog, 3 January. Available online.

Goffman, Erving. 1967. "Where the Action Is." In *Interaction Ritual,* 149–270. New York: Random House.

Goldberg, Steven T. 2001. "He Never Saw the Sun: Day Traders Who Became Addicted to Buying and Selling Stock." *Kiplinger's Personal Finance Magazine* (August). Available online.

Goodman, Robert. 1995. *The Luck Business: The Devastating Consequences and Broken Promises of American's Gambling Explosion.* New York: Free Press.

Grant, Jon E., and Suck Won Kim. 2001. "Demographic and Clinical Features of 131 Adult Pathological Gamblers." *Journal of Clinical Psychiatry* 62: 957–62.

Griffiths, Mark D. 1998. "Internet Addiction: Does It Really Exist?" In *Psychology and the Internet: Intrapersonal, Interpersonal, and Transpersonal Applications,* edited by J. Gackenbach, 61–75. New York: Academic Press.

——. 2005. "Does Gambling Advertising Contribute to Problem Gambling?" *International Journal of Mental Health & Addiction* 3 (2): 15–25.

——. 2008. "Internet Gambling: Psychosocial Impact." Slide show presented at the National Conference on Problem Gambling, Long Beach.

——. 2009a. "Online Computer Gaming: Advice for Parents and Teachers." *Education and Health* 27: 3–6.

——. 2009b. "Professional Practice: Internet Gambling in the Workplace." *Journal of Workplace Learning* 21 (8): 658–70.

Griffiths, Mark D., and Andrew Barnes. 2008. "Internet Gambling: An Online Empirical Study among Student Gamblers." *International Journal of Mental Health and Addiction* 6: 194–204. Available online.

Griffiths, Mark D., and Jonathan Parke. 2002. "The Social Impact of Internet Gambling." *Social Science Computer Review* 20 (3): 312–20. Available online.

Griffiths, Mark D., Jonathan Parke, Richard Wood, and Jane Rigbye. 2010. "Online Poker Gambling in University Students: Further Findings from an Online Survey." *International Journal of Mental Health and Addiction* 8 (1): 82–89.

Griffiths, Mark D., Heather Wardle, Jim Orford, Kerry Sproston, and Bob Erens. 2009. "Sociodemographic Correlates of Internet Gambling: Findings from the 2007 British Gambling Prevalence Survey." *CyberPsychology and Behavior* 12: 199–202.

——. 2010. "Gambling, Alcohol, Consumption, Cigarette Smoking and Health: Findings from the 2007 British Gambling Prevalence Survey." *Addiction Research and Theory* 18 (2): 208–33.

Griffiths, Mark D., and Robert T. Wood. 2000. "Risk Factors in Adolescence: The Case of Gambling, Videogame Playing, and the Internet." *Journal of Gambling Studies* 16 (2/3): 199–225.

Gupta, Rina, and Jeffrey Derevensky. 1996. "The Relationship between Gambling and Video Game Playing Behavior in Children and Adolescents." *Journal of Gambling Studies* 12 (4): 375–94.

——. 1997. "Familial and Social Influences on Juvenile Gambling Behavior." *Journal of Gambling Studies* 13 (3): 179–92.

——. 1998. "Adolescent Gambling Behavior: A Prevalence Study and Examination of the Correlates Associated with Problem Gambling." *Journal of Gambling Studies* 14 (4): 319–45.

———. 2000. "Adolescents with Gambling Problems: From Research to Treatment." *Journal of Gambling Studies* 16: 315–42.

Guttentag, Daniel. 2010. *Gambling by Ontario Casino Employees: Gambling Behaviours, Problem Gambling, and Impacts of the Employment.* Waterloo: University of Waterloo.

Hagan, Kate. 2010. "Gambling Linked to One in Five Suicidal Patients." *The Age* (Melbourne), 21 April.

Hall, Lyle, and Rob Scarpelli. 2010. *2010 Survey of the Canadian Gaming Industry.* HLT Advisory and Canadian Gaming Association. Available online.

Hammersley, Richard, and Marie Reid. 2002. "Why the Pervasive Addiction Myth Is Still Believed." *Addiction Research and Theory* 10 (1): 7–30.

Han, Doug Hyun, Yang Soo Kim, Yong Sik Lee, Kyung Joon Min, and Perry F. Renshaw. 2010. "Changes in Cue-Induced, Prefrontal Cortex Activity with Video-Game Play." *Cyberpsychology, Behavior, and Social Networking* 13 (6): 655–61.

Hancock, Linda, Tony Schellinck, and Tracy Schrans. 2008. "Gambling and Corporate Social Responsibility (CSR): Re-Defining Industry and State Roles on Duty of Care, Host Responsibility and Risk Management." *Policy and Society* 27: 55–68.

Hardoon, Karen K., and Jeffrey Derevensky. 2002. "Child and Adolescent Gambling Behavior: Current Knowledge." *Clinical Child Psychology and Psychiatry* 7 (2): 1359.

Hardoon, Karen K., Rina Gupta, and Jeffrey Derevensky. 2004. "Psychosocial Variables Associated with Adolescent Gambling: A Model for Problem Gambling." *Psychology of Addictive Behaviors* 18 (2): 170–79.

Harrison, Bach. 2003. *Nebraska Risk and Protective Factor. Student Survey.* Nebraska Partners in Prevention. Available online.

Harter, James, Frank Schmidt, and Corey L. Keyes. 2003. "Well-being in the Workplace and Its Relationship to Business Outcomes: A Review of the Gallup Studies." In *Flourishing: The Positive Person and the Good Life*, edited by Corey L. Keyes and Jonathan Haidt, 205–24. Washington D.C.: American Psychological Association.

Hartman, Bob. 2006. "Internet Gambling Industry Growth to Reach $528 Billion by 2015." Casino Gambling Web, 12 December. Available online.

Helfant, Ian M. 2002. *The High Stakes of Identity: Gambling in the Life and Literature of Nineteenth-Century Russia.* Evanston: Northwestern University Press.

Henriksson, Lennart E. 2001. "Gambling in Canada: Some Insights for Cost-Benefit Analysis." *Managerial and Decision Economics* 22: 113–23.

Hewig, J., N. Kretschmer, R. Trippe, H. Hecht, M. Coles, C. Holroyd, and W. Miltner. 2010. "Hypersensitivity to Reward in Problem Gamblers." *Biological Psychiatry* 67 (8): 781–83.

HFM Prevention Council. n.d. *Problem Gambling: It Doesn't Just Affect You. It Affects Your Family, Your Friends and Your Community.* Pamphlet.

Hing, Nerilee, and Helen Breen. 2005. "Gambling amongst Gaming Venue Employees: Counsellors' Perspectives on Risk and Protective Factors in the Workplace." *Gambling Research* 17 (2): 25–26.

HLT Advisory. 2010. *2010 Economic Impact of the Canadian Gaming Industry.* Toronto: Canadian Gaming Association.

Hodgins, David C., Chrystal Mansley, and Kylie Thygesen. 2006. "Risk Factors for Suicide Ideation and Attempts among Pathological Gamblers." *American Journal on Addictions* 15 (4): 303–10.

Holtgraves, Thomas. 2009. "Gambling, Gambling Activities and Problem Gambling." *Psychology of Addictive Behaviors* 23 (2): 295–302.

Hoskins, Gary, and Colleen Tessier. n.d. *Gambling and the Workplace.* Centre for Addiction and Mental Health (CAMH). Available online.

Howell, D. 2005. "Alberta Oil Workers Share $54m Lotto Win." *Ottawa Citizen*, 28 October: A3.

Huang, J., and R. Boyer. 2007. "Epidemiology of Youth Gambling Problems in Canada: A National Prevalence Study." *Canadian Journal of Psychiatry* 52 (10): 657.

Huang, J.H., D.F. Jacobs, Jeffrey L. Derevensky, Rina Gupta, and Tom S. Paskus. 2007. "A National Study on Gambling among US College Student-Athletes." *Journal of College Health* 56 (2): 93–9.

Huggins, Mike J. 2000. "More Sinful Pleasures? Leisure, Respectability and the Male Middle Class in Victorian England." *Journal of Social History* 33 (3): 585–600.

Humphrey, Chuck. 2008. *Summary: Australian Interactive Gambling Act 2001.* Available online.

International Centre for Youth Gambling Problems and High-Risk Behaviors. 2010. *Tools for Youth Gambling Problem Prevention.* Available online.

———. n.d. *Materials for Youth Gambling Problem Prevention.* Available online.

Ipsos Reid and Canadian Gaming Association (CGA). 2010. "Internet Gaming in Canada: Perceptions and Behaviour." Slide show. Available online.

Ipsos Reid Public Affairs and Gemini Research. 2008. *British Columbia Problem Gambling Prevalence Study.* Vancouver, BC, and Northampton, MA: Gaming Policy and Enforcement Branch, British Columbia Ministry of Public Safety, and Solicitor General. Available online.

Itzkowitz, D.C. 1988. "Victorian Bookmakers and Their Customers." *Victorian Studies* 32 (1): 7–30.

Jackson, D. 2010. "N.S. Stays Out of Online Gambling." *Chronicle Herald*, 6 October. Available online.

Jacobs, Durand F. 2000. "Juvenile Gambling in North America: An Analysis of Long-Term Trends and Future Prospects." *Journal of Gambling Studies* 16: 119–51.

———. 2005. "Youth Gambling in North America: Long Term Trends and Future Prospects. In *Gambling Problems in Youth*, edited by Jeffrey L. Derevensky and Rina Gupta, 1–26. New York: Springer.

James, Darlene. 2003. *Gambling in Alberta: Policy Background Paper.* Edmonton: Alberta Health Services. Available online.

Jayashanker, G. 2007. "Is Investing on the Stock Market Gambling?" Associated Content, 1 October. Available online.

John, Deborah R. 1999. "Consumer Socialization of Children: A Retrospective Look at Twenty-Five Years of Research." *Journal of Consumer Research* 26: 183–213.

Jones, P. 2009. "Screening for Suicide Risk with Gamblers." Slide show. Behavioral Health and Family Studies Institute.

KAAP. 2008. "Youth Gambling: Recreation with Risk." Slide show handout. Kansas Coalition on Problem Gambling. Available online.

Kallick-Kaufmann, Maureen. 1979. "The Micro and Macro Dimensions of Gambling in the United States." *Journal of Social Issues* 35: 7–26.

Kaminer, Yifrah, Joseph Burleson, and Agnes Jadamec. 2002. "Gambling Behavior in Adolescent Substance Abuse." *Substance Abuse* 23: 191–98.

Kang, Yong Soon, Patrick T. Long, and Richard R. Perdue. 1996. "Resident Attitudes toward Legal Gambling." *Annals of Tourism Research* 23 (1): 71–85.

Karleff, I. 1998. "Cybergambling: Where She Stops, Nobody Knows." *National Post*, 5 December: D01.

Kassinove, Jeffrey I., and Mitchell Schare. 2001. "Effects of the 'Near Miss' and the 'Big Win' on Persistence at Slot Machine Gambling." *Psychology of Addictive Behaviors* 15 (2): 155–58.

Kavanagh, T. 1994. "Gambling, Chance and the Discourse of Power in Ancien Régime France." *Renaissance and Modern Studies* 37: 31–46.

Kelley, Robin, Peter Todosichuk, and Jason J. Azmier. 2001. *Gambling@Home: Internet Gambling in Canada*. Gambling in Canada research report no. 15. Calgary: Canada West Foundation. Available online.

Kenny, E. 1998. "All Gambling Profits Urged for Charities Alberta Government Takes Too Much." *Globe and Mail*, 21 July: A2.

Korn, David. 2000. "Expansion of Gambling in Canada: Implications for Health and Social Policy." *Canadian Medical Association Journal* 163 (1): 61–64.

———. 2004. *Gambling Policies in Ontario Intercollegiate Athletics*. Guelph: Ontario Problem Gambling Research Centre.

Korn, David, Tim Hurson, and Jennifer Reynolds. 2005. *Commercial Gambling Advertising: Possible Impact on Youth Knowledge, Attitudes, Beliefs and Behavioural Intentions*. Guelph: Ontario Problem Gambling Research Centre, 1–64.

Korn, David, and Martha Murray. 2005. *Gambling Policies in Ontario Intercollegiate Athletics*. Ontario Problem Gambling Research Centre Available online.

Korn, David, and Lorne Tepperman. 2005. *At Home with Gambling*. Guelph: Ontario Problem Gambling Research Centre. Available online.

Kulig, J., and D. MacKinnon. 2005. "Aboriginal Casinos." *Optimum Online*. Available online.

Kyer, C. Ian, and Danielle Hough. 2002. "Is Internet Gaming Legal in Canada: A Look at Starnet." *Canadian Journal of Law and Technology* 1 (1). Available online.

LaBrie, Richard, Sara Kaplan, Debi LaPlante, Sarah Nelson, and Howard Shaffer. 2008. "Inside the Virtual Casino: A Perspective Longitudinal Study of Actual Internet Casino Gambling." *European Journal of Public Health* 18 (4): 410–16.

LaBrie, Richard, Howard Shaffer, Debi LaPlante, and Henry Wechsler. 2003. "Correlates of College Student Gambling in the United States." *Journal of American College Health* 52: 53–62.

Ladouceur, Robert. 1996. "Prevalence of Pathological Gamblers in Canada and Related Issues." *Journal of Gambling Studies* 12 (2): 129–42.

Ladouceur, Robert, D. Dubé, and A. Bujold. 1994. "Prevalence of Pathological Gambling and Related Problems among College Students in the Quebec Metropolitan Area." *Canadian Journal of Psychiatry* 39 (5): 289–93.

Ladouceur, Robert, C. Jacques, S. Chevalier, S. Sévigny, and D. Hamel. 2005. "Prevalence of Pathological Gambling in Quebec in 2002." *Canadian Journal of Psychiatry* 50: 451–56.

Ladouceur, Robert, and Chantal Mireault. 1988. "Gambling Behaviors among High School Students in the Quebec Area." *Journal of Gambling Behavior* 4: 3–12.

Ladouceur, Robert, Caroline Sylvain, and Patrick Gosselin. 2007. "Self-Exclusion Problem: A Longitudinal Evaluation Study." *Journal of Gambling Studies* 23: 85–94.

Laframboise, Donna. 2000. "Gambling Is a Public Health Issue." *National Post*, 29 August: A13.

Lange, Mark A. 2001. "'If You Do Not Gamble, Check This Box': Perceptions of Gambling Behaviors." *Journal of Gambling Studies* 17 (3): 247–54.

LaPlante, Debi, Anja Schumann, Richard A. LaBrie, and Howard Shaffer. 2008. "Population Trends in Internet Sports Gambling." *Computers in Human Behaviour* 24: 2399–414.

Le, Gianna, Michael Liao, Stella Lee, and Kent Woo. 2010. *Youth Gambling in the 21st Century: Prevalence, Impact and Interventions*. Problem Gambling Prevention: NICOS Chinese Health Coalition. Available online.

Leeds, Mike, and George Diemer. 2010. "Point Shaving in NCAA Basketball: Corrupt Behaviour or Statistical Artifact?" DETU Working Paper 1009, Department of Economics, Temple University. Available online.

Lem, Sharon. 2010. "Gambling Addiction Controlled His Life." *Edmonton Sun*, 6 September. Available online.

Lemmens, Jeroen, Patti Valkenburg, and Jochen Peter. 2011. "The Effects of Pathological Gaming on Aggressive Behavior." *Journal of Youth and Adolescence* 40 (1): 38–47.

Lesieur, Henry R. 1984. *The Chase: Career of the Compulsive Gambler*. Rochester, VT: Schenkman Books.

———. 1998. "Costs and Treatment of Pathological Gambling." *The Annals of The American Academy* 556: 153–71.

Lesieur, Henry R., and Sheila B. Blume. 1987. "The South Oaks Gambling Screen (SOGS): A New Instrument for the Identification of Pathological Gamblers." *American Journal of Psychiatry* 144 (9): 1184–88.

Lesieur, Henry R., and Richard J. Rosenthal. 1991. "Pathological Gambling: A Review of the Literature (prepared for the American psychiatric association task force on DSM-IV committee on disorders of impulse control not elsewhere classified)." *Journal of Gambling Studies* 7 (1): 5–39.

Lester, David. 1994. "Access to Gambling Opportunities and Compulsive Gambling." *Substance Use & Misuse* 29 (12): 1611–6.

Levin, Aaron. "Leaving Las Vegas May Reduce Odds of Suicide." *Psychiatric News* 44 (3): 21. Available online.

Liau, Albert K., Angeline Khoo, and Peng Hwa Ang. 2008. "Parental Awareness and Monitoring of Adolescent Internet Use." *Current Psychology* 27 (4): 217–33.

Lin, Teh Joo, and Ang Yiying. 2009. "Most Problem Gamblers Get Hooked at Early Age." *The Straits Times*, 19 August. Available online.

Lockwood, Penelope, and Ziva Kunda. 1997. "Superstars and Me: Predicting the Impact of Role Models on the Self." *Journal of Personality and Social Psychology* 73: 91–103.

Looney, Ed. 2003. *Stock Market Gambling*. Council on Compulsive Gambling of Jersey, 14 July. Available online.

Lussier, I., Jeffrey Derevensky, Rina Gutpa, Tanya Bergevin, and Stephen Ellenbogen. 2007. "Youth Gambling Behaviours: An Examination of the Role of Resilience." *Psychology of Addictive Behaviors* 31: 165–73.

MacAfee, M. 2000. "Quebec's Gambling CD-ROM Unsuitable for Kids, Critics Say." *Globe and Mail*, 24 February: A5.

Markle, Glen. 2003. *Sports Participation: Gambling Situations and Learning Opportunities: An Exploratory Investigation*. Ontario Problem Gambling Research Centre. Available online.

Marshall, K., and H. Wynne. 2003. *Fighting the Odds*. Statistics Canada Catalogue no. 75-001-x1E. Ottawa: Statistics Canada. Available online.

McBride, J. and Jeffrey Derevensky. 2009. "Internet Gambling among Youth: Cause for Concern!" Slide show. Available online.

McBride, J., Jeffery Derevensky, and Rina Gupta. 2007. "Youth Gambling and the Internet: A Preliminary Examination." Poster presented at the National Council on Problem Gambling annual conference, Kansas City.

McCarthy, Michael. 2007a. "College Kids Caught in Gambling Madness." *USA Today*, 28 March. Available online.

———. 2007b. "Gambling Madness Can Snag Court Fans." *USA Today*, 28 March. Available online.

———. 2007c. "Student Gamblers Take Terrible Risks." *USA Today*, 27 March. Available online.

———. 2011. "Point-Shaving Remains a Concern in College Athletics. Gamblers Seek Ways to Lure Players into Game-Fixing Fold." *USA Today*, 9 May. Available online.

McDonald, Marci. 2000. "Betting the House." *U.S. News and World Report* 129 (15): 44.

McKibbin, Ross. 1979. "Working Class Gambling in Britain 1880–1939." *Past and Present* 82: 147–78.

McMullan, John L., and Delthia Miller. 2007a. "All In! The Commercial Advertising of Offshore Gambling on Television." *Journal of Gambling Issues* 22: 230–51.

———. 2007b. "The Commercial Advertising of Gambling in Nova Scotia." *Nova Scotia Gaming Corporation* (May): 1–183.

———. 2009. "Wins, Winning and Winners: The Commercial Advertising of Lottery Gambling." *Journal of Gambling Studies* 25 (3): 273–95.

McMullan, John L., and Jason Mullen. 2001. "What Makes Gambling News?" *Journal of Gambling Studies* 17 (4): 321–52.

Meerkamper, Eric. 2006. *Decoding Risk: Gambling Attitudes and Behaviours amongst Youth in Nova Scotia.* Nova Scotia Gaming Corporation. Available online.

Melemis, Steven M. n.d. "What is Addiction?" http://www.AddictionsAndRecovery.org.

Messerlian, Carmen, Andrea Byrne, and Jeffrey Derevensky. 2004. "Gambling, Youth and the Internet: Should We Be Concerned?" *The Canadian Child and Adolescent Psychiatry Review* 13 (1): 3–6. Available online.

Messerlian, Carmen, Jeffrey Derevensky, and Rina Gupta. 2005. "Youth Gambling Problems: A Public Health Perspective." *Health Promotion International* 20: 69–79.

Milstone, C. 2001. "Kids Being Encouraged to Gamble, Researchers Say." *National Post*, 9 July: D02.

Monaghan, Sally. 2008. "Review of Pop-up Messages on Electronic Gaming Machines as a Proposed Responsible Gambling Strategy." *International Journal of Mental Health and Addiction* 6: 214–22.

Moodie, Crawford, and Frances Finnigan. 2005. "Prevalence and Correlates of Youth Gambling in Scotland." *Addiction Research and Theory* 14 (4): 365–85.

Moodie, Crawford, and Gerard Hastings. 2009. "Social Marketing and Gambling: A Critical Perspective." *Addiction* 104: 692–93.

Moore, Susan, and Keis Ohtsuka. 1999a. "Beliefs about Control over Gambling among Young People, and Their Relation to Problem Gambling." *Psychology of Addictive Behaviors* 13 (4): 339–47.

———. 1999b. "The Prediction of Gambling Behavior and Problem Gambling from Attitudes and Perceived Norms." *Social Behavior and Personality* 27 (5): 455–66.

Moore, Thomas L. 2008. *Oregon Gambling Programs Evaluation Update 2008.* Salem, OR: Department of Human Services, Addictions and Mental Health Division. Available online.

Moran, Susan, Henry Wechsler, and Nancy Rigotti. 2004. "Social Smoking among US College Students." *Pediatrics* 114 (4): 1028–34.

Morasco, B.J., K.A. VomEigen, and N.M. Petry. 2006. "Severity of Gambling Is Associated with Physical and Emotional Health in Urban Primary Care Patients." *General Hospital Psychiatry* 28: 94–100.

Morrow, Crossdale and Associates Inc. n.d. Company website. http://morcro.ca.

Morton, Suzanne. 2003. *At Odds: Gambling and Canadians 1919–1969.* Toronto: University of Toronto Press.

Munting, Roger. 1989. "Betting and Business: The Commercialisation of Gambling in Britain." *Business History* 31: 67–68.

Nation, Maury, Cindy Crusto, Abraham Wandersman, Karol L. Kumpfer, Diana Seybolt, Erin Morrissey-Kane, and Katrina Davino. 2003. "What Works in Prevention: Principles of Effective Prevention Programs." *American Psychologist* 58 (6-7): 449–56.

National Center for Responsible Gaming (NCRG). 2009. *A Call to Action: Recommendations for Science-Based Policies and Programs.* Available online.

———. 2010. "Evaluating Self-Exclusion as an Intervention for Disordered Gambling." *Increasing the Odds* 5. Available online.

National Collegiate Athletic Association (NCAA). 2008. National Study on Collegiate Sports Wagering and Associated Health Risks. Available online.

National Council on Problem Gambling (NCPG). 2011. REAP: Sport Gambling Facts and Statistics. Available online.

———. n.d. *National Problem Gambling Awareness Week.* Available online.

———. n.d. *Problem Gambling Information: Educational Material.* Available Online

National Gambling Impact Study Commission (NGISC). 1999. *Final Report.* Available online.

———. 1999. *Final Report.* Available online.

Nelson, Sarah E., Debi A. LaPlante, Allyson J. Peller, Anja Schumann, Richard A. LaBrie, and Howard J. Shaffer. 2008. "Real Limits in the Virtual World: Self-Limiting Behavior of Internet Gamblers." *Journal of Gambling Studies* 24 (4): 463–77.

Nelson, Sarah E., J.H. Kleschinsky, R.A. LaBrie, S. Kaplan, and H.J. Shaffer. 2010. "One Decade of Self-Exclusion: Missouri Casino Self-Excluders Four to Ten Years after Enrollment." *Journal of Gambling Studies* 26 (1): 129–44.

Nelson, Toben, Richard LaBrie, Debi LaPlante, Michael Stanton, Howard Shaffer, and Henry Wechsler. 2007. "Sports Betting and Other Gambling in Athletics, Fans, and Other College Students." *Research Quarterly for Exercise and Sport* 78 (4): 271–83.

New Brunswick. Department of Finance: Lotteries Commission of New Brunswick. 2007. *Responsible Management, Responsible Play in a Responsible Environment.* Fredericton: Department of Finance. Available online.

Nibert, David. 2000. *Hitting the Lottery Jackpot: Government and the Taxing of Dreams.* New York: Monthly Review Press.

Nickerson, Norma P. 1995. "Tourism and Gambling Content Analysis." *Annals of Tourism Research* 22 (1): 53–66.

Nieves, Evelyn. 1997. "Our Towns: Taste of Hope at Restaurants Casinos Hurt." *New York Times,* 23 March.

———. 2009. "Our Towns: Taste of Hope at Restaurant Casinos Hurt." *New York Times,* 23 March: 39.

Northwest Territories Bureau of Statistics. 2002. *2002 NWT Alcohol and Drug Survey.* Available online.

Nova Scotia Legislature. 2010. *Casino Regulations Made under Section 127 of the Gaming Control Act.* Province of Nova Scotia. Available online.

Nower, Lia, Rina Gupta, Alex Blaszczynski, and Jeffrey Derevensky. 2004. "Suicidality and Depression among Youth Gamblers: A Preliminary Examination of Three Studies." *International Gambling Studies* (4) 1: 69–79.

Odegaard, S., A. Peller, and H. Shaffer. 2005. "Addiction as Syndrome." *Paradigm* 9 (3): 12–22.

Oei, Tian P.S., and Namrata Raylu. 2004. "Familial Influence on Offspring Gambling: A Possible Mechanism for Transmission of Gambling Behavior in Families." *Psychological Medicine* 34: 1279–88.

Olson, Phillip. 2009. "Stock Market vs. Gambling!" Sports Rumble. Available online.

Ontario Lottery and Gaming Corporation (OLG). 2008. *Casino Niagara*. Available online.

Oregon Department of Human Services. 2011. "Problem Gambling and the Workplace." Available online.

Orme, Cynthia, Glenda Northey, and Phil Townshend. 2010. "Internet Gambling: Discussion Paper on Internet and Other Forms of Remote Gambling." *Gambling and Public Health Alliance International*. Newsletter. July. Available online.

Oster, S., and T. Knapp. 1998. "Sport Betting by College Students: Who Bets and How Often?" *College Student Journal* 32 (2).

Otteman, Timothy. 2008. "Gambling with Their Lives: College Students and Sports Wagering." PhD diss., Central Michigan Univ. Available online.

Out-of-Home Marketing Association of Canada (OMAC). 2006. *Online Gambling Guidelines Canada*. Available online.

———. 2010. Online Gambling Guidelines Canada. Available online.

Papoff, Katharine M., and Joan E. Norris. 2009. "Instant Ticket Purchasing by Ontario Baby Boomers: Increasing Risk for Problem Gamblers." *Journal of Gambling Studies* 25 (2): 185–99.

Patton, David, David Brown, Jastej Dhaliwal, Curt Pankratz, and Brian Broszeit. 2002. *Gambling Involvement and Problem Gambling in Manitoba*. Addictions Foundation of Manitoba.

Paul, Robert J., and James B. Townsend. 1998. "Managing Workplace Gambling—Some Cautions and Recommendations." *Employee Responsibilities and Rights Journal* 11 (3): 171–86.

Pelisek, Christine. 2005. "The Gamblers Index." *LAWeekly*, 8 December. Available online.

Perkins, Dave. 2009. "Sports Betting Is No Long Shot." *Toronto Star*, 8 February. Available online.

Perkins, Tara. 2006. "Canada Chided for Lax Online Gaming Policy." *Toronto Star*, 6 November. Available online.

Petry, Nancy M., Frederick S. Stinson, and Bridget F. Grant. 2005. "Comorbidity of DSM-IV Pathological Gambling and Other Psychiatric Disorders: Results from the National Epidemiologic Survey on Alcohol and Related Conditions." *Journal of Clinical Psychiatry* 66: 564–74.

Peukert, Peter, Sonja Sieslack, Gottfried Barth, and Anil Batra. 2010. "Internet and Computer Game Addiction: Phenomenology, Comorbidity, Etiology, Diagnostics and Therapeutic Implications for the Addictives and Their Relatives." *Psychiatrische Praxis* 37 (5): 219–24.

Picard, André. 2011. "Government-Sanctioned Online Gambling: Short-Sighted and Morally Bankrupt." *Globe and Mail*, 20 April. Available online.

Porter, G., V. Starcevic, D. Berle, and P. Fenech. 2010. "Recognizing Problem Video Game Use." *Australian and New Zealand Journal of Psychiatry* 44 (2): 120–28.

Porter, John. 1965. *The Vertical Mosaic*. Toronto: University of Toronto Press.

Poulin, Christiane, and David Elliot. 2007. *Student Drug Use Survey in the Atlantic Provinces 2007*. Halifax: Dalhousie University, Community Health and Epidemiology. Available online.

Priest, Lisa. 2009. "The Million-Dollar Club: Losing Big, Losing Often." *Globe and Mail*, 5 October. Available online.

Problem Gambling Institute of Ontario (PGIO). 2010. *Youth and Gambling: Prevention*. Available online.

Productivity Commission, Government of Australia. 1999. *Australia's Gambling Industries: Inquiry Report.* Available online.

Public Sector Gaming Study Commission (PSGSC). 2000. *Final Report.* Available online.

Rassmussen, Brent. 2007. "Living Paycheck to Paycheck." CNN.com, 4 April. Available online.

Rehbein, F., M. Kleimann, and T. Mössle. 2009. "Excessive Video Game Playing and Video Game Addiction in Adolescence: Results of a German Nationwide Survey." *Die Psychiatrie: Grundlagen & Perspektiven* 6 (3): 140–46.

Reith, Gerda. 2002. *The Age of Chance: Gambling and Western Culture.* New York: Routledge.

———. 2007. "Gambling and the Contradictions of Consumption: A Genealogy of the 'Pathological' Subject." *American Behavioral Scientist* 51 (1): 33–55.

Responsible Gambling Council (RGC). 2010. *Negative Impacts.* Available online.

———. n.d. *kts2 Overview.* Available online.

———. n.d. http://www.responsiblegambling.org.

Rex, Justin, and David J. Jackson. 2008. "The Options for Internet Gambling in Canada." *The American Review of Canadian Studies* 38: 222. Available online.

Roberts, John M., Malcolm J. Arth, and Robert R. Bush. 1959. "Games in Culture." *American Anthropologist* 61 (4): 597–605.

Rosecrance, John. 1985. "Compulsive Gambling and the Medicalization of Deviance." *Social Problems* 32 (3): 275–84.

Rossol, Josh. 2001. "The Medicalization of Deviance as an Interactive Achievement: The Construction of Compulsive Gambling." *Symbolic Interaction* 24 (3): 315–41.

Sadinsky, Stanley. 2005. *Review of the Problem-Gambling and Responsible-Gaming Strategy of the Government of Ontario.* Ontario: Ontario Ministry of Health and Long-Term Care. Available online.

Samson, Adam. 2009. "Student Creates Web Site for Legal Sports Betting." QuarterBets Blog, 23 March. Available online.

Saum, William. 1999. "Sports Gambling in College: Cracking Down on Illegal Betting." *USA Today Magazine.* Society for the Advancement of Education. Available online.

Schellink, Tony, and Tracy Schrans. 2002. *Atlantic Lottery Corporation Video Lottery Responsible Gaming Feature Research: Final Report.* Halifax: Focal Research Consultants.

Schellinck, Tony, Tracy Schrans, G. Walsh, and J. Grace. 2002. *2002 Seniors Survey— Prevalence of Substance Use and Gambling among New Brunswick Adults Aged 55+.* New Brunswick Department of Health and Wellness. Halifax: Focal Research Consultants. Available online.

Schwabish, Jonathan A. 2005. "Regulating Underground Industry: An Economic Analysis of Sports Betting." *New York Economic Review* Fall: 65–77. Available online.

Schwartz, David G. 2006. *Roll the Bones: The History of Gambling.* New York: Gotham Books.

Schwartz, H. 1977. "Games, Timepieces, and Businesspeople." *Diogenes* 99: 60–79.

Seelig, Michael Y., and Julie H. Seelig. 1998. "'Place Your Bets!' On Gambling, Government and Society." *Canadian Public Policy* 24: 91–106.

Séguin, Monique, Richard Boyer, Alain Lesage, Alexandre McGirr, Amnon Suissa, Michel Tousignant, and Gustavo Turecki. 2010. "Suicide and Gambling: Psychopathology and Treatment-Seeking." *Psychology of Addictive Behaviors* 24 (3): 541–47.

Shaffer, Howard J., Anthony. N. Donato, Richard A. LaBrie, Rachel C. Kidman, and Debi A. LaPlante. 2005. "The Epidemiology of College Alcohol and Gambling Policies." *Harm Reduction Journal* 2 (1): 1.

Shaffer, Howard J., and Matthew N. Hall. 2000. "Updating and Refining Prevalence Estimates of Disordered Gambling Behaviour in the United States and Canada." *Canadian Journal of Public Health* 92 (3): 168–72.

Shaffer, Howard J., Matthew N. Hall, and Joni Vanderbilt. 1999. "Estimating the Prevalence of Disordered Gambling Behavior in the United States and Canada: A Research Synthesis." *American Journal of Public Health* 89: 1369–76.

Shaffer, Howard J., Richard A. LaBrie, and Debi LaPlante. 2004. "Laying the Foundation for Quantifying Regional Exposure to Social Phenomena: Considering the Case of Legalized Gambling as a Public Health Toxin." *Psychology of Addictive Behaviors* 18 (1): 40–48.

Shaffer, Howard J., Debi A. LaPlante, Richard A. LaBrie, Rachel C. Kidman, Anthony. N. Donato, and Michael Stanton. 2004. "Toward a Syndrome Model of Addiction: Multiple Manifestations, Common Etiology." *Harvard Review of Psychiatry* 12 (6): 367–74.

Shepellžfgr Research Group. 2007. "Employee Engagement and Health: An EAP'S Role and Perspective." Available online.

Simon, Derek. 2010. "A Quick and Dirty Look at Sports Gambling." Financial Edge, 10 March. Available online.

Sirakaya, Ercan, Dursun Delen, and Hwan-Suk Choi. 2005. "Forecasting Gaming Referenda." *Annals of Tourism Research* 32 (1): 127–49.

Skinner, Harvey, Sherry Biscope, Martha Murray, and David Korn. 2004. "Dares to Addiction: Youth Definitions and Perspectives on Gambling." *Canadian Journal of Public Health* 95 (4): 264.

Sklar, Alissa. 2007. "Guest Columist." *NCAA Don't Bet On It.* Newsletter. November. Available online.

Skolnik, Sam. 2011. *High Stakes: The Rising Cost of America's Gambling Addiction.* New York: Beacon Press.

Slutske, Wendy S., Kristina M. Jackson, and Kenneth J. Sher. 2003. "The Natural History of Gambling Problems from Age 18 to 29." *Journal of Abnormal Psychology* 112: 263–74.

Smith, Garry J. 1992. "Sucker Bet or Sure Thing: A Critical Analysis of Sports Lotteries." *Journal of Gambling Studies* 8 (4): 331–49.

———. 2004. Review of *At Odds: Gambling and Canadians, 1919–1969*, by Suzanne Morton. *The Canadian Journal of Sociology* 29 (4): 614–17.

———. 2009. "Sports Betting in Canada." *International Sports Law Journal* 1: 106–11. Available online.

Smith, Garry J., and Colin S. Campbell. 2007. "Tensions and Contentions: An Examination of Electronic Gaming Issues in Canada." *American Behavioral Scientist* 51 (1): 86–101.

Smith, Garry J., David Hodgins, and Robert J. Williams, eds. 2007. *Research and Measurement Issues in Gambling Studies.* New York: Elsevier.

Smith, Garry J., and Robert Paley. 2001. "Par for the Course: A Study of Gambling on the Links and a Commentary on Physical Skill-Based Gambling Formats." *International Gambling Studies* 1 (1): 103–34.

Smith, Garry, and Dan Rubenstein. 2009. *Accountability and Social Responsibility in Ontario's Legal Gambling Regime.* Report prepared for the Ontario Problem Gambling Research Centre (OPGRC).

Smith, Garry J., Donald Schopflocher, Nady el-Guebaly, David Casey, David Hodgins, Robert Williams, and Robert Wood. 2011. "Community Attitudes towards Legalized Gambling in Alberta." *International Gambling Studies* 11 (1): 57–79.

Smith, Garry J., and Harold J. Wynne. 2002. *Measuring Gambling and Problem Gambling in Alberta: Final Report Using the Canadian Problem Gambling Index (CPGI)*. Calgary: Alberta Gaming Research Institute. Available online.

Snyder, Michael. 2010. "The Middle Class in America Is Radically Shrinking. Here Are the Stats to Prove It." Yahoo Finance, 15 July. Available online.

Society of Human Resource Management (SHRM). 1999. *Gambling in the Workplace Survey*. Available online.

Sorensen, Chris. 2010. "A Game of High Scores and High Stakes." Macleans.ca, 22 July. Available online.

Spelvins, Katie, Shab Mireskandari, Kymbra Clayton, and Alex Blaszczynski. 2010. "Prevalence of Adolescent Problem Gambling, Related Harms and Help-Seeking Behaviours among an Australian Population." *Journal of Gambling Studies* 26 (2): 189–204.

Srikanthan, T. 2007. "Gambling by Teens on Rise, Study Says; From Online Poker to Betting on Sports, More on Rolling the Dice on Risky Behavior." *Toronto Star*, 25 January: A15.

St-Pierre, Renée A., Jeffrey L. Derevensky, Rina Gupta, and Isabelle Martin. 2011. "Preventing Lottery Ticket Sales to Minors: Factors Influencing Retailers' Compliance Behaviour." *International Gambling Studies* 11 (2): 173–91.

Stevens, Rhys. 2001/2005. *Legalized Gambling in Canada*. Edmonton: Alberta Gaming Research Institute. Available online.

———. 2006. *Social and Economic Costs and Benefits of Gambling*. Edmonton: Alberta Gaming Research Institute.

Stevens, Rhys, and Maureen Beristain. 2004. "Canadian Guide to Gaming Industry Resources." *Reference Services Review* 32 (3): 320–28.

Stevens, Rhys, and Brian Soebbing. 2009. "The Integrity of Game Outcome in Professional Sportsbetting Markets: An Interview with Brian Soebbing." *Gambling Research Reveals* 8 (2): 1–3. Available online.

Stinchfield, R., and K.C. Winters. 2004. "Adolescents and Young Adults." In *Pathological Gambling: A Clinical Guide to Treatment*, edited by J.E. Grant and M.N. Potenza, 69–81. Washington, D.C.: American Psychiatric Association.

Stock, C. 2007. "Gambling Money the Lifeblood of Sports Groups." *Edmonton Journal*, 19 February. Available online.

Stockwell, Tim, Paul J. Gruenewald, John W. Toumbourou, and Wendy Loxley. 2005. *Preventing Harmful Substance Use: The Evidence Base for Policy and Practice*. New York: Wiley.

Stueck, Wendy. 2010. "Non-profits Take Aim at Gambling Revenues." *Globe and Mail*, 7 October. Available online.

Sutton-Smith, Brian, and John M. Roberts. 1970. "The Cross-Cultural and Psychological Study of Games." In *The Cross-Cultural Analysis of Sport and Games*, edited by G. Lueschen, 100–8. Champaign, IL: Stipes Publishing Company.

Suurvali, Helen, David C. Hodgins, and John Cunningham. 2010. "Motivators for Resolving or Seeking Help for Gambling Problems: A Review of the Empirical Literature." *Journal of Gambling Studies* 23: 231–43.

Sychold, Martin. 2006. *Study of Gambling Services in the EU Internal Market: Progress and Preliminary Findings*. Amsterdam. Available online.

Tavares, Hermano, Monica L. Zilberman, David C. Hodgins, and Nady El-Guebaly. 2005. "Comparison of Craving Between Pathological Gamblers and Alcoholics." *Alcoholism: Clinical and Experimental Research* 29 (8): 1427–31.

Telegraph Staff. 2008. "Fry's Executive Allegedly Stole $65m to Pay Gambling Debts." *The Telegraph*, 23 December. Available online.

Tepperman, Lorne. 2009. *Betting Their Lives: The Close Relations of Problem Gamblers.* Toronto: Oxford University Press.

Toplak, Maggie E., Eleanor Liu, Robyn MacPherson, Tony Toneatto, and Keith E. Stanovich. 2007. "The Reasoning Skills and Thinking Dispositions of Problem Gamblers: A Dual-Process Taxonomy." *Journal of Behavioral Decision Making* 20: 103–24.

Tremblay, George, Loreen Huffman, and Ronald Drabman. 1998. "The Effects of Modeling and Experience on Young Children's Persistence at a Gambling Game." *Journal of Gambling Studies* 14: 193–210.

Turner, Nigel E., John Macdonald, Mark Bartoshuk, and Masood Zangeneh. 2008. "Adolescent Gambling Behavior, Attitudes, and Gambling Problems." *International Journal of Mental Health Addiction* 6 (2): 223–37.

Turner, Nigel E., Jamie Wiebe, Agata Falkowski-Ham, Jon Kelly, and Wayne Skinner. 2005. "Public Awareness of Responsible Gambling and Gambling Behaviours in Ontario." *International Gambling Studies* 5 (1): 95–112.

United States General Accounting Office (US GAO). 2000. *Impact of Gambling: Economic Effects More Measurable Than Social Effects.* Report to the Honorable Frank R. Wolf, House of Representatives. Available online.

University at Buffalo. 2005. "Study Ties Risk of Problem Gambling with Proximity to Casinos and Other Gambling Opportunities." *Science Daily*, 29 June. Available online.

Valentine, Gill. 2008. *Literature Review of Children and Young People's Gambling.* Gambling Commission. Available online.

Valentine, Leanne. 2008. "Exposure to Gambling-Related Media and Its Relation to Gambling Expectancies and Behaviors." PhD diss., Georgia State University.

van Rijn, N. 1998. "Towns Hit Jackpot with Casinos Host Regions See Big Boost in Tourism." *Toronto Star*, 8 August: A8.

Van Rooij, Antonius J., Tim M. Schoenmakers, Ad A. Vermulst, Regina J.J.M. Van Den Eijnden, and Dike Van De Mheen. 2010. "Online Video Game Addiction: Identification of Addicted Adolescent Gamers." *Addiction.* 106 (1): 205–12.

Vandermaas, Mark. 2008. *The Separation of Gambling from Social Costs in Canada.* Unpublished paper, Department of Sociology, Univ. of Toronto.

Volberg, Rachel A., and Matt Wray. 2007. "Legal Gambling and Problem Gambling as Mechanisms of Social Domination?" *American Behavioral Scientist* 51: 56–85.

Vrecko, Scott. 2008. "Capital Ventures into Biology: Biosocial Dynamics in the Industry and Science of Gambling." *Economy & Society* 37 (1): 50–67.

Walker, Douglas M. 2007. "Problems with Quantifying the Social Costs and Benefits of Gambling." *American Journal of Economics and Sociology* 66 (3): 609–45.

Walsh, K. 2007. "Gambling Theme a New Trend in Reality TV." *International Centre for Youth Gambling Problems & High-Risk Behaviors Newsletter* 9: 7. Available online.

Walton, D. 2003. "Everybody's Got Their Eyes on $30-Million Prize." *Globe and Mail*, 11 October: A7.

Wanner, Kristy. 2010. "Reducing Gambling-Related Harms among College Students and Other Young Adults: Recommendations in Action: Examples from the Trenches." Presented at the 10th annual National Center on Responsible Gaming Conference on Gambling and Addiction, Las Vegas.

Wanner, Kristy, and Tom Paskus. 2010. "Hedging Your Bets: How Athletes and Teams Can Be Affected by Gambling Behavior." Poster presented at the annual meeting of the Association for Applied Sport Psychology, Providence.

Ward, Peter W. 1978. *White Canada Forever: Popular Attitudes and Public Policy Toward Orientals in British Columbia*. Montreal: McGill-Queen's University Press.

Wardle, Heather, Kerry Sproston, Jim Orford, Bob Erens, Mark Griffths, Rebecca Constantine, and Sarah Pigott. 2007. *British Gambling Prevalence Survey 2007*. National Centre for Social Research (Great Britain), National Centre for Social Research, Gambling Co. Available online.

Wardman, D., Nady el-Guebaly, and David Hodgins. 2001. "Problem and Pathological Gambling in North American Aboriginal Populations: A Review of the Literature." *Journal of Gambling Studies* 17 (2): 81–101.

Weinstein, Aviv Malkiel. 2010. "Computer and Video Game Addiction—A Comparison between Game Users and Non-Game Users." *The American Journal of Drug and Alcohol Abuse* 36 (5): 268–76.

Welte, John W., Grace M. Barnes, and Joseph H. Hoffman. 2004. "Gambling, Substance Use and Other Problem Behaviors among Youth: A Test of General Deviance Models." *Journal of Criminal Justice*. 32: 297–306.

Welte, John W., Grace M. Barnes, Marie-Cecile O. Tidwell, and Joseph H. Hoffman. 2008. "The Prevalence of Problem Gambling among U.S. Adolescents and Young Adults: Results from a National Survey." *Journal of Gambling Studies* 24 (2): 119–33.

———. 2009. "Association between Problem Gambling and Conduct Disorder in a National Survey of Adolescents and Young Adults in the United States." *Journal of Adolescent Health* 45 (4): 396–401.

Wenzel, Robert, ed. 2010. "The Middle Class in America Is Radically Shrinking." EconomicPolicyJournal.com, 9 September. Available online.

Wiebe, Jamie, Brian Cox, and Agata Falkowski-Ham. 2003. *Psychological and Social Factors Associated with Problem Gambling in Ontario: A One Year Follow-Up Study*. Ontario Responsible Gambling Council. Available online.

Wiebe, Jamie, and Michael Lipton. 2008. *An Overview of Internet Gambling Regulations*. Guelph: Ontario Problem Gambling Research Centre. Available online.

Wiebe, Jamie, Phil Mun, and Nadine Kauffman. 2006. *Gambling and Problem Gambling in Ontario 2005*. Toronto: Responsible Gambling Council. Available online.

Wiebe, Jamie, and Rachel A. Volberg. 2007. *Problem Gambling Prevalence Research: A Critical Overview*. Canadian Gaming Association. Available online.

Wilkins, Glenn. 2010. "The Skinny on Sports Lotteries" Canoe.ca, 20 October. Available online.

Williams, Robert J., Jurgen Rehm, and Rhys Stevens. 2011. *The Socio-Economic Impact of Gambling*. Canadian Consortium for Gambling Research. Available online.

Williams, Robert J., Beverly L. West, and Robert I. Simpson. 2007a. *Prevention of Problem Gambling: A Comprehensive Review of the Evidence*. Guelph: Elsevier Publishing. Available online.

———. 2007b. "Prevention of Problem Gambling." In *Research and Measurement Issues in Gambling Studies*, edited by G. Smith, D. Hodgins, and R.J. Williams, 399–435. San Diego: Elsevier.

———. 2008. *Prevention of Problem Gambling: A Comprehensive Review of the Evidence 2008*. Guelph: Ontario Problem Gambling Research Centre.

Williams, Robert J., and Robert T. Wood. 2007. "The Proportion of Ontario Gambling Revenue Derived From Problem Gamblers." *Canadian Public Policy* 33 (3): 367–88.

Wilson, Mark. 2003. "Chips, Bits, and the Low: An Economic Geography of Internet Gambling." *Environment and Planning* 35: 1245–60.

Winters, Ken. 2011. "Adolescent Brain Development: Implications for Understanding Youth Gambling NCRG Webanair Series." Presented August 24, 2011. Available online.

Winters, Ken C., and Matt G. Kushner. 2003. "Treatment Issues Pertaining to Pathological Gamblers with a Comorbid Disorder." *Journal of Gambling Studies* 19 (3): 261–77.

Winters, Ken, Randy D. Stinchfield, Andria Botzet, and Nicole Anderson. 2002. "A Prospective Study of Youth Gambling Behaviors." *Psychology of Addictive Behaviors* 16 (1): 3–9.

Wood, Robert T., and Robert J. Williams. 2007. "Problem Gambling on the Internet: Implications for Internet Gambling Policy in North America." *New Media and Society* 9 (3): 169–91.

———. 2009. *Internet Gambling: Prevalence, Patterns, Problems, and Policy Options.* Guelph: Ontario Problem Gambling Research Centre. Available online.

Wood, Robert T., Rina Gupta, Jeffrey L. Derevensky, and Mark Griffiths. 2004. "Video Game Playing and Gambling in Adolescents: Common Risk Factors." *Journal of Child and Adolescent Substance Abuse* 14 (1): 77–100.

Wood, Robert T., Robert J. Williams, and Paul K. Lawton. 2007. "Why Do Internet Gamblers Prefer Online Versus Land-Based Venues? Some Preliminary Findings and Implications." *Journal of Gambling Issues* 20: 235–52.

Wray, Matt, Matthew Miller, Jill Gurvey, Joanna Carroll, and Ichiro Kawachi. "Leaving Las Vegas: Exposure to Las Vegas and Risk of Suicide." *Social Science & Medicine* 67 (11): 1882–88.

Wu, Anise M.S., and Eva M.W. Wong. 2007. "Disordered Gambling among Chinese Casino Employees." *Journal of Gambling Studies* 24 (2): 207–17.

Wu, C.R., and K.J. Zhu. 2004. "Path Analysis on Related Factors Causing Internet Addiction Disorder in College Students." *Chinese Journal of Public Health* 20: 1363–64.

Wynne, Harold J. 2002. *Gambling and Problem Gambling in Saskatchewan.* Ottawa: Canadian Centre on Substance Abuse. Available online.

Wynne, Harold J., and Howard J. Shaffer. 2003. "The Socio-Economic Impact of Gambling (SEIG) Framework: The Whistler Symposium." *Journal of Gambling Studies* 19 (2): 111–21.

Wynne, Harold J., Garry J. Smith, and Durand F. Jacobs. 1996. *Adolescent Gambling and Problem Gambling in Alberta.* Edmonton: Alberta Alcohol and Drug Abuse Commission.

YMCA of Greater Toronto. *YMCA Youth Gambling Awareness Program.* 2010. Available online.

Young, K. 2009. "What Is Internet Addiction?" Slide show. Available online.

Yuan, Kai, Wei Qin, Guihong Wang, Fang Zeng, Liyan Zhao, Xuejuan Yang, Peng Liu, Jixin Liu et al. 2011. "Microstructure Abnormalities in Adolescents with Internet Addiction Disorder." *PLoS One* 6 (6). Available online.

Zacharias, Jan. n.d. *Internet Gambling: Is It Worth the Risk?* British Columbia: Problem Gambling Program. Available online.

Zangeneh, Masood, Mark D. Griffiths, and Jonathan Parke. 2008. "The Marketing of Gambling." In *In the Pursuit of Winning: Problem Gambling Theory, Research and Treatment*, edited by Masood Zangeneh, Alex Blaszczynski, and Nigel Turner, 135–54. New York: Springer Publishing.

Zimmer, L. 1986. "Card Playing among the Gende: A System for Keeping Money and Social Relationships Alive." *Oceania* 56 (4): 245–63.

Index